10—

A Darker Shade of Pale

A DARKER SHADE OF PALE

A Backdrop to Bob Dylan

WILFRID MELLERS

New York
OXFORD UNIVERSITY PRESS
1985

First published in 1984 by Faber and Faber Limited,
London, England

Published in 1985 in the United States by Oxford University Press, Inc.,
200 Madison Avenue, New York, NY 10016

British Library Cataloguing in Publication Data
Mellers, Wilfrid
A darker shade of pale
1. Dylan, Bob
I. Title
784.5'0092'4 ML420.D98
ISBN 0–571–13345–2

Library of Congress Cataloging in Publication Data
Mellers, Wilfrid Howard, 1914–
A darker shade of pale.
Discography: p. Bibliography: p. Includes index.
1. Dylan, Bob, 1941– . 2. Music, Popular (Songs, etc.)—
United States—History and criticism. I. Title
ML420.D98M4 1985 784.4'924 85-272
ISBN 0-19-503621-2
ISBN 0-19-503622-0 (pbk.)

Printing (last digit): 9 8 7 6 5 4 3 2 1

Printed in the United States of America

Contents

Contents

PART II: BOB DYLAN
Freedom, Belief and Responsibility

Illustrations

To Robin

Acknowledgements

Grateful thanks are due to Bob Dylan and his publishers for permission to quote extracts from his lyrics as detailed below. All rights in these are reserved by their publishers.

'Boots of Spanish leather' copyright © 1963 Warner Bros Music
'With God on our side' copyright © 1963 Warner Bros Music
'Blowin' in the wind' copyright © 1962 Warner Bros Music
'When the ship comes in' copyright © 1963, 1964 Warner Bros Music
'A hard rain's a-gonna fall' copyright © 1963 Warner Bros Music
'It's alright Ma (I'm only bleeding)' copyright © 1965 Warner Bros Music
'Subterranean homesick blues' copyright © 1965 Warner Bros Music
'Love minus Zero/no limit' copyright © 1965 Warner Bros Music
'Gates of Eden' copyright © 1965 Warner Bros Music
'Like a rolling stone' copyright © 1965 Warner Bros Music
'Ballad of a thin man' copyright © 1965 Warner Bros Music
'Rainy day women #12 & 35' copyright © 1966 Dwarf Music
'One of us must know (sooner or later)' copyright © 1966 Dwarf Music
'Most likely you go your way (and I'll go mine)' copyright © 1966 Dwarf Music
'Obviously five believers' copyright © 1966 Dwarf Music
'I dreamed I saw St Augustine' copyright © 1968 Dwarf Music
'Ballad of Frankie Lee and Judas Priest' copyright © 1968 Dwarf Music

Acknowledgements

'Dear Landlord' copyright © 1968 Dwarf Music
'Down along the cove' copyright © 1968 Dwarf Music
'I'll be your baby tonight' copyright © 1968 Dwarf Music, sub-published by B. Feldman & Co. Ltd, reproduced by permission of EMI Music Publishing Ltd
'Tell me that it isn't true' copyright © 1969 Big Sky Music
'Quinn the eskimo' copyright © 1968 Dwarf Music
'Sign on the window' copyright © 1970 Big Sky Music
'Dirge' copyright © 1973 Ram's Horn Music
'Simple twist of fate' copyright © 1974 Ram's Horn Music
'Idiot wind' copyright © 1974 Ram's Horn Music
'Shelter from the storm' copyright © 1974 Ram's Horn Music
'Buckets of rain' copyright © 1975, 1976 Ram's Horn Music
'Black Diamond bay' copyright © 1975 Ram's Horn Music
'Romance in Durango' copyright © 1975 Ram's Horn Music
'Mozambique' copyright © 1975 Ram's Horn Music
'One more cup of coffee (valley below)' copyright © 1975 Ram's Horn Music
'No time to think' copyright © 1978 Special Rider Music
'Is your love in vain?' copyright © 1978 Special Rider Music
'Where are you tonight' copyright © 1978 Special Rider Music
'Changing of the guards' copyright © 1978 Special Rider Music
'Slow train' copyright © 1979 Special Rider Music
'When you gonna wake up' copyright © 1979 Special Rider Music
'Do right to me baby (do unto others)' copyright © 1978 Special Rider Music.

The extract from 'Brother to Dragons' by Robert Penn Warren is copyright 1953 by Robert Penn Warren and is reprinted by permission of Random House, Inc., and the William Morris Agency.

The author would like to thank the Leverhulme Trust for a research grant enabling him to visit the United States during the writing of this book. Grateful thanks are also due to Jill Burrows and Roger Ford for their help in preparing the manuscript for publication, and to Roxane Streeter for the picture research.

Introduction

With the Beatles, Bob Dylan is the most prodigiously talented performer to emerge from the pop scene during the critical sixties. The significance of Dylan and the Beatles is mirrored in their durability. Though one of the Beatles is dead and others are moribund, their music survives to make renewed impact on fresh generations of young people, while Dylan, who started at the same time, has turned 40 but is still active and still evolving. For more than twenty years Dylan has been a spokesman for the young, promulgating a message and a way of life. A singing poet-composer, he is a quasi-folk musician, an artist and a commercial operator–in all of which roles he has become the mythic representative of a generation and a culture.

The aim of this book is to examine the nature and meaning of his myth both intrinsically and also in relation to his heritage–which to a degree he shares with us. Part I explores the legacy of white American folk, country and pop music from the late nineteenth century to the mid-twentieth century when Dylan was born. Part II considers what Dylan did with this heritage, and why his individual contribution turned out to be 'universal'. The universality of his meaning is in depth as well as breadth, though of course it is true that his songs have been heard by millions of people rather than, like real folk songs, by hundreds.

A waste and howling Wildernesse
Where none inhabited
But hellish Fiends and brutish men
That Devils worshipped.

Michael Wigglesworth: *Devil's Den*, 1662

And you that are young now, may live to see the Enemy as much impeached by that place, and your friends yea Children, as well accommodated to that place, as any other. You shall have made this *Island*, which is but as the *Suburbs* of the old world, a Bridge, a Gallery to the new; to joyne all to that world that shall never grow old, the Kingdom of Heaven.

John Donne: A Sermon preached before the
Honourable Company of the Virginian
Plantation, 13 November 1622

Our father does not know the minds of Indians: their minds are invincible; they are strongly attached to other things. We don't say to what their minds are most strongly inclined; but of this we are confident, that they are not disposed to embrace the Gospel: for here we are upon the spot, with open ears, ready to receive such Intelligence. As to your expectations of a favourable answer from the Oncondagas, we must desire you to cut off your hope, and not to protract it to any further length; for we know by experience that hope deferred is very painful.

Reply of the Indians to an address by Dr Eleazar
Wheelock, transcribed by David Avery, 1771

Two worlds — one black, one white; and to receive
Souls of their own colour, two heavens exist;
But must we, to make sense of it, believe
In two gods, or in one grey Dualist?

Edward Lowbury, 1978

Foreword

WHITE, RED AND BLACK IN THE AMERICAN EXPERIENCE

To define the nature of American folk culture is implicitly to define America. Races grow more amorphous and less homogeneous, more complex and less pure, in proportion to their increase in size. The notion of racial purity may become, perhaps always is, a shibboleth; certainly it is so in reference to the American peoples who, gravitating from old Europe to a new world, had no generic identity. In studying the artefacts of the American folk one may therefore legitimately begin obliquely, and by indirection find direction out. For before the American people existed, the Americas were not an uninhabited and uninhabitable waste. The original Americans were the Amerindians, savage tribes (in the eyes and ears of white settlers from Europe) who had lived through several thousand years over several thousand square miles of the vast American continent. The Indians' way of life and the rituals and arts in which it was incarnate evolved, inevitably, from the wide, wild world that succoured them. Based of necessity on hunting–and therefore on territorial rights, and therefore on war–the Indians' tenets were severe, stoic and self-dependent, with a religious relationship to nature and its seasonal processes.

Of course the aboriginal Americans had no real connection with India, having been dubbed *los Indios* because of Columbus's ignorance of geography. The Indians were puzzled as to why they were so called–by the French and English as well as by the Spaniards. More commonly the French and English dismissed them as *sauvages* or savages, rooting them in the wild woods far from the amenities of civilization. All the Europeans projected on to the natives a dual and contradictory identity. On one hand they were regarded as pristine inhabitants of a pre-lapsarian Golden Age, 'handsome and goodly, mannerly and civil', 'gentle, loving and faithful, void of all guile and treason';[1] on the other as barbarians and infidels, black of mind and heart, 'ferocious and cowardly to an excessive degree'.[2] At best, the Good Indian was what man might providentially have been in a state of nature; at worst, the Bad Indian was anarchical, probably soulless, an arch-fiend who copulated at random and observed 'no sort of law' about anything. 'Beyond the fact that they have no church,' asked Amerigo Vespucci, 'no religion and are not idolators, what more can I say of them?'[3] A great deal, it seems, for Vespucci goes on volubly to accuse the Indians–as a generic race, regardless of any ethnic or cultural subdivisions–of cannibalism, libidinousness and perversion. Later the French chronicler André Thévet calls them a 'marvellously strange, wild and brutish people, without faith, without law, and without civility'.[4] In more than one sense the native Americans were beyond the pale, being non-Christian and therefore impervious to white European values. Even Thomas Hobbes, a man of no mean intellect, cited the Amerindians as proof that the life of 'unaccommodated man' was 'solitary, poore, nasty, brutish and shorte'. John Locke more succinctly remarked that 'in the beginning all the World was *America*'.

Given the monogenetic origin of the human race according to Genesis, the native Americans ought not to have been there; no less tricky to explain away was the existence of beasts unknown to Noah. As Sir Thomas Browne put it:

There is another secret, not contained in the Scripture . . . and

[1] Arthur Barlowe, 1584, reprinted in David Quinn (ed.), *Ronoake Voyages*, vol. 104; quoted in Robert F. Barkhofer, jun., *The White Man's Indian*, New York, 1978.

[2] *The Journal of Christopher Columbus*, translated by Cecil Jane, London, 1960.

[3] Amerigo Vespucci, 1504, quoted in Northrup (ed.), *Vespucci Reprints, Texts and Studies*, vol. 5, Princeton, 1916.

[4] André Thévet, *The New Found World*, 1568, translated by Thomas Hackett, quoted in Barkhofer, *The White Man's Indian*.

> that is not only how the distinct pieces of the world and divided Ilands should be first planted by men, but inhabited by Tygers, Panthers and Bears. How America abounded with beasts of prey, and noxious animals, yet not contained in it that necessary creature, a Horse. By what passage those, not only Birds, but dangerous and unwelcome Beasts came over: How there be creatures there, which are not found in the triple continent; all which needs be stranger unto us, that hold but one Arke, and that the creatures began their progresse from the mountain of Ararat.[5]

Since it was difficult to square biblical with geographical and anthropological evidence, the early authorities put their trust in God and followed Joseph de Acosta in maintaining that the 'first men of these Indies' must have come from Europe or Asia because Holy Scripture teaches that all creatures are descended from Adam and the animals of the Ark. Not surprisingly, later authorities were wary of formulating a definitive theory of Indian origins, and were inclined to list alternative possibilities without adjudicating between them. As early as 1607 Gregorio Garcia remarks that:

> The Indians proceed neither from one Nation or peoples, nor went to those parts from only one part of the Old World, nor did the Settlers walk or sail by the same road or voyage nor in the same time, nor in the same manner. But actually they proceeded from various Nations, from which some came by Sea, forced and driven by Storms, others by art of Navigation looking for those Lands, of which they had heard. Some came by land.[6]

Wherever they came from, they could trace their origin to some dark race whose existence in the East could be biblically accredited. Garcia lists Carthage, Ophir, Greece, China, Atlantis, the wandering tribes of Tartars and, especially, the ten Lost Tribes of Israel. The Jewish connection was given shifty biblical authority in the apocryphal First Book of Esdras, a passage from

[5] Sir Thomas Browne, *Religio medici*, 1642, *Works*, G. Keynes (ed.), London, 1964.

[6] Gregorio Garcia, *Origen de los Indios*, 1607/1729, quoted in Huddleston, *Origins of the American Indians*, Texas, 1967.

Kings and a reference in Isaiah to 'the coastlands afar off'; and Garcia supports this with empirical evidence of similarities between Indian and Hebraic customs, behaviour and physical characteristics. The Lost Tribes, though factually no better attested than the ancient Iberians, the Carthaginians, or even the Chinese or the inhabitants of Atlantis, were appealing candidates since, being lost, they could be assumed to have forgotten the true God. Wandering over the face of the earth, they could have degenerated into the savagery perceived in the Amerindians, whose plight, though desperate, need not be hopeless. The conversion of the Jews might ultimately take place in a new world; the Indians, though 'more brutish than the beasts they hunt' and 'captivated by Satan's tyranny', might yet be reclaimed for Christ. Spanish missionaries made some attempts to Christianize the Indians, who discovered affinities between cannibalistic Roman rituals and their own and who, in the early seventeenth century, composed some passable imitations of Palestrinian polyphony. Similarly the English Puritans at Jamestown optimistically collaborated with the Indians in agricultural ventures, offering Western know-how in exchange for Indian experience.

But a heavy blow to this reciprocity was dealt in 1622 by the Openchancanough Massacre, of which Edward Waterhouse wrote, in indigestibly explosive syntax:

> Our hands which before were tied with gentlenesse and faire usage are now set at liberty by the treacherous Violence of the Sausages [sic] so that we, who hitherto have had possession of no more ground than their Waste, and our purchase at a valuable consideration to their own contentment, gained; may now by right of Warre and Law of Nations, invade their Country, and destroy them who sought to destroy us.[7]

From that moment the Indians' notions of the nature and purpose of life seemed antipathetic to those which the medley of white men had brought from the European civilizations they had wilfully or will-lessly disinherited. Only the Bad Indian was real, and the only Good Indian was a dead one. The *image* of the

[7] Edward Waterhouse, *Relation of the Barbarous Massacre*, 1622, quoted in Barkhofer, *The White Man's Indian*.

Good Indian survived in the Enlightenment's Rousseau-inspired vision of social amelioration: but only as a dream of what might have been. The few good Indians who counteract the bad in James Fenimore Cooper's *Last Mohican* cycle are, in relation to the 'guileless truth' of his white deerstalking hero, Natty Bumpo, wish-fulfilments who speak and behave like upper-class Christian gentlemen. And although Longfellow's *Hiawatha* was immensely popular in the mid-nineteenth century, it owed its appeal to its unabashed romanticism. The story was set, to an archaic metre, in a legendary past before the white man had impinged; moral consciousness was therefore unnecessary and inappropriate.

It is not surprising that the white man's view of his own new world, as evinced by the symbolic figure of the White Pioneer himself, should have shared this paradoxical duality. From one point of view Daniel Boone–a genuine backwoodsman who became mythologized–was regarded as a harbinger of civilization, taming the wilderness in order to bless it with the benefits of culture and technology; from another he was seen as congenital Adamic man, fleeing the shams of civilization in order to find himself in communion with nature and a transcendent godhead, rather than with the God of a defined creed. No sooner had Daniel decided on some spot where he wanted to rest a while than some 'damned Yankee' would establish a claim a mere hundred miles away, forcing him to trek even further West.

Neither of these backwoodsman stereotypes bore much relation to the actuality. Man alone in the wilderness did not normally reflect the divinity of a beneficent universe; nor did contact with European technology turn the West into a land of milk and honey, the goal of man's civilized endeavour, bringing the wheel of the great world cultures full circle, from India and China, to Persia, Greece, Rome, Spain and Britain, to the perennially United States. Two supreme nineteenth-century American writers of fiction pierced to the depths of the paradox. Herman Melville, writing of the White Steed in the famous chapter on 'The Whiteness of the Whale' in *Moby Dick,* describes it as 'a most imperial and archangelical apparition of that unfallen, western world, which to the eyes of the old trappers and hunters revived the glories of those primeval times when Adam walked majestic as a god, bluff-browed and fearless as this mighty steed'; but he adds that 'this spiritual whiteness, this divineness, had that in it which, though commanding worship, at the same time enforced a certain nameless terror'. In many of its visible aspects the American world might seem to be 'formed in love'; 'the invisible spheres', however, 'were formed in fright'.

Complementarily, Henry James wrote, in *The Europeans,* of the terrifying gulf that yawned between the hope inherent in the open American landscape and the horrors it induced in people's souls: in the dark of which the esteemed values of 'Europe' proved impotent. Thomas Jefferson's agrarian dream of the Garden of the West faded with the land-hungry migrations of the 1840s, when 'civilized', westward-thrusting men, bruised by privation and hardship, descended to abominations beside which 'savage' excesses paled into insignificance. The notorious Donner party, trekking to California, was reduced, within sight of the Promised Land, to the cannibalism with which the Indians were charged. The Janus view of the Indian as noble savage and bestial brute came home with a vengeance, and the more the white invader felt threatened, the more he found in the Red Indian a focus for his fear. The Indian came to represent not merely an otherness out there, but also the dark undercurrents that, as the far from unique horrors of the Donner migration showed, lurked beneath even the whitest skin. There were Reds under the bed long before commies were invented; and in so far as the red man was a scion of the devil, to purge him from the continent and from white consciousness and conscience became a religious duty. He was ripe for 'divine slaughter at the hands of the English'–for 'the glory of God and the advancement of the beaver trade'.

Casuistry came to the aid of white intellectuals in explaining away, if not justifying, the Indians' extinction. It was not the white man's fault if his admirable application and industry frightened the birds and beasts from the virgin forests and plains. That the Amerindians had to follow the creatures or starve was unfortunate, but in no sense was it a consequence of white malignancy. The Indian was doomed not so much by the assault of white muskets as by disseminated white diseases and by the privations of perpetual migration. He had to move West ahead of the white settlers; even if the cultivator's civilization had been offered to him he could not, being by nature a hunter, have profited from it. Dispossessed of his heritage and deprived of the buffalo on which his subsistence depended, the red man was effaced from the emergent white world: a world on and with which his life and artefacts had virtually no influence or even contact. Only as the twentieth century draws to its turbulent close have we become aware that the Red Indian endures. It is true that, as Francis Parkman pointed out a hundred or more years ago:

> The buffalo is gone, and of all his millions nothing is left but bones. Tame cattle and fences of barbed wire have supplanted his vast herds and boundless grazing grounds. The wild Indian is turned into an ugly caricature of his conqueror; and that which made him romantic, terrible and hateful, is in large measure scourged out of him. The slow cavalcade of horsemen armed to the teeth has disappeared before parlour cars and the effeminate comforts of modern travel.[8]

But it is also true, as Parkman goes on to point out, that 'no exertions of the missionaries Jesuit or Puritan, of the old world or the new', could ever seduce the Indian's 'dormant mind from its beaten track. Never launching into speculation or conjecture, he proferred his comprehensive solution of the incomprehensible: "It is a great medicine."' And so it has been and yet may be, for the Red Indian has left a stain on the vaunted American Way of Life. His *dispossession* is endemic to the American experience. As William Carlos Williams has put it: 'Every American is an Indian without a home.' The Indians' dispossession is the aboriginal darker shade on the white man's pale.

Yet those white settlers were not, most of them, congenitally wicked men; some even thought they were acting in everyone's best interest. What so grossly distorted their judgement was the Indians' incompatibility with the white man's concept of life. This made the white man afraid; and fear, as usual, brought other problems in its wake. For although the white man had

[8] Francis Parkman, *The Oregon Trail*, New York, 1849–1892.

conquered by means of his rudimentary technology, that technology was found to be inadequate to subdue the wilderness in which the Indian had survived through continuous adaptation to it. Having killed or driven off the indigenous populace, whose experience of local conditions might have benefited him, the white European was vulnerable. Only by the imposition of an alternative labour force could the values of 'civilization' function in the Old-New World.

Slaves were imported from another supposedly savage race: temperamentally more amenable, perhaps, than the stoically resourceful Indians, and certainly easier victims because, cruelly uprooted from their native traditions, they were dumped into a world even more alien to them than it was to the white settlers. Again, the white man's religion was used to justify physical oppression. Black Africans were not at first assumed to be irremediably of the devil's party, as were the Indians; but they were regarded as bestial rather than human, and therefore as commodities to be bought and sold. Advertisements appeared announcing:

> Negroes for sale: A girl about twenty years of age (raised in Virginia) and her two female children, one four and the other two years old, remarkably strong and healthy, never having had a day's sickness with the exception of smallpox, in her life. The children are fine and healthy. She is very prolific in her generating qualities and affords a rare opportunity to any person who wishes to raise a family of strong and healthy servants for their own use.

Moreover, if it were considered feasible that these black cattle might aspire to human status, being potentially redeemable by and for Christ, it was clearly the white man's duty to enslave them in order that they might be converted. As agrarian communities became 'civilized', exploited black Africans became the lubricant for the creaky machine of white affluence. The African was granted, as was the Indian, a dual and contradictory mythic identity; simultaneously he represented the beast within us and the innocent child we once were. If as beast he must be suppressed, as child he is a reminder of what has been surrendered: on both counts he is to be feared. To exploit him cancels the potency of his image. Since the black African's destiny has from the earliest days been interlaced with that of the white American it differs markedly from that of the Red Indian, whose fate it was to be effaced; and since the interaction of the white and black American will be a recurrent theme of this book, both sociologically and musically, it is unnecessary to discuss it further here. The *exploitation* of the black African was no less fundamental to the American experience than was the Red Indian's *dispossession*. This is the second darker shade on the white man's pale.

In 1893 Frederick Jackson Turner propounded a view of American history as the story of the western frontier which, in Turner's phrase, marked the borderline between savagery and civilization. As long as the sober theory of Jeffersonian agrarian democracy sustained the dream of the Garden of the West, American man could believe that the great American desert could, with each push westward, be redeemed. That the plough would itself bring rain was hardly a scientific fact, though with the advance of industrialization science could, to a degree, have changed the course of nature. But it did not turn out like that. The dream was always too simple-minded, and industrialization, inadequately understood and controlled, only added its own dangerous turbulence to that already inherent in nature itself. The white American came late but hard to a consciousness of his twofold, red-black guilt. Ralph Waldo Emerson's 'plain old Adam, the single genuine self against the whole world', finds himself in need of absolution. Henry Thoreau at Walden 'got up early and bathed in the pond; that was a religious exercise'. Nathaniel Hawthorne in *The New Adam and Eve* makes Adam say, 'We must again try to discover what sort of world this is, and why we have been sent thither.' Hawthorne can still ask, in *The Marble Faun,* whether it may have been 'that very sin–into which Adam precipitated himself and all his race' that was the 'destined means by which, over a long pathway of toil and sorrow, we are to attain a higher, brighter, and profounder happiness than our lost birthright gave'. A generation later Henry James Sr makes the same point in remarking that 'the first and highest service which Eve renders Adam is to throw him out of Paradise! Nothing could be more remote from distinctively human attributes, or from the spontaneous life of man, than this sleek and comely Adamic condition.' But neither James nor Horace Bushnell, who in his *Nature and the Supernatural* of 1858 bluntly described the state of Adamic innocence as 'utterly forbidding and hopeless', had high hopes of the American Adam's growth to maturity. He would be left, in the words of the greater Henry James's lament, with 'no state, in the European sense of the word, and indeed barely a specific national name. No sovereign, no court, no personal loyalty, no aristocracy, no church, no clergy, no army, no diplomatic service, no political society.' There is of course a positive aspect to that condition which James ignores or even disavows; but the American experience, in the eyes of sensitive observers, was never to recover its visionary gleam. Walt Whitman, 'chanter of Adamic songs', strode 'through the new garden to the West, the great cities calling'; but Alexis de Tocqueville leaves us with a chilling view of man alone in the wilderness: 'Taken aloof from his country and age, standing in the presence of God and Nature . . . man springs from nowhere, crosses time and disappears forever into the bosom of God; he is seen but for a moment, wandering on the verge of two abysses, and there he is lost.' Ironically enough, both James's and de Tocqueville's views of white American man are precisely the same as the view the early settlers took of the aboriginal Indian.

The iconographer E. McClung Fleming[9] has fascinatingly demonstrated how the interaction of red, white and black strands in the American image is evident in the symbols that came to represent the United States in cartoons, caricatures, coins, medals, stamps, and in decorative devices. The earliest of them, appearing first around 1620 and surviving well into the eighteenth century, is that of the Indian princess: a handsome, tawny young woman in her mid-twenties, naked to the waist, plumed with Indian feathers and usually accompanied by eagle and rattlesnake, symbols of the wild wastes. Often she is armed with bow and arrows, sometimes with a club; always she parleys amicably with some benevolent representative of Western civilization, such as Benjamin Franklin or George

[9] E. McClung Fleming, 'Symbols of the United States', in *Frontiers of American Culture*, Purdue University Studies, Purdue Press, 1968.

Washington. Her open-eyed aspiration is presumably deemed appropriate to men and women in a new world, potentially reborn in noble savagery, though the irony of the image, in view of the Indians' dismal fate, grew heavier as the years rolled on. Not surprisingly, the image of the Indian Princess faded during the eighteenth century, being replaced by a European Goddess of Liberty whose prototype, moulded by Jefferson's vision of the Noble Husbandman, was Graeco-Roman. She retains links with the Indian Princess in being a plumed goddess whose headdress resembles, even if it is not made of, eagle feathers; in growing more opulent she has lost her innocence, though her nobility is, if anything, enhanced. Ironically enough, a little black African boy, garlanded in American Indian feathers, often appears as her attendant page. The plumed Goddess of Liberty has come to represent the Jeffersonian dream of Graeco-Roman civic virtues re-created in a pastoral Arcadia, yet dependent on slavery for its operation.

By the late eighteenth century the Goddess of Liberty has merged into the figure of Columbia, named after Columbus, whose historic mission fuses a return to Eden (Whitman's *Passage to India*) with the ideal of freedom and of the national prosperity that makes that ideal a practical possibility. Columbia preserves something of the idealistic optimism of the Indian princess, though she is now divested of feathers, bow and arrows and rattlesnake, her stately beauty crowned only by a laurel wreath or liberty cap. Her Graeco-Roman majesty looks more sleekly comfortable as agrarian are reinforced by mercantile and industrial values.

In the final stage idealism weakens, as mother goddesses are superseded by the perkily democratic American male. He is thrown up by the civil war era, in the person of Brother Jonathan, clean-shaven, top-hatted, stripe-trousered, armed with 'segar' and slave-whip. Oddly enough, he resembles the black-*faced* minstrel-show entertainer–which is one way of sweeping blackness under the carpet. Something of this subterfuge survives in the late nineteenth-century image of Uncle Sam, who combines rural simplicity with urban cunning; draped in a dollar bill, he's a Jacksonian transformation of Jefferson's Noble Husbandman. Generally, he can be considered as a comic character, when set against the noble self-righteousness of Columbia or the noble innocence of the Indian princess. The American image seeks and finds, as de Tocqueville had said it would, a lowest common denominator.

The American experience is of its nature polyglot and polyethnic, for immigration involved many races other than the British. Slavic, Russian, Polish, French, German, Italian and Spanish groups from Europe tended, however, to keep themselves to themselves, zealously cultivating homes from home. Over the years elements from these cultures–not to mention non-European elements from Japan, China, Asia and India–must have seeped into the mainstream; and in a few cases peripheral ethnic groups–for instance French Louisianan and Spanish Texan-Mexican–interact directly, and become part of white American culture. This complicates the matter of American identity, but does not alter the fact that the central American tradition derived from white British stock, modified not so much by the global village character of the ethnic infiltrations as by those twin shadows, red and black, the former cast by the aboriginal inhabitants of the American continent, the latter by the labour force deliberately imported from 'barbarous' parts by the white settlers. White American culture, with its British roots, was untouched by the red shadow for several centuries. But the Negro's black shadow overcast the white man's pale from the beginning of their interaction, even though the white man, at first unknowing, resented it, while the black man, at last knowing, has come to repudiate it. It is thus impossible to trace the evolution of white American folk music without investigating the inextricable entanglement of white culture with black; and if the red shadow, like the Indian himself, has been all but invisible, this does not mean that its presence has not been felt. This is a theme I shall return to later. First I shall explore the ancestral roots from which white American culture directly sprang.

Those roots were in the British old world, and especially in those Celtic elements of it which have most strongly preserved their identity through the passage of time. Throughout I shall work by way of commentary on a number of specified recordings. For the most part the reference will be to a particular track, though the whole of the disc, and much other peripheral material, may often be relevant. Without the sound of the music the book cannot be fully understood. Most, though not all, of the recordings are readily available, and their details are set out in the discography.

PART I

THE BACKDROP
From the Appalachians to Nashville

Kentucky was filled with the ghosts of its slaughtered inhabitants: how could the white man make it his home?

W. H. Perrin: *History of Christian County*, 1884.

Then to new Climes the Bliss shall trace its way,
And Tartar Desarts fill the rising Day;
From the long Torpor startled China wake;
Her chains of misery rous'd Peruvia break;
Man link to man; with bosom bosom twine;
And one great Bond the house of Adam join:
The sacred Promise full completion know;
And peace, and Piety, the world o'erflow.

Timothy Dwight: *Greenfield Hill*, 1794

It spoke
Of a fair time yet to come, but soon
If we might take man's hand, strike shackle, lead
him forth
From his own monstrous nightmare–then his
natural innocence
Would dance like sunlight over the delighted
landscape,
And he would need no saint or angel then
To tread the monsters . . .
But that was then, not now.
For now all has been made clear to me, and I know
now
It is the monsters slain that are innocent . . .
And as for heroes, yes every one . . .
but plays the sad child's play
And old charade where man puts down the bad
and then feels good–
It is the sadistic farce by which the world is
cleansed.
And is not cleansed, for in the deep
Hovel of the heart that Thing lies
That never will unkennel himself to the
contemptible steel.

Robert Penn Warren: *Brother to Dragons*, 1953

1

The Word and the Body: The Legacy of the Old World

One of the more positive aspects of our current disillusion with Western civilization is a recognition that only a microscopic proportion of man's creative endeavour has depended on literacy. We are less confident than we used to be that the glories of post-Renaissance culture obliterate the 'primitive' artefacts of so-called folk and savages, let alone the often unnotated and unnotatable poetry, dance and music of the great Oriental civilizations. The significance of jazz throughout the twentieth century may lie in the fact that it is an aural and oral activity surviving alongside and creatively compromised by industrial technocracy. That there is so little useful writing about jazz–or for that matter about the folk-song revival and the semi-improvised pop music of the young–may be endemic. Oral art is, of its nature, resistant to commentary and analysis.

That we can no longer ignore oral traditions has now become accepted, and the publication in 1960 of Albert B. Lord's *The Singer of Tales* was a decisive part of that process. Lord, following the example of his teacher Millman Perry, attempted to approach the oral cultures of Homer and of medieval epic by way of fieldwork within still-flourishing Yugoslav traditions; and in so doing asked questions about the nature and function of poetry, music and dance which were no less fundamental for being neglected. We in Britain are beginning to ask the same questions, even though in our industrial society oral culture survives mainly in forms modified, and in some instances degraded, by literary and visual concepts. None the less there are still precarious outposts of the old, heroic oral tradition in the remoter areas of Ireland and Scotland, if no longer in Wales. Scotland in particular offers opportunities to study the relationship between the oral and the literary, the popular and the polite. Comment on the fundamentals of this ancient folk art will reveal why it was strong enough to be reborn, with the settlers, on the other side of the Atlantic.

Not surprisingly, the further we travel from the centres of civilization, the closer we approach the ancient heroic world. Let us consider a few examples, all recorded comparatively recently. 'Robh thu'sa' bheinor'[1] is a waulking song sung, in Gaelic, by Mary Morrison and a group of old women on the isle of Barra; they sing to aid their labour as they pound homemade cloth, 'waulking' it round in a sunwise direction against a board. A fragment such as this cannot adequately represent a performance that has no beginning, middle or end, and in which even the words are devoid of chronological sequence. We may, however, gain some insight into what is happening by describing the song's technique. The melody is entirely monophonic, so there is no awareness of the duality–the tensions and pressures–of 'Western' harmony. Further, the line is basically pentatonic; and pentatonic phrases, moving by whole-tone steps and minor thirds, are the most acoustically natural of melodic shapes since they derive most directly from permutations of the fifths and fourths of the harmonic series. This is why pentatonic formulae prevail in folk music in all cultures at all stages of evolution and are spontaneously uttered by young children, even those living in complex societies moulded by industrialism, by literacy and, in musical terms, by harmonic concepts. In pentatonic tunes the semitonic leading note of modern diatonic or chromatic scales, pressing upwards towards harmonic consummation, is almost never encountered. They therefore have little sense of temporality; they are not trying, like Western man, to 'get somewhere' but live in an existential present, affirming an identity with nature, even with the cosmos, cradling us on the unconscious deep, winging us into the air. They attempt neither to assert one man's will over others, nor to boss nature.

Since this is a work song, the initial phrase is brief and

[1] *Music of Scottish Tradition, Volume 3: Waulking Songs from Barra.*

insidiously reiterated, its rhythm lively and easily memorable. The tune, bandied antiphonally between the leader and the group as in the work songs of many primitive peoples, is an extension of the body's movements; yet through repetition it carries the singers beyond the body's thrall. It at once affirms and transcends the physical, inducing a state of trance, even *ecstasis,* when the women begin to yell a magical 'music of the vowels' which is beyond literate sequence and consequence. Whether the words–usually invented by the women workers and handed down from generation to generation–are about the natural or the supernatural they always obliterate barriers between physical activity and metaphysical experience. A medley of sense and nonsense evades chronology and coherent narration; there are no distinctions between present, past and future, or between chronometrical and mythological time. 'The silver whistle',[2] for instance, refers to a legendary king, a Prince Charles, and a 'renowned minister', thereby equating, in poetic imagery, a timeless myth, a historical past, and a topical and local present. What the women create at their toil, without the slightest intention of being overheard, is a functional art that is magical in the sense defined by R. G. Collingwood:

> Magic is a representation where the emotion evoked is an emotion evoked on account of its function in practical life. . . . Magical activity is a kind of dynamo supplying the mechanism of practical life with the emotional current that drives it. Hence magic is a necessity for every sort and condition of men. A society which thinks, as ours thinks, that it has outlived the need for magic, is either mistaken in that opinion, or else it is a dying society, perishing for lack of interest in its own maintenance.[3]

As one might expect, waulking songs are dateless. Many of the words suggest a seventeenth-century origin, others clearly refer to recent events; the tunes are usually much older than the words. It would seem that the melodies evolve very slowly from an ancient heritage, while the words are in part empirically improvised and in part fragmentarily recalled from multifarious runes and incantations of the past. In so far as they are magical

[2] Ibid. [3] R. G. Collingwood, *The Principles of Art*, London, 1937.

as well as functional, waulking songs are not radically distinct from songs associated with play or sleep, in both of which the mind's subconscious levels surface. Dandling and 'diddling' songs such as the 'Bressay lullaby',[4] or 'Portnockie's girl',[5] sung by Elisabeth Barclay and Blanche Wood, are merrier than waulking songs, but spring no less from the invocatory word and from bodily movement, carrying the infant and us outside time. Similarly, two magic songs that are also lullabies, 'The Mermaid song'[6] and 'The Fairy lullaby',[7] sung in Gaelic by Kitty Gallagher and Maire O'Sullivan, call on the same pentatonic contours as we find in the waulking songs, though the rhythm is naturally more tranquil if no less insidious. Sometimes lullabies turn into rowing songs, for the lulling of the cradle may carry us gently over the unconscious waters; often lullabies become heroic ballads, since the mother praises the potential deeds of her child. The lullaby was deeply honoured in the heroic world. It is not merely functional but carries us through the Gates of the Dream–as is borne out by the meandering tune and hypnotically disembodied vocal production of Flora MacNeil's exquisite performance of 'Cairistiona'[8]–simultaneously a lullaby, a rowing song and a heroic lament, for a dead girl is being rowed over the waters to her final rest.

The work song and the lullaby cannot of their nature allow much scope for metrical flexibility or complexity of ornamentation, though unexpected stresses and grace notes may be introduced to point a muscular movement or to encourage an entrancing lilt. In 'Tha thide, agam eirigh',[9] however, rhythmic flexibility and melismatic ornament are a highly developed modification of the pentatonic line. What Angus McIver, of the isle of Lewis, is singing is at once a love song and an epic elegy. So, although this song has no specific relation to a function in practical life, it too exists in a world of once-upon-a-time in which chronology is meaningless. The love of man for maid, and the sudden destruction of love by death, is a tale told 'since time was', and the singer has 'all the time in the world' in the telling of it. The girl is evoked in vivid immediacy; at the same

[4] *Columbia Library of Folk Music, Volume 1: Scotland.* [5] Ibid.
[6] *Columbia Library of Folk Music, Volume 6: Ireland.* [7] Ibid. [8] Ibid.
[9] *Music of Scottish Tradition, Volume 2: Music from the Western Isles.*

time her life and death are elemental. This bears not only on the monodic pentatonicism the song shares with the waulking songs and lullabies, but still more on the relative length and asymmetry of the clauses, spiralling onwards without seeking resolution; and on the ornamentation which seldom relates directly to the words. This is still more evident in the more literary tradition of the Ossianic ballad, improvised in accord with exacting metrical rules. In Mrs Archie Macdonald's version of the Fenian ballad, 'Latha dha'n Fhinn am Beinn langraidh',[10] for instance, the ornamentation suggests a parallel with the runic decoration on Celtic crosses: both seek release from the consciousness of crucifixion in whatever form it may take. Visually, the ornamentation is a paean to the prodigal beauty of the natural world; aurally the decoration twitters and quavers like birds, beasts and insects, like the purling stream or the wind in the trees.

When the old tradition is explicitly Christianized the magically runic effect is, perhaps paradoxically, still more potent. 'Tha do Rioghachd làn do, ghlọir',[11] sung by Mrs Murdina Macdonald, is a Gaelic evangelical hymn sung to a tune that is a permutation of an ancient love song. The effect of the marvellous melody–I choose the adjective advisedly–depends on its absorption of Christian heritage into the heroic pagan world. Christianity deepens consciousness with conscience; that heavier burden makes liberation the more ecstatic. Although rooted in Gaelic folk poetry, these hymns were inspired by the evangelical fervour of the eighteenth century, so that the import of the words, in which biblical imagery is rife, is now crucial–to use an appropriate word. But there is still no *expressive* interrelationship between musical ornament and verbal meaning; and the tunes that are adapted to the words are often secular and usually of some antiquity. In length of line, in rhythmic plasticity and in richness of ornament, the monodic pentatonic folk sources are here veering towards art: the music significantly invites comparison both with plainchant, the original doctrinal music of the Christian Church, and with the melodies of the troubadours, sophisticated poet-composers who sang of love frustrated and transcended, in monodic styles related both to

[10] Ibid. [11] Ibid.

plainchant and to the religious cantillation of Oriental cultures.

The similarity to the musical techniques of the Orient, patent in this hymn and latent in our earlier examples, is physiological as well as psychological and philosophical: it embraces the methods of vocal production–penetrative, nasal, without opulent vibrato, at once natural and supernatural rather than (in the strict sense) pathetic–and also the styles of performance–unhurried, still, tranced and trance-inducing. The parallel is reinforced if we turn from the vocal to the instrumental music of the heroic world, at least in the classic form of the Great Music for the highland pipes, popularly known as pibroch. This complex art was given definitive form in the sixteenth century, though its origins certainly go back to the fourteenth century, and probably much earlier. It is highly sophisticated and not strictly speaking a folk art, but a technique of oral composition by way of improvised variation on given formulae, which may or may not be notated. Even the technique of instruction by way of a series of conventionalized vocables was and still is oral. Whether or not Scots bagpipes have antique links with central European and Oriental bagpipes, there are unmistakable parallels, both technically and philosophically, between pibroch and the classical instrumental musics of India. The pibroch opens with an *urlar* or ground; continues with a *siabhal* or a 'moving' of the figuration; flows into a *taorluath* or a sequence of variations; and culminates in a *crunluath* or 'crown of dexterity'. This is a concept similar, if not precisely analogous, to the sections within which an Indian sitar player establishes his pre-ordained *raga* and cumulatively improvises variations on it, passing through a series of stages with elaborately codified techniques and experiential, almost doctrinal, references.

In both Indian musics and pibroch the pitch series seems to have been derived originally from vocal sources, and both employ microtones suggested by the inflexions of the spoken language in order to intensify the modality. In both cases these melodic techniques were then adapted to the instrument, which has more than vocal agility; and pibroch, no less than classical Indian musics, pays back its dues to song, for the pibroch vocables are employed as material for vocal improvisation. Most of the famous pibroch tunes eventually had words adapted to them, and in this form–first in Gaelic, then in English–entered the song canon. It would seem that in the old Gaelic culture the Great Music of instrumental pibroch must have been closely related to the bardic tradition of praise song and lament; and it survives in that form to the present day. Ten generations of MacCrimmons have been hereditary bards and pipers to the Macleods, and we can hear their great lament for the laird sung by most of today's finest Gaelic singers, from Mrs Archie Macdonald,[12] to Jeannie Robertson,[13] to Jean Redpath,[14] to a young girl like Isla St Clair.[15] All these singers have derived their versions of the lament from its instrumental form, sometimes from the ground itself, sometimes from one of its variations. It is music indeed bardically heroic: as becomes still more evident if one juxtaposes the vocal laments with their instrumental prototypes.

There is no recorded instrumental version of this melody; but there is one of a famous pibroch[16] composed by one of the MacCrimmons in honour of Donald Lagan, who died in 1645, reputedly at the age of 102. From this example it is clear that pibroch intensifies the qualities of the vocal music so closely affiliated with it. The immense slowness and spaciousness of the phrases is similar, and monodic pentatonicism is inherent in the instrument as in the unaccompanied voice. The nasal tone of the pipes resembles that of the singers, only it is heroically louder; the pipers' grace notes have a vocal source, though the singers in turn have learned to emulate the pipes' virtuosity. The only basic difference between vocal and instrumental style is that the pipes carry a drone–a musical image of eternity in pibroch no less than in classical Indian musics. The presence of the drone tends to deepen the tragic grandeur of the music, for although it does not modify the monodic nature of the line, it does generate tension, analogous to the jazz musician's 'dirt',[17]

12 Ibid.

13 *Jeannie Robertson: The Great Scots Traditional Ballad Singer.*

14 *Jean Redpath.* 15 *Isla St Clair Sings Traditional Scots Songs.*

16 *Scottish Bagpipe Music played by Pipe Major John A. MacLellan.* See also three versions of 'MacCrimmon's Sweetheart', played by Seumas MacNeill (*The Classical Music of Highland Pipers*), and John Burgess's version of 'The Battle of the Birds' (*John Burgess, King of Highland Pipers*).

17 Singing or playing dead on pitch may be considered clean; singing or playing slightly off the note is by analogy dirty, though this is the expressive point.

between its unending resonance and the tune's dissonantly clashing grace notes. There is a rhythmic complement to this in the muscular energy of the Scotch snap, the savage thrust of which is counteracted by the fact that the drone is unmoving. Thus both dissonant pain and bodily ferocity are sublimated in the length of line, and in the tortoise-like pace with which line flowers into ornament. Though northern pibroch is a long way from both India and from post-Renaissance Christian Europe, it is in the deepest sense a transcendental experience. The reality of its harsh initial motives is non-temporally sublimated as the variations slowly, almost imperceptibly, create ecstasy without development.

Gaelic song existentially celebrates an eternal present in the world of nature. The numinous utterance of pibroch does the same on a grander scale, for the pipes–with the drones tuned slightly off to make them more penetrative–were meant to be played in the great outdoors, with God or the gods as audience. But this Great Music is an almost forgotten survival from the heroic world. For the most part the pipes were, by the eighteenth century, restricted to the Little Music, which is military or social, for marching or dancing mortals rather than for putatively immortal heroes. The Little Music was and is essentially functional, like the waulking songs, only for play instead of work. Though the tunes of reels and strathspeys are still usually monodic and pentatonic, their fast triple rhythms are symmetrical, adapted to the body rather than the spirit. The dancers worship the earth in stamping their feet on her, though they deny temporality in the continuity of the patterns they create. Pipe dances often had words written to them, again emphasizing the interdependence of vocal and instrumental technique.

Particularly fine music may be created in a cross between the Little and the Great Musics: as when Billy Pigg[18] (if we may cross the border into Northumbria) creates classical pibroch-like variations on a folk song that liltingly dances. On this splendid disc Billy Pigg strings these pibroch-like folk-song variations along with a jig of his own composition, within the conventional formula for the dancing Little Music, and with a slow air,

[18] *Billy Pigg the Border Minstrel.*

'Dargai', composed by Scott Skinner. The jig is of a type now more familiar as fiddle music, while the slow air is in fact folk-styled violin music in a notated tradition. During the eighteenth century, indeed, the pipes were gradually ousted by the fiddle as an instrument for dancing to; and folk fiddle could easily cross the barrier to become the violin of polite society.

What is remarkable is that even after mainland Scotland had been absorbed into 'Europe' her fiddle music retained memories of the heroic strain. In the remote Shetlands especially, fiddle music[19] reveals its distant Scandinavian ancestry. 'Grieg's Pipes' and 'Black Jock', as played by Andrew Polson, preserve the raw, open sonority of the fiddle's Shetland predecessor, the *gue*, which is in turn comparable with the Norwegian *hardanger* fiddle; while 'Auld swarra', a slow air from Walls, played by Tom Anderson, is as wild as any bagpipe music. Though fiddle tunes naturally tend to be more arpeggiated and harmonically triadic, and therefore jollier, than vocal or pipe tunes, they may also use the open strings to evoke a sense of space. Social in banding together communities of lonely people, they may also suggest the vulnerability of social institutions against the immensity of air, sea and sky.

Something of this quality must have penetrated the music of the mainland fiddlers, who were amateurs of artisan if not labouring class. A figure such as James Oswald became associated with the urban vogue for violin music, especially that of Handel; yet, although he was a literate musician who composed courtly minuets embellished with Corellian 'graces', he employed the traditionally reedy tone of the folk fiddler, while the tunes of his elegant dances preserved modal (often pentatonic) contours indistinguishable from his adaptations of traditional pipe reels. This fusion of popular fiddle and polite violin reached an apex in the music of the great Niel Gow,[20] the master of eighteenth-century mainland tradition. Though his tunes are academically violinistic in technique, he still composed monodically, and the gapped scales of folk tradition preserve, beneath the elegance, the music's earthy virility. He often used the so-called 'double tonic'–oscillations between two keys a tone

[19] *Music of Scottish Tradition, Volume 4: Shetland Fiddle Music.*
[20] *A Tribute to Niel Gow by Ron Gonella.*

apart–which, the practice of Elizabethan virginalists suggests, derived from a modal partiality for the flat seventh of the scale. Archaic though this convention is, it still crops up occasionally in the playing of today's folk-fiddling virtuosi, though they play Gow's tunes with too beautiful a tone and with anachronistic piano accompaniment. None the less genteel tone and harmonic support were latent within the original music–which is why it fascinates as a hybrid between worlds popular and polite. When Bobby Harvey plays Gow's heartfelt slow air, 'Farewell to whiskey',[21] the arty presentation and the chromatic harmony cannot destroy the noble arch of the melody: however celebrated and materially successful Gow may have become in genteel society, it is impossible to forget that he was the son of a village weaver.

This is notated and printed music which exhibits a debt to Corelli and which was relished by middle-class and even by aristocratic patrons. None the less its melancholy grandeur brings a hint of the heroic tradition into a Scottish eighteenth-century drawing room. And if Scots fiddle music absorbed elements from European art music, which it in turn enriched, the opposite process occurred with the music of the Established Church. In the High Renaissance, Scots church music had been professional, complex, sophisticated, a European rather than local phenomenon. Knox and Presbyterianism stifled that brilliance, substituting, where music was permitted at all, a restricted diet of a few syllabic chants more dreary than austere, culled from the Reformed Churches. This time congregations–the folk–got their own back by way of *ad hoc* improvisation. They annulled the flagging pulse of the chant by adding twiddling embellishments, which they appropriately called 'quavers', at the ends of the lines; and the embellishments, calling on memories of old hymnic chants, grew so extended that the original tunes were hardly recognizable. Again appropriately, these folk psalm settings came to be known as 'Long Tunes'. So spontaneous was the return to folk sources that a precentor at Greenock, bored with his umpteenth repetition of one of the sanctioned Reformed chants, jumped from the middle of Psalm 107 into 'The Ballad of Sir Patrick Spens' without noticing the

[21] *Aye on the Fiddle: Bobby Harvey.*

difference. The congregation followed him blithely; and might do so today, for congregational psalm singing in antiphony with the pastor is still practised, most effectively in remote areas, but relatively uncorrupted even in sizeable towns. There could be no finer tribute to the toughness of the heroic tradition's tentacular roots.

When Murdina and Effie Macdonald, of the isle of Lewis, sing Psalm 118 to the eighteenth-century psalter tune, *Coleshill*,[22] they omit leading notes and so render the melody near-pentatonic. Murdina's complex tracery resembles her style in the unaccompanied psalm referred to earlier; but the addition of a second part makes the effect both wilder and grander, and contains the essence of Scots psalter singing, which is not congregational singing where 'everyone sings in a body, as with one mouth . . . but rather individual people who in the singing fellowship reserve the freedom to bear witness to their relation to God on a personal base'.[23] Such music can be extended to antiphony between precentor and congregation, for example, when Alasdair Graham and his flock sing Psalm 79 to the tune *Martyrs*.[24] There are obvious affinities between this music and the examples of heroic tradition mentioned earlier. First, the line is monophonic and basically pentatonic, though it may also embrace heptatonic elements, perhaps because of the legacy of ecclesiastical modality. Then, as in some primitive musics, there is an extension of linear unity into a dialogue between pastor and congregation. He, as God's representative, utters the psalmic Word which is God's voice, using a nasal, quasi-Oriental vocal production; in responding to him with orally acquired 'Long Tunes', the congregation seeks unity with the divine. Since this is religious, not social, music the rhythm is uncorporeal; the line modally soars from the rhythms natural to chanted Gaelic, achieving a levitatory ecstasy that denies the pulse of time, far more dangerously than does plainchant.

Since mortal beings are not, however, divine but fallibly human, the congregation does not often manage to sing in true

22 *Music of Scottish Tradition, Volume 6: Gaelic Psalms from Lewis.*
23 Thorkild Knudson, quoted in the sleeve note to *Music of Scottish Tradition, Volume 6: Gaelic Psalms from Lewis.*
24 *Music of Scottish Tradition, Volume 6: Gaelic Psalms from Lewis.*

unison or in Milton's 'Perfet Diapason' of the octave. What results is unconscious folk heterophony that sometimes fortuitously becomes organum–processions of parallel fourths and fifths–as the singers adapt the melody to the pitch most convenient to their voices. The ululating heterophony produces, as with many 'savage' peoples, a fuzz-buzz effect from its coruscation of indeterminate pitches; and this intensifies the sense of slightly frenzied aspiration. Though the singers start from their own voices in the natural world, they are seeking an experience of the numinous–which may be why they tend to pitch the chant high, or occasionally very low. Although they may themselves be naturals, they seek the supernatural–and seemingly find it, in the heart of big cities as well as in remote islands. When Murdo Macleod and his congregation of under-30-year-olds sing Psalm 107 to the tune *New London*, from a psalter of 1635,[25] the tempo is somewhat brisker, the ornamentation less extended, yet the bases of the traditional style are preserved, even in the heart of industrial Glasgow, in 1974.

This extraordinary act of worship prompts the question: is such music a people's riposte to a crabbed creed, a lowering landscape, a life of toil? Does the physical ecstasy flower out of spiritual penury? Without wishing to turn the clock back on essential material advancement, one finds a quality in this music–pentatonically innocent, ignorant of progressively sharpened *leading* notes and of *dominant* sevenths–which evokes the numinous in a way that is now lost–or at least forgotten. Admittedly, without leading notes and dominant sevenths a Beethoven would have been impossible; and I do not quarrel with the view that what Beethoven represents is humanity's supreme and most inwardly heroic achievement. But there can never be many Beethovens; and every so often it is salutary to recall a world in which common men were capable of their own smaller heroism, creating music, poetry and dance to which questions of value and of moral choice are not pertinent, but which remind us of springs of being we have ceased to be aware of: what it feels like to be one with sea and sky; to find ourselves, even in the grime of Glasgow, 'rolled round in earth's diurnal course,/With rocks, and stones, and trees'.

[25] Ibid.

The toughness of primitivism was necessary to the American wilderness, and most of the traditions and conventions mentioned here recur in an American context. The pentatonic monody of the waulking songs is basic to the American monody of deprivation; monophonic religious cantillation and heterophonic religious community singing are more crudely reborn; and although there is no direct American complement to the music of Gaelic pipes, drone-based ostinati on various stringed instruments may serve a similar function as an accompaniment to singing. In secular song and dance magic vocables are used in American children's games, as they are in those of the Old World; and the Scots and Irish tradition of fiddle music, itself derived from the Little Music for pipes, was transferred direct to American soil, and adapted to the banjo. The starkness of conditions in the New World meant that all these ancient techniques could serve functions comparable with those they had served in the heroic world. Moreover, because the American wilderness was so rapidly industrialized, those veerings and shiftings between folk and art conventions which, in the Old World, evolved over centuries, can be detected in the United States within a very short period. This is why the physiological, psychological, philosophical and sociological meanings of the legendary old music are a necessary prelude to the evolution of white folk musics in America.

2

The Old Heritage in the American Grain

THE MONODY OF DEPRIVATION

White American folk music self-evidently had, for the most part, British origins: Cecil Sharp claimed to have collected in the remoter Appalachian Mountains monodic songs which survived there in purer form than in the old country, apart from in darkest Ireland and starkest Scotland. Yet Sharp was not really justified in describing the life his Appalachian agrarians lived and the language they spoke as comparable with those of Elizabethan England. The first Elizabethans lived in rural communities, in direct contact with a distant past and in intimate relationship with a thriving urban culture. They were motivated by inherited values and shared experience. Life was often hard but it had the compensation of spiritual solidarity, from which flowered the techniques of monodic folk song and, to a lesser degree, dance. The songs' modal formulae, usually rooted in an instinctive pentatonicism, allowed for rhythmic flexibility and for richly melismatic ornament. Their circular rather than linear structures–their evasion of sharpened leading notes and cadential dominants–implied a life lived affirmatively, in mythological rather than chronological time, in relation to seasonal process and the turning earth.

Transplanted into American soil, British folk music underwent an inevitable transmutation: evolutionary elements were fostered at the expense of antique virtues. Migration on an appreciable scale began only in the seventeenth century, and increased dramatically during the eighteenth and nineteenth centuries. Even during the seventeenth century, when Britishers braved the unknown for the sake of their dissident religious beliefs, the old, intuitive fusion of Christian and pagan culture which had permeated the folk arts had already fallen into abeyance. The onset of industrialization, during the eighteenth and nineteenth centuries, forged links between the melodic styles of the rural order and harmonic and metrical techniques derived from an urban society–especially from the evangelical hymn and the music-hall ditty. Such cross-fertilization was encouraged by conditions in the New World. The settlers lived in direct rapport with nature; they had no choice in the matter. None the less, their relationship with nature differed from that of an agrarian peasantry stabilized by historical continuity and by contact with a vigorous civilization. The New World settlers, rather than living on and by the land, were obliged to become predators subduing it. If they were to survive they had to be remorseless, and their Puritan Nonconformity became proportionately the narrower. This had consequences for the character and quality of the music they made, whether it was a simple transplant of the old music into an alien soil or a re-creation of it, mingling memories of the past with hopes for the future.

British settlers were disseminated along the East Coast but were most strongly established in the South, where the climate was amenable. Even today rural music-making, especially in the Carolinas, Tennessee, Kentucky and Virginia, demonstrates the roots of oral tradition in the context of day-to-day life. Modern notions about correct vocal technique are no more pertinent to such 'music of necessity' than they are to the musics of the Amerindians and Afroamericans: style, structure and technique are here the consequence of social function. The white as well as the black man hollered, often wordlessly, in the empty fields, to solace his solitude, or to communicate from a distance with other solitaries, making a shaky gesture towards comfort and conformity. We can listen to Leonard Emanuel[1] and Red Buck Estes,[2] taped as late as 1961 and 1975, hollering and hooting in Sampson County of North Carolina. The poor white man whooped and yodelled, 'eephed' and 'hoodled' in

[1] *I'm on My Journey Home.* [2] Ibid.

imitation of birds and beasts and comically cretinous humans, as demonstrated by Lindy Clear[3] in 1956 and Jimmie Riddle[4] in 1971. Spelling was taught mnemonically in catchy chants, such educational ventures being scarcely distinguishable from the nonsense rhymes and runes with which amenable children were amused and recalcitrant ones pacified. Auctioneers cried their wares in monotonic incantation, exploiting the hypnogenesis of reiterated metrical pattern and of regularly alternating pitch. Square-dance leaders yell their calls in a style that, although not singing in the conventional sense, employs regular alternations of pitch and often complex metrical organization.[5] In the calling of Neil Morris, for instance, speech accent and body rhythm are inseparable. This is an art that, with the growing popularity of square dancing, has outrun its functional purpose. It has become an attraction in itself, on which the success of a junketing may depend.

An element of gameyness, even of exhibitionism, has crept into the performance of all these functional musics, as compared with the original Negro hollers, wrested out of direr necessities. Yet the techniques–the use of the slide, the portamento, the glottal stop, the changes of gear between natural voice and falsetto–are unchanged; and when we turn to the singing of folk songs, we find that the same functional techniques remain pertinent. Speaking, crying and yelling are not eschewed in song; on the contrary, the vocal techniques associated with work and play in everyday life are employed to intensify lyricism. We have seen that the impersonality of the Anglo-Irish-Scots tradition was such as to allow for vagaries of passion and pain; objectivity was the means whereby anguish was rendered endurable. Everyman's experience became, through unnotatable distonations of pitch and subtleties of nuance and ornament, momentarily particularized. Occasionally something approaching the old tradition occurs in North Carolina ballad singing, as in Nick Maylor's performance of the ubiquitous 'Barbara Allen'. By way of the nasal glide, the scoop, extravagant vibrato, the elongation of syllables and the ornamental device known as 'feathering', Maylor gives dramatic emphasis to particular words and incidents in the story,

[3] Ibid. [4] Ibid. [5] Ibid.

which he at the same time renders archetypal rather than personal through his bold, high-pitched delivery. Emotional identification is discouraged, but passion is not discredited.

Dangerous though it may be to generalize about musics so widespread and so multi-faceted, we may risk the suggestion that more normally monodic songs of the old tradition were modified, when sung in the New World, in one of two complementary ways, which can be regarded as the positive and negative poles of the same experience. I will discuss the negative pole first, for reasons which will become self-evident. Fortitude and endurance were necessary virtues in confronting the wilderness, in which social groups were small and defensively isolated. So, when 'poor white' American folk sing dolorous words and tunes, their manner tends to be not merely impersonal but also laconic. Holding on stoically for grim life often deprives the traditional tunes of their lyrical warmth; sometimes pain is so 'distanced' that the music sounds like a pretence that suffering may be discounted. Almeda Riddle,[6] a justly celebrated Ozark singer still performing around her home at Heber Springs, Arkansas, is a good example of this. When she sings what she calls a 'classic ballad' such as 'Lady Margaret', she is meticulous about the story-line, singing the fullest and usually the most poetic version of the words she can muster. The tunes, however, she takes at a brisker pace than did her British forebears, singing in the traditionally incantatory style, but in a regular, even plodding rhythm. Such ornamentation as she employs serves further to distance the experience, the curious upward roulades at the ends of the phrase being almost dismissive. The breaks in vocal register, which are not merely a consequence of the querulousness of old age, have a similar effect, and again show the partiality of old-style white American singers for the falsetto voice, which they employ with far more relevance than did their British ancestors. The later history of falsetto in American folk and pop musics suggests that it may be, if not escapist, at least an attempt to gain release from pain.

Granny Riddle calls on similar techniques whether she is singing authentic old ballads or the hymns and parlour songs

[6] *Almeda Riddle: Ballads and Songs from the Ozarks.*

she has appropriated. A song's classic status is attributable not so much to its age and origin as to its venerability, the respect and affection in which it is held by the community. This is a pale survival of the Red Indian's view that a song is to be valued not for its aesthetic appeal but for its social and therapeutic efficacy. Granny Riddle would find irrelevant, even meaningless, any critical discrimination of musical qualities *per se*. Sung by her, a folk hymn such as 'The old churchyard' retains traces of archaic modality though its source is in evangelical hymnody; a parlour ballad such as 'My old cottage home' is unambiguously diatonic and metrically structured, though sung in the same incantatory, nagging rhythm and with the same impersonally bleating intonation as a genuine old ballad. The odd breaks in the line (after the word 'old', for instance) destroy not only verbal meaning but also the cosy lilt of the Stephen Fosterish tune. What comes out is uneasy, even disturbing; it is not radically different from the effect of her singing of 'Lady Margaret' or 'Rare Willie'. She wouldn't maintain that the old songs are necessarily superior; nor, in her performance, should we. The songs that have become classics have lasted because they were the ones that did most for people in a life that was physically arduous and emotionally exhausting. Almeda Riddle's songs testify to the durability of the human spirit.

Such rhythmic uneasiness and such intonational strain–the consequence of a life deficient in material and perhaps spiritual comfort–is not confined to singers as austere as Granny Riddle. Another Carolina singer, Goldie Hamilton, has a vocal timbre much sweeter than Riddle's, and habitually relishes the lyrical qualities of the tunes, especially the older ones. Yet when she sings the beautiful love song, 'Sweet wine',[7] her lyricism sounds aloof in its rhythmic fortuity, the more so because the words are supposed to be sung by a man. In the singing of Dillard Chandler,[8] the basic white Southern American idiom comes out as a cross between Granny Riddle's linear starkness and Goldie Hamilton's lyricism. Recounting the most dastardly human behaviour or the most savage acts of an indifferent deity, he sings the ballad of 'Little Mattie Groves' with a laconicism that

[7] *I'm on My Journey Home.*
[8] *Old Love Songs and Ballads from the Big Laurel.*

might be taken for cynicism, did it not uncompromisingly accept the fact that life is nasty, brutish and short. Passion becomes more overt when he sings love songs rooted in his American environment. None the less his version of 'The sailor being tired' is, if deeply moving, deflating rather than enlivening: literally so, since the pentatonic phrase, beginning on a painfully sustained note, teeters under its own weight, like a primitive tumbling strain.[9] Like Almeda Riddle, Chandler does not differentiate in performing style between lyrical songs like 'Awake, awake' and gloomily introverted hymns like 'Hicks farewell'; the former asserts human resilience, the latter bolsters human survival, but each state, coexisting, implies the other. Dillard Chandler's songs, no less than Almeda Riddle's, are a way of life, even a technique for living. Chandler, singing traditional ballads of considerable antiquity, often insisted that the characters referred to in the songs were related or personally known, if not to himself, at least to his forebears. Always, the past is *presented*: on one occasion when Chandler sang 'Little Mattie Groves', some of his audience maintained that Mattie should have fought back harder against the tyrannous husband and should have run off with the girl; others thought it would have been wiser to have 'snuck off'. One or the other of those alternatives would be adopted, should the event recur tomorrow as–the implication is–it well might.

The ubiquity of old ballads in the Appalachians may be partly attributable to a defensive conservatism in the adventurous pioneer. Faced with the hazardous unknown, he clung where he could to a familiar past; and did so the more when nature's unknown was, as industrialism encroached, modified by a clash of cultures. Even in rural areas old ballads coexisted with hymns, parlour songs and music-hall ditties; in areas undergoing industrialization, folk communities reacted with varying degrees of assimilation and rejection, integration and disintegration, support and disjunction–to use the terms coined by the sociologist Herbert Blumer. Thus songs from the Kentucky

[9] The term 'tumbling strain', coined by the ethnomusicologist Curt Sachs, denotes a phenomenon prevalent in all primitive musics: a singer initiates a phrase on a high note, from which he tumbles down, usually through a fourth, though sometimes through as much as an octave, with an effect of uncontrolled libido.

and Virginia mining areas, where conditions for the workers under small-time *laissez-faire* capitalism were and to a degree still are oppressive, tended to deal with new socio-economic issues in conservative, even archaic, musical styles. Aunt Molly Jackson,[10] for instance, came from Dillard Chandler's Laurel country but moved as a child to the Kentucky mining area, her father being driven by economic necessity. Her mother died when Molly was 6; her father, remarrying within a year, added another eleven children to his quiver; Molly herself was married at 14 and was twice a mother by the age of 17. Yet despite or because of the hardship of her life, Molly made up copious songs, usually adapting old tunes garnered in her childhood to new words related to her own life and the life of her community. Often her songs amount to protest numbers; for a period in the thirties she achieved political notoriety and served a spell in prison.

Whether she adapted old tunes or made up her own, she favoured melodies of a primitively pentatonic type, presented with exiguous grandeur. 'Lonesome jailhouse blues' is not in form a blues though it has affinities with a black field holler, which she must have heard both in her rural childhood and in Kentucky. The black holler in turn had its roots in a pre-pentatonic African tumbling strain; and Aunt Molly's lacerating vocal production thus makes patent a stark reality which, in Dillard Chandler's declining lament in 'The sailor being tired', had remained latent. The savagery of Aunt Molly's songs has become an act of rebellion rather than of perdurable acceptance–which is why she can, in singing 'I love coal miners, I do', reinvigorate folk modality with an unremitting beat that suggests black gospel music or work song, and hints at the urban music hall. But Aunt Molly always sang unaccompanied, and her most overtly political songs tended to be the most musically primitive; nor did she distinguish between the political and the evangelical motive, as in 'The lone pilgrim' or 'A little talk with Jesus'. The religious songs evoke no metaphysical consolation; having a little talk with Jesus serves the same purpose as solidarity with one's oppressed fellows. Jesus is simply a legendary friend who, unlike most flesh-and-blood friends, never fails.

[10] *Aunt Molly Jackson.*

Sarah Ogan Gunning,[11] a younger relative of Aunt Molly, from the same Kentucky mining area, sometimes uses traditional tunes, as does Aunt Molly, but more commonly invents her own, within the archaic modal tradition. Her words usually deal with material and spiritual deprivation, but do not directly seek political solutions. This may be because the evangelical tradition is a more positive force in her songs than it is in Molly Jackson's. Her vocal timbre, though still rasping, is more lyrically continuous, her rhythm swings more potently, as she creates a haunting synthesis of folk sources with social comment and personal experience. Although her father worked in the mines, he had started out as a farmer and minister, and Gunning's most characteristic songs are a secular modification of old-style Baptist and new-style Holiness music, as can be heard in 'Just the same today' or the grim conversation piece, 'O death'. Her most remarkable songs are the most personal: 'I have letters from my father', for instance, has its roots in a white spiritual of the group related to 'Wondrous love', though its searing intensity comes from the relevance of its biblical imagery to her own community and from her obviously deep relationship to her father.

In this monody of deprivation the flatness, the rasping tone, the lack of vocal bloom become themselves a kind of lyricism, embracing more than the mere will to endure. It should not be surprising that the style has survived virtually until the present day, for the relative affluence that has come to most white American peoples bypassed the hillbillies marooned in the creeks of the Carolinan, Virginian and Kentucky mountains; industrial exploitation added to, rather than alleviated, their penury. The land was gouged and scarred, the streams polluted, animal life decimated, human life materially and spiritually impoverished. Yet out of deprivation men and women wrested a music which, if niggardly, attained nobility. The archetypically named Virginian miner Nimrod Workman[12] finds his material both within ancient traditions and in the world that surrounds him. He sings the ancient Scots 'Ballad of Lord Bateman', whom he appropriately translates into Lord

[11] *A Girl of Constant Sorrows: Sarah Ogan Gunning.*
[12] *Nimrod Workman: Mother Jones' Will.*

Baseman; since the tale concerns the imprisonment of the weak and poor by the rich and powerful it is relevant to Workman's own situation, into which it is reborn through his pinched, nasal tone, his painful elongations and dislocations of rhythm, and his piercing distonations of pitch. To 'Lord Daniel' he gives the same minimal treatment; nor does his manner change when he sings a white American hymn of the nineteenth century, 'The city four square', substituting his bleak monody for the conventional homophony, and imbuing the originally four-square tune with the incantatory quality of epic lament.

In 'Rock the cradle and cry' he creates a poor white lullaby that effects a minimal but deeply expressive distillation of conventions more richly used in lullabies of the Old World; in 'Sweet Rosie' and 'Darling Cory' he fuses the lyricism of a folk source with the tawdrier vivacity of the music hall, yet attains an intensity of timbre and a long-spanned control of the paragraph that approaches the heroic. His own impressive 'Coal black mining blues' and 'Black lung song' have the fervour of black gospel music and the harsh reality of the blues, pitch black in pentatonic ululation and rhythmic flexibility, yet inseparable from the white penuries to which he is committed. When he sings white evangelical hymnody ('I want to go where things is beautiful') or even a sentimental parlour song ('The drunkard's lone child') he preserves the same uncompromising monodic grandeur. What Workman calls 'Christian songs' are not escapist but part and parcel of his life, fortifying its harshness without promise of celestial absolution. As with Aunt Molly Jackson, evangelism tempers militancy without erasing bitterness. Both owe something to Baptist tradition in that its disapproval of instruments (especially the fiddle, associated with the dancing devil) encourages them in their severe monophony, on which the force of their songs depends.

POOR WHITE FOLK AND HOMOPHONY FOR WORSHIP

Although the severe monodic style of a Nimrod Workman or an Aunt Molly Jackson is at the base of the American experience, it is obvious from their songs that they, in common with the other settlers, were *religious* Nonconformists. It is therefore logical that the deprived country idiom should not be restricted to monophonic isolation. Each man or woman may have been alone in the wilderness; but individuals could band together, adapting the harmonic as well as melodic stylizations of primitive hymnody to their raw, new land. What had begun in the old country as an educational venture, reinforcing the solidarity of common men by moral and technical disciplines, returned now to God and nature as Southern men and women improvised harmonic concordance. Just as the Scottish Presbyterians had expressed dissent from the Established Church in the near-togetherness of heterophony around a few sanctioned psalm tunes, so the Revd Ike Caudill, in Mount Olivet Regular Baptist Church in the Kentucky mining town of Blackley, leads his congregation into comparably uneasy congruence.[13] The lines of the eighteenth-century hymn–composed originally, not surprisingly, in Welsh by William Williams–are incanted by the preacher and echoed by the congregation in long-drawn melismata, producing a heterophony as awesome as it is wild. Grandpa Ipsom Ritchie leads his large congregation at Lick Branch, Kentucky, into similar communal *ecstasis*,[14] declaring that, having been 'a long time travelling here below', it is about time they took off. In one sense the sound is extremely earthy, for the multiple pitches of the unison that doesn't quite make it produce a sonority as harsh, gritty and frightening as the earthly life most of the singers had to lead. In another sense, however, there is a heavenly quality in the singers' mere attempt at unity: the melodies fly the more wingedly the more the instinctive organum of their parallel fourths, fifths and occasionally thirds seeks to efface the disparities between individual men and women in the oneness they achieve in praising God.

Such harmony as results from the concatenation of preacher and God-inspired community is here fortuitous, as it almost certainly was in the original organum of Europe's medieval monks. But since nineteenth- and twentieth-century Americans

[13] *The Gospel Ship: Baptist Hymns and White Spirituals from the Southern Mountains.*
[14] *I'm on my Journey Home.*

had behind them an established, diatonic harmonic tradition, even though they were not formally trained in it, it is obvious that sooner rather than later they would explore the interrelationships between this tradition and the modal monody and heterophony they created instinctively. From this compromise sprang the tradition of fa-so-la singing, which flourished in New England from the mid-eighteenth century, and is not extinct even today. Here the boundaries between art music and folk music are even more than usually insecure. In the eighteenth and early nineteenth centuries the Yankee tunesmiths or hymnodists notated and published their compositions, and comprised the first, powerfully impressive, school of American creative musicians. In this music what, in academic terms, would be considered mistakes were a source of musical strength, whether in simple homophony or in one of William Billings's more elaborate 'fuguing tunes'. Elements of folk improvisation survived, and the notation gives an inadequate, even a misleading, notion of the heard sound. The hollow texture, the sturdy rhythm and the mingle of folk-derived modality with diatonic triads usually in root position, give to the music a fervent nobility proportional to its non-professionalism. This music just makes the grade as art music,[15] though the hymn-making movement was so socially functional and so widely popular that it proliferated into areas closer to folk music than to art. The normal historical process is inverted: shape-note notation–an aural technique related to tonic *solfège*–had to be invented so that the music could be disseminated among the musically, and often verbally, illiterate.

So American hymnody, which came to fruition in the townships of New England, moved back into the rural wilderness, especially in the South and West. Many of Billings's and the other New Englanders' tunes were spread by travelling singing teachers, who themselves made up similar tunes. As they were carried through thinly populated regions of the vast continent, their primitive features were reasserted. The melodies tended to revert from the New Englanders' bass-rooted SATB to three-part

[15] *Old Harp Singing of Eastern Tennessee, White Spirituals from the Sacred Harp* and see Wilfrid Mellers, *Music in a New Found Land*, London, Faber and Faber, 1964, pp. 7–17.

settings; their modal character was reinforced by contact with the agrarian folk songs still sung in the South, as in the justly celebrated 'Wondrous love'. Similarly, the New Englanders' fumbling if often inspired attempts at eighteenth-century harmonization gave way to an intuitive folk organum, as in the strange version of 'Holy manna' published in *Southern Harmony*, in which Jean-Jacques Rousseau's original diatonic tune has been purged to pure pentatonicism, and the harmony minimalized to (usually parallel) fourths and fifths. This looks crude on paper because the temptation is to compare it with more familiar four-part hymnic harmony. But it is not 'paper' music; it is unexpectedly notated folk art that sprang empirically from the sound made by massed voices. In performance the sonority is impressive: the more so because the New Englanders' habit of allowing men or women to sing any part–up or down according to sex–was, in remoter rural areas, adopted with total spontaneity. The consequent octave doublings give the sound its awe-inspiring resonance. Nor is it possible to predict which part will be most prominent, as that depends on the number of people who decide to sing each part.

Shape-note tunes proliferated rapidly; as they appealed to the illiterate, they were irresistible fodder for the Revivalist sects that mushroomed in each state. The empiricism of the shape-note method encouraged singers to make up their own versions of the tunes on the spur of the moment, so that a wild heterophony often resulted–not unlike the heterophony of Scottish congregational singing, but more savage because it derived from metrical movement rather than from syllabic chant. This was the musical equivalent of the physical excesses of Revivalist fervour: according to contemporary descriptions this seems to have been not altogether distinct from 'barbaric' voodoo ritual. Although the fathers of the Puritan Churches disapproved of dancing as an agent of the devil, there is no doubt that in the South white shape-note tunes were one of the sources for the black American's spirituals; together, white and black Christians sought instinctive refuge from Calvinistic fire and brimstone. Throughout the nineteenth century shape-note hymns, allied to black gospel music, were part of the roots of the American folk art that is jazz. Only in the twentieth century–in some of the music of composers such as Charles Ives, Henry Cowell, Aaron Copland, Roy Harris and Virgil Thomson–does shape-note hymnody affect the evolution of art music. It says much for the subterranean vigour of this indigenous music that–preserved in teaching manuals such as *Kentucky Harmony, Sacred Harp, Harp of Columbia* and *Southern Harmony* (at first in the traditional three parts, but later with an alto added)–it should still be performed, in much the same manner, in the remoter regions of the southern states.

These performances are, and always were, for the most part by large gatherings of people, often in the open air. Fa-so-la hymns were also performed by small choirs and even by solo voices, as in the Denson Quartet's version of a mid-nineteenth-century hymn, 'I'm on my journey home'.[16] George Pullen Jackson, the major historian of this music, called the Densons 'the Deans of the white Spiritual', for the family has been arranging and composing *Sacred Harp* hymnody since 1844. This development was in part a product of commercial manipulation: as music printing proliferated among rapidly expanding urban communities, a market was stimulated for religious music adapted to domestic use. Publishers printed hymns and hired, and even promoted, groups to popularize them, especially at organized singing conventions. Naturally many new songs were called for; and even the old songs, performed by solo voices, sound sweeter, more synchronized in rhythm and in pitch, than the congregational hymns. The Densons still cultivated a jazz-flavoured rhythmic drive and employed folk-like vocal mannerisms such as the scoop. These empirical techniques, anathema to academic musical respectability, tend to be ironed out in more sophisticated versions of gospel close harmony, such as the Southland Ladies Quartette's 1930 performance of 'Don't put off salvation too long'.[17] However, despite the vocal polish and observance of 'polite' diction, there are anomalies even here: the portamento is not entirely evaded, and the disposition of parts is odd, as the notated bass line is sung, in this all-women ensemble, an octave up.

The relationship between amateur and professional elements in gospel music is complex and fascinating. The original shape-

[16] *I'm on My Journey Home.* [17] Ibid.

note singers, though often verbally illiterate, could sight-sing from their own notation, and did so at their singing conventions. However, many of the sophisticated gospel groups sang by ear, especially during the thirties and forties, when they were able to pick up their styles from radio and recordings. Many groups, dissatisfied with the convention publishers, who often rewarded the singers only with copies of the printed songbook, set up as their own entrepreneurs. In freeing themselves from Revivalist rigour they also became receptive to a variety of secular influences. The Homeland Harmony Quartet in the forties responded to the potential gospel implications of piano boogie, as it had been practised twenty years earlier by Arizona Dranes; while the Sons of the Pioneers appropriated smooth-harmony cowboy style in a number such as 'Riding the range for Jesus'. Commercially speaking, at least, the white gospel group won its battle with congregational fa-so-la, and the Homeland Harmony Quartet's 'Gospel boogie', copyrighted in 1947, claimed, with some degree of exaggeration perhaps, to have sold more than two million copies on disc. Although this was hardly a commercial operation on the scale of an Elvis Presley, it does indicate how the singing of small vocal groups, though an evolution from congregational fa-so-la singing which in turn derived from folk heterophony and monody, moved in a radically different direction.

Evangelical folk heterophony, like the monody of deprivation, was a negative pole of the New World's re-creation of its traditional sources. The groups, on the other hand, inevitably veer towards the positive pole, for their music is more vigorously metrical and involves the togetherness of streamlined harmonic congruence. The lonesomeness of individual lines seeks the cosiness and stability of the triad: a socio-musical panacea that is explicitly spelled out when, during the Depression years, the Evening Breezes Sextet of Vivian, West Virginia, employ their gospel idiom to deal briskly, in 'The coal-loading machine', with the hard realities of mining life. Ultimately such an approach affects congregational singing too: as is evident when the congregation of Ridgecrest Baptist Church in North Carolina sing a hymn by Robert Lowry, written in 1867 to words by Isaac Watts, at a Sunday school convention in 1971.[18] Though there is much in this performance that is empirical, it is no more folk music than are the group arrangements discussed above. The words themselves, exhorting us to cast aside the trammels of mortality and to *march* (like soldiers) to 'fairer worlds on high', invite an ethical choice. Choice involves consciousness and possibly conscience; clearly such attitudes cannot live in the existential present in which folk song thrives, since the consequences of choice can be perceived only in time. The music paradoxically encourages us to relinquish the very values it asserts: both metrically, in that the swinging 6/8 march pulse is as regularly time-dominated as a pendulum; and harmonically, in that the vocal lines are marshalled into congruence and, supported by the massive sonority of organ and the percussive hammering of piano, are driven towards cadence and temporal resolution. *Our* hymns, unlike the monodic incantations of the folk, do not transcend the world, the flesh and the devil but rather attempt to control–in psychological terms to repress–them by an imposition of the human will, through which alone chaos may be evaded.

This evasion of guilt extends beyond the range of folk-affiliated music. In secular contexts, however, the bypassing of tragedy was soon under way, and at first glance appears to be at the opposite pole from the deadpan approach to the realities of a rudimentary life. The Monody of Deprivation gives way to the White Euphoria, which is to depend ultimately on instrumental resource. It would not have been feasible, however, were there not a positive aspect in both religious and secular terms to American vocal monody.

[18] *Brighten the Corners where you are: Black and White Urban Hymnody.*

3
The White Euphoria

THE MONODY OF INNOCENCE

The most thorough-going manifestation of the monody of innocence is undoubtedly provided by the music of the Shakers –whose positive qualities sprang, in no discreditable sense, from self-righteousness. The most extreme of separatist sects, they believed that the millennium had arrived in the person of Mother Anna Lee, who was Christ reincarnate. Secure in their belief, the original band of twelve disciples established communities in New England and New York in the early years of the eighteenth century and sustained, in the teeth of hostility, traditions of morality, craft, architecture and music. Ideologically, they disapproved of sex as a betrayal of spiritual purity, yet they managed to propagate themselves; and although they stemmed from the English Quakers, unlike them, they were never quietists. Anna Lee urged her followers to 'put your hands to work and your hearts to God', adding that there are 'no sluts nor slovens in heaven'. She had a vision of America: 'I saw a large tree, every leaf of which shone with such brightness as made it appear like a burning torch. I knew that God had a chosen people in America; I saw some of them in a vision, and when I met them I knew them.' Despite, or perhaps because of, the theoretical belief in total celibacy, the chosen people could be male or female. Anna Lee was succeeded by the elders James Whitaker and Joseph Meacham, and her most illustrious heir was the handsome and intellectually distinguished Lucy Wright, who disseminated light and righteousness from 1796 until her death in 1821. Under her guidance the Shakers 'travelled' and 'travailed' to resolve the tension between themselves and their alien land. Their triumph was both utilitarian and aesthetic.

Equivocation between the world and the spirit is nowhere more striking than in the Shakers' music, which is exclusively vocal as instruments were considered by them, as by many puritanical sects, to be the property of the devil. The words, inevitably, are religious; and the melodies are all monodic, since harmony was suspected of sensuality. Words and music were not composed but 'received', sometimes direct from God, sometimes from departed elders, and then 'given'. Thus received and given, the words and tunes naturally echoed the turns of phrase of Wesleyan hymnody, and the contours and rhythms of traditional, often secular, folk songs. The Shakers were so named because as they sang they shook, generating a frenzy that, according to contemporary and local opinion, accorded ill with their professed celibacy. Their self-justification was that they shook in order to shake *off* sin and stamped their feet in order to trample sensuality and the devil underground:

Shaking here, and shaking there,
People shaking everywhere.
Since I have my sins confessed,
I can shake among the rest.

We'll be shaken to and fro
Till we let old Adam go;
When our souls are born again,
We unshaken will remain.

If this is having it both ways, the cunning compromise seems to have born dividends in musical as well as material and spiritual terms. Sister Mildred Barker,[1] singing with the United Society of Shakers at Sabbathday Lake, Maine, has a voice that is purely penetrating, without the rasp typical of the singers dealt with in *The Monody of Deprivation* (pp. 44–52). The verse is usually in rhyming couplets, sometimes with internal rhymes; and each

[1] *Early Shaker Spirituals from Sabbathday Lake, Maine.*

couplet is repeated, probably to get the message across, but also to invite symmetrical bodily gyrations. Even when Shaker songs were not shaken to, they were marched or danced to, in an act of corporate solidarity, since ''Tis the union of each other/ That makes believers strong.' And so it does, as Sister Mildred sings with a steady, swinging pulse, whether it be a marching song like 'The rolling deep' (originally 'received' by Eldress Polly Lawrence in 1826), which adapts its tune from the old Scots *Drumdelgie;* or a hymn like 'The Gospel is advancing', which has ancient Gaelic musical origins; or a song such as 'Bow down O Zion', which has no specific relation to an older tune, though it stems from long-established traditions of folk modality. This hymn is one of the large number 'received' by Elder Otis Sawyer, who was musically active in Mildred Barker's community around 1870.

In many hymns and marching songs bodily movement is written into the text. The beautiful ''Tis the gift to be simple'– familiar through Aaron Copland's use of it in his *Appalachian Spring*–states that

> . . . when true simplicity is gained,
> To bow and to band we shan't be ashamed,
> To turn, to turn, will be our delight,
> Till by turning, turning we come round right.

The symmetry of the tune embodies the meaning of the words, inviting balanced movements that reflect spiritual grace in fleshly form: a grace evident too in the functional elegance of Shaker furniture, tools, household implements and dress. None the less, though Mother Lucy Wright's ministry had tended to curb the Shakers' more exuberant expression of devotional zeal, songs survive which 'take out of me all that is carnal' by treading 'nimble steps' at a brisk pace and with evident relish. Several numbers have a lilt that sounds almost feckless, making use of nonsense refrains and vocables simply to stimulate body movement, as in 'On Zion's holy ground' and 'Little children'. Occasionally the Shakers sang free-rhythmed pieces that seem to derive from reading biblical prose aloud, as in 'I looked and lo! a lamb', which transforms an eighteenth-century New England anthem into monodic incantation. More usually, however, the positive and innocent qualities of Shaker music consist in the simplicity of its unadorned modal contours, the open style of its vocal production, and the almost habitual association of symmetrical modal melodies with dance movement.

While Shakers offer the most extreme example of this tendency in monodic religious music, they are not unique. Andrew Rowan Summers,[2] for instance, a New Englander, sings fa-so-la hymns and carols in a style that preserves folk modality but maintains, over a dulcimer drone, a slow, swinging beat. His vocal tone is lyrically virginal, as though untouched by the harsh realities implicit in Sarah Ogan Gunning's lacerating or Nimrod Workman's bleak timbre. This may be because his beautiful voice had been rudimentarily trained, but a comparably mellifluous lyricism appears, especially in secular contexts, in singers whose folk origins are in no way suspect. A case in point is Sara Cleveland,[3] whose grandparents emigrated from Ireland to the United States in the mid-nineteenth century. Born in 1905, she now lives at Brant Lake, New York, and has a repertory of well over two hundred songs, many of them old ballads of Irish and Scots extraction. The innocence of her performance, like that of Andrew Rowan Summers, comes mostly from the bell-like purity of her voice, still only slightly affected by the tremulousness of old age. All the ballads – a song of unfaithful love and of remorse like 'To wear a green willow', a song of rape like 'Queen Jane', a magic ballad like 'Molly Bawn', or even a version of the grisly 'Lord Randal' – are sung with floating lyricism, fairly slow but in long-spanned, freely lilting paragraphs. Sometimes Sara Cleveland colours a word by a slight distonation of pitch – the 'over' in the last line of 'To wear a green willow', or the puns on 'time' and 'thyme' in 'The maiden's lament' (a fusion of 'The sprig of thyme' with the closely related 'Seeds of love'). The total effect of her pristine lyricism is to liberate; and this is scarcely less true of her adaptations of more recent songs from the music hall and from the Grand Ole Opry, or of the songs she makes up herself, usually from fragments of traditional material.

[2] *Hymns and Carols: Andrew Rowan Summers.*

[3] *Sara Cleveland: Ballads and Songs of the Upper Hudson Valley.*

Certainly there is nothing deprived about this delicately blooming monody; yet the innocence of the presentation does not deny experience. Clearly, however, innocence *could* be a denial, and often is so: American versions of old ballads frequently defuse passion and violence not in therapeutic lyricism but by deflation, by treating them humorously, even parodistically, or even by transforming them into children's ditties. Fortitude against hazardous odds may lead to a cockiness that, if endearing, is also slightly inane. Singing the tunes rather fast, tempering their modality to diatonicism, ironing out their metrical irregularities, may lead to a cheeriness almost irritatingly relentless. Though one *goes on*, and deserves credit for it, such going on may itself become an evasion of reality, as when Ben Mandel turns the sinister ballad 'Two brothers'[4] into a kiddies' rune, with a comically incongruous final stanza that punctures any pretension to tragedy, or even any hint of the supernatural. Similarly Jean Ritchie sings the grim ballad 'Lord Lovell'[5] with bright, lucent tone, and to a text and tune that render it blithely insouciant.

Not surprisingly, this positive evolution in American folk music becomes associated with the development of instrumental, and therefore harmonic and rhythmic, resource. The settlers took with them the fiddles that had been used at home to create body music for communal get-togethers; in the rigorous conditions of their new life this body music grew more aggressive and ultimately more virtuosic. Primitive folk dulcimers (used by Andrew Rowan Summers for the drones supporting his hymns and carols) gave way to guitar, mandolin and banjo, all plucked string instruments capable of extreme agility. When Jean Ritchie sings 'Old Bangum' to her own dulcimer accompaniment she affects a manner so jovial that the tune's origin in the ancient ballad of Lord Eglamour (or Sir Lionel in Child's version) is scarcely recognizable. Not only is the tune burlesqued, the words too divest the epic tale of its heroism and supernaturalism, leaving only a backwoods fight between a man and a boar and an ambiguous association with a wild woman, these events being set inconsequently within a nonsense refrain. Similarly

[4] *Brave Boys: New England Traditions in Folk Music.*

[5] *Child Ballads in the Southern Mountains, Sung by Jean Ritchie.*

Hedy West's accompanied version of 'Little Mattie Groves'[6] doesn't alter the text as much as Dillard Chandler's stern version mentioned above; but its jaunty speed and its diatonically harmonic refashioning of the ferocious tale make its manner comic, even satirical, especially in the two final stanzas. Indeed it is not so far in spirit from her version of 'Old Smokey', a tune which incorporates snatches of several old ballads such as 'The inconstant lover', but ends up as an indigenously American lonesome tune suggestive of minstrel show and music hall. In similar vein the North Carolina singer Frank Proffitt denatures that ancient ballad of passion and poison, 'Lord Randal',[7] by croaking it deadpan, accompanied by triadic concords on banjo, smoothing the ruffled brow of care. He can't quite convert it into the lickety-spit jauntiness he habitually favours, but does his best to deprive it of its sting. Of course an element of self-deception is involved: it isn't true that murder is no longer a threat if it can be laughed at, or that nastinesses cease to exist if swept under the carpet.

The domesticating effect of accompaniment on American secular song has a complement in instrumentally accompanied gospel music. I have related unaccompanied vocal hymnody to the monody of deprivation, and have described the process whereby the wildness of folk heterophony and homophony was tamed into social conformity in the quartet arrangements of the thirties and forties. This process is accelerated by the use of banjo or guitar accompaniment, which substitutes sociability for the religious impulse. This can be heard even in Walter and Lola Caudwell's 1934 version of 'Bright and morning star':[8] although the male and female voices sing primitively an octave apart, with imperfect co-ordination of both rhythm and pitch, and with folk-style ornamentation and scoops, it is clear that the performers would welcome synchrony if they could attain it. Harry and Jeanie West,[9] who hail from Virginia and North Carolina respectively, achieve synchrony unambiguously. Their duet singing of hymns derived from eighteenth- and

[6] *Hedy West: Pretty Saro and Other Appalachian Ballads.*
[7] *Frank Proffitt: Northern Carolina Songs and Ballads.*
[8] *I'm on My Journey Home.*
[9] *White Gospel Songs, Sung by Harry and Jeanie West.*

nineteenth-century tradition is always accompanied by banjo or sometimes mandolin, guitar or dobro. Any hint of modality is banished from the simple harmonic structure; voices are dovetailed, often in parallel thirds; antiphony, if employed, is neatly symmetrical. The style of performance does not vary, whether they are singing traditional hymns like 'Amazing grace', white spirituals like 'Campin' in Canaan's ground', moralizing numbers like 'Only one more step', or newly created pieces like 'I'm only on a journey here'. In all these songs there is a link with folk tradition in that the voices are not prettified but preserve a hard edge suggesting that the hymns' self-righteous certitudes, having been hard won, are worth respect. None the less, the experience lacks any sense of the numinous, and the habituation of the moderate tempo and the cosiness of the harmony are unshaken by the introduction of fire-eating biblical quotations or topical references in the text. The unfailing–one might uncharitably say remorseless–clitter-clatter of the banjo generates enthusiasm as Harry West shout-sings the message, which Jeanie embroiders and echoes with arabesques of assent, representing the voice of the people. The total effect is to encourage acceptance of one's arduous lot, and so to reinforce the white euphoria. But if the development of instrumental resource tends to denature the spirituality of religious folk music, it brings positive compensations to secular contexts, where, in country music for scraped and plucked strings, it inculcates a therapy of corporeal assent.

A THERAPY OF CORPOREAL ASSENT: MUSIC FOR SCRAPED AND PLUCKED STRINGS

White American country fiddle music has well-established roots in the Old World, as the settlers took with them both their instruments and the repertory of dance tunes played on them. Basically, the country fiddle, in America as in Scotland and Ireland, is an ordinary violin employed in styles more typical of the functional techniques of Europe's Middle Ages and Renaissance than of the lyrically expressive techniques of the seventeenth, eighteenth and nineteenth centuries. The fiddle, for the white American country player as for the medieval or Renaissance peasant, was an instrument for moving to. Played held against the chest, with a flat bridge and sometimes an arched bow, it was adept at marking metrical accents and at reinforcing sonority by the use of open-stringed drones; but was inefficient at sustaining melody stimulating to the soul rather than to cavorting legs, arms and trunk. What it was designed to do, it did brilliantly, potently complementing the monody of deprivation. The singing of an Aunt Molly Jackson or a Nimrod Workman pares the Old World's experience to its barest bone, holding on to it for grim life; the fiddling of the early string bands abandons everything to the hedonism of the present moment, manifest in our whirling limbs. Such music embodies innocence, as Nimrod Workman's embodies experience, but it is not necessarily escapist–if only because the music's sheer speed may entail an element of danger.

Southern fiddle styles varied regionally, though all betray their roots in old Scots and Irish tradition. Especially close to the Old World is Luther Strong's performance of 'The last of Sizemore',[10] even though this version of a Scots A major reel, commemorating a local hanging, dates from as recently as 1937. The drone-dominated texture and the wailing pentatonic arabesques in the Kentuckian AEAE tuning preserve much of the wildness, even the mystery, of ancient Scots, especially Shetland style. More usually, Kentucky style fosters the white euphoria by presenting the tunes very fast, with a tone at once sweet and open. Alva Greene's version of 'Hunky dory'[11] is typical of this merry domesticity, which is boosted not only by drones, but by 'fiddlesticks'–a rhythmic ostinato played on fiddle strings with a set of knitting needles. A further process of domestication is revealed in a version of 'That's my rabbit',[12] made by the Walter family, who came from Nicholasville in Kentucky. The fiddle tune is accompanied by 'found' instruments such as jug and washboard as well as by domestic piano and guitar. Even the most famous of Kentucky fiddlers, Arthur Smith, whose virtuosity brought him some national celebrity during the thirties, did not allow his pyrotechnics seriously to

[10] *That's my Rabbit: Traditional Southern Instrumental Styles.*
[11] Ibid. [12] Ibid.

threaten homeliness. Although Smith played traditional reels he was especially partial to rags picked up from radio and recordings. Rag was the southern black man's attempt at a 'civilized' music competing with that of his masters; in his 'Peacock rag'[13] Arthur Smith imbues a Kentucky fiddle tune with something of rag's dandified elegance.

Charming though this is, old-time fiddle music fascinates most when it most chances its wildly whirling arm. The obscure Carter Brothers offer an appropriately tipsy version of 'Give the fiddler a dram',[14] in which the excitement derives from their failure to co-ordinate their lines. Technical virtuosity may imply some degree of emotional complexity too, for one cannot walk a tightrope without a tremor of fear lest one might fall off. The Carter Brothers' 'mistakes' prove not to be errors since they are the core of the music's forcefulness. Similarly, when the Georgian Fiddlin' John Carson[15] sings to his fiddle, his vocal style–whether he is singing an old ballad like 'The honest farmer' or a relatively new lonesome railway train number like 'I'm nine hundred miles from home'–is traditionally scrawny, while the fiddle part, raucous if sustaining in open-stopped chords and bagpipe-like drones, is far from jolly. However, when he lets loose with his fiddle and uses his voice mainly for intermittent shouts or for calling the numbers in a square dance–as he does in 'Corn licker and barbecue', 'Sugar in the gourd', 'Engineer on the Mogul', or in his extraordinary, dervish-like, Mixolydian version of 'Cotton-eyed Joe'–the music's ostensible subservience to social function becomes a corybantic release, comparable with the excesses of gospel music. The near-crazy zest of the performance produces a music that is not merely a merry noise for dancing to, but is also a simultaneously social and personal ritual act. White fervour acquires something of the immediate reality of the black blues: indeed black influence permeated white instrumental music irresistibly, whether or not the players were willing to admit to it. It is evident in the work of all the Georgian fiddle bands that

13 Ibid.

14 *Echoes of the Ozarks, Volume 1: Arkansas String Bands 1927–1930.* See also *Old Time Music at Charlie Ashley's.*

15 *Fiddlin' John Carson: The Old Hen Cackled, the Rooster's Gonna Crow.* Carson was the first country musician to be recorded commercially.

flourished in the twenties and thirties, such as the Hometown Boys, the Georgian Organ Grinders and, most notably, Earl Johnson's Clodhoppers,[16] who give a breathtaking performance–very fast, with bouncing spiccato and inebriated slides–of the popular nineteenth-century number, 'Sourwood mountain'. Johnson himself had some training as a straight violinist–unlike Fiddlin' John Carson, an empiricist whose mistakes were the essence of his genius. None the less Johnson's relative technical competence did not affect the folk fervour of his music; it reinforced rather than dampened his exuberance.

In a neighbouring state, Louisiana, we find a minor tributary of euphoric country fiddle music which seems poles apart from the rabid Georgians; and is so, in that the Acadians were originally French Canadians, exiled in the eighteenth century as a consequence of the British–American wars. In Louisiana's amiable climate they continued to speak French or a French patois, and cultivated a smilingly relaxed music that matched their new environment. Their music, perhaps because they were 'foreigners' at a comparatively late stage in the development of polyglot American culture, is the most eclectic on the continent: folk songs stemming from seventeenth- and eighteenth-century France and old French contredanses merge unselfconsciously with southern American mountain songs, absorbing Negro blues, Tex-Mex tangos, cowboy songs and Tin Pan Alley hits *en route*. The Cajuns, as they came to be pronounced in their new land, favoured the French valse and two-step, yet both are often served with a Spanish or Latin American sauce, and are liable to be metamorphosed into jigs that sound like continental versions of Irish reels, or into American hoedowns, which had in any case absorbed the European quadrille, schottische and polka. Vocal production is more French and Latin American than North American: high and slightly fierce, in contrast to the relaxed instrumental sonorities of guitars, banjos, and French café accordions. Melodically, the fiddle remains the lead instrument. A Floyd LeBlanc, a Wallace 'Cheese' Reed or an Austin Pitre plays waltzes, jigs, stomps and breakdowns in a bright, sharp style affected by the southern American country fiddling heard in the neighbouring states,

[16] *Georgia Fiddle Bands.*

but with a warmth and vivacity that are no less clearly European.[17] Wallace Reed's 'French jig', 'Waltz of the wayside', 'Rabbit stomp' and 'Empty bottle stomp' are mildly virtuosic performances that are none the less eupeptic. Cajun music seems to be oblivious of pain and danger–which means that its charm needs a social context. The players have no doubt that wine and women should accompany this song.

Cajun fiddle music is perhaps American only by adoption and by courtesy. But if it is regarded as the opposite pole to the wild Georgian and Arkansas fiddle music, the most rewarding American fiddling could be said to effect a compromise between Georgian savagery and Louisianan amiability. The Kessinger Brothers of West Virginia favoured, indeed still do favour, a moderate, jogging tempo in comparison with the whirligig Georgians, and a tone which, although penetrating, is pure and sweet. What prevents their music from degenerating into cosiness is an occasional omitted or added beat, giving the music an uneasy edge. In the Kessinger tradition is the work of a much younger man, J. P. Fraley,[18] most active in his native East Kentucky during the sixties and seventies. With guitar accompaniment by his wife Annadeene, he creates a lyrical line as pure as the Kessingers', but still more expressive in its irregular rhythms–no less subtle than the *notes inégales* of classical French tradition–and in its microtonally distorted pitch. Although the music sounds American rather than Scots, the relatively slow performance of 'Wild rose of the mountain' preserves, or re-creates, much of the haunting, other-worldly quality of the ancient tradition. But this was not, of course, music of the future or even of the present. Fraley's music is an anachronism, a creation of revivalist fervour, remarkable none the less for the immediacy with which it is presented.

Although American fiddle music had deep roots in the Scots and Irish traditions which Fraley resuscitates, it was from the start as ethnically varied as the continent that produced it; and became more so as the fiddlers increasingly collaborated with the plucked string players on clawhammer banjo, guitar and mandolin. This development is neatly illustrated by a comparison

[17] *Music of the Louisiana Acadians.*

[18] *J. P. and Annadeene Fraley: Wild Rose of the Mountain.*

of the two finest string bands flourishing in the twenties and thirties. Gid Tanner and his Skillet Lickers,[19] playing 'Skillet licker breakdown' or 'Back up and push' in 1931, create a 'rip roarin' free for all' directly in the tradition of the Georgian fiddle bands. Clayton McMichen and Lowe Stokes fiddle with short, stabbing bow strokes, both emulating and stimulating body movement; Fat Norris's banjo functions mainly as a rhythmic instrument; Gid Tanner sings high and strained, often in falsetto; while blind Riley Puckett fills in with his celebrated, empirically plucked, three- or four-chord runs on guitar. Old folk songs, Yankee military tunes, hymns and minstrel-show dances equally are grist to their fast-pounding mill, and the genres are not differentiated. The countrified abandon characteristic of the Skillet Lickers is more tightly–and more artistically–controlled by Charlie Poole and his North Carolina Ramblers playing, a year earlier, 'Milwaukee blues'.[20] The piece is in fact not a blues but a story song with the familiar railway background, the regular progress of the train being represented by Fred Harvey's steady guitar bass–which could hardly be further removed from Riley Puckett's double- and quadruple-time capers. Odel Smith's fiddle, played with relatively long bow strokes, is bluely expressive rather than merely an impulse to bodily movement. Charlie Poole's banjo similarly functions as a melody instrument, not simply as rhythmic support. It is from the sophisticated interplay between the two melodic parts and the beat that the jazzy, urban impact of the resolutely diatonic music derives. Although Georgian savagery has been disciplined, the jazzy flavour retains a hint of danger.

The banjo seems to have been transported from Africa to the West Indies in the late seventeenth century, and was established in the United States by about 1870. It became popular through being used as the instrument of white black-faced minstrels, who presumably were emulating the black slaves they heard on the plantations. Little is known about the music enslaved blacks played on their banjos, but there seems little doubt that southern mountain whites acquired their 'frailing' technique (in which the strings are struck downwards with the back of the fingernails, the thumb being dropped out)

[19] *Bluegrass for Collectors.* [20] *Going Down the Valley.*

directly from late nineteenth-century minstrel shows. Slightly later, probably influenced by the guitar, finger-picking technique (in which the tune is picked out by a finger or plectrum, while two other fingers chitter in a rapid drone) was introduced. The melodic line comes out as sharp, hard, and agile. Some banjos were equipped with a fifth string or chanterelle, used mostly for drones. The five-string banjo could be readily adapted to the Scots and Irish fiddle tunes which were the staple repertory of dance music. This was a superficial reason for the instrument's popularity with mountain whites; a deeper reason was that the banjo's relatively easy virtuosity fostered the white euphoria. It was not fortuitous that the banjo had been so basic a part of the black-faced minstrel shows wherein white men attempted to laugh away the threat of blackness.

So the banjo, appropriated by whites, was an equivocal instrument. In that it encouraged the use of drones it could be accommodated to old-fashioned modal melodies; in that it was metrically percussive and capable of extreme agility it provoked mirth, usually in fast, square-rhythmed, diatonic dances. When Mr and Mrs Henry Judd of Irving, Kentucky, perform a representative banjo song like 'Granny went to meeting with her shoes on',[21] the music can be related to country fiddle style, although its comfortable gait and its amiable nonsense words bring the song closer to the parlour than to outdoor festivity. Parlour solos were written for banjo, calling on a three- or four-finger plucking style similar to that of the classical guitar. Pieces like Jutis Begley's 'Run banjo'[22] or Pete Steele's 'Spanish fandango'[23]–originally improvised but, then, by popular demand, notated in sheet form–are jolly low-class salon music rather than folk art; and although the first of the great banjo men, Uncle Dave Macon,[24] sometimes sang and played traditional tunes like the folk fiddlers, he was, with his plug hat, gates-a-jar collar and flashing gold tooth, basically a minstrel-show and vaudeville entertainer. Born in Tennessee in 1870 he was active as an entertainer almost to the day of his death in 1952. A spiritual like 'Shout Monah, you shall be free', a country waltz version of 'Over the mountain' with yodelling refrain, an

[21] *That's my Rabbit.* [22] Ibid. [23] Ibid.

[24] *Uncle Dave Macon, the Dixie Dewdrop.*

anti-evolution song like 'The Bible's true', a rehash of a work song like 'Hold that wood-pile down', a banjo solo version of the hymn 'Will there be any stars in my crown?' or even a song of the Depression years like his own 'All in down and out blues', are scarcely differentiated in style of performance. All are briskly extrovert, relying more on personal charisma than on musical ability. Nor is there much difference in kind between the virtuosity he displays in a novelty number like 'Tennessee red fox chase' (a comedy technique borrowed directly from the fiddlers) and the exuberance with which he puts over a hot gospel number such as 'From Jerusalem to Jericho'.

Although Dave Macon drew heavily on minstrel-show material which must have had black roots, that darker shade is scarcely discernible in his eupeptically white music. It becomes increasingly evident, however, as banjo tradition matures, admitting within its machine-gun virtuosity an element of danger comparable to that of the fiddlers. The legendary Dock Boggs,[25] who came from the South Virginia mountains, worked in the mines as a truck driver until the toll on his health prompted him to become a semi-professional musician. Most of the songs he sang seek release from toil in what might seem to be escapism were it not that the songs fail to make him happy. Like the Negro blues, which he clearly listened to attentively, Dock Boggs's music is in part therapy. His 1963 version of a song of the Depression years which he labels 'Country blues' is played in a style dating back to the early thirties. Verbally, the number gloomily celebrates the joys of sex, drink and gambling, appending an evangelistically moral coda; musically, the wailing pitch and wandering rhythm have an affinity with the field holler, giving a suppressed passion to the nagging numbness or vacuous inanity typical of a Dave Macon. In becoming niggerly the music ceases to be niggardly; Boggs maintains that he learned his own 'Down south blues' from an old 'race' record from which he made a banjo accompaniment, before adding his own words. 'My old horse died' borrows from both black blues and minstrel music; 'Pretty Polly' begins as amiable country music but grows jazzier as it gains momentum. The positive aspects of black influence can be heard in an instrumental

[25] *Dock Boggs.*

number, 'Coal creek march', in effect a banjo rag in the usual two-step convention: fairly virtuosic (and therefore precarious) in figuration, often stridently if fortuitously dissonant, with exhilarating cross-rhythms in the coda.

Even when playing in the merry manner Dock Boggs remains, as do all the banjo soloists, totally impassive. The faster the banjoists' fingers fly, and they can flicker very fast, the more deadpan is their demeanour. It is as though they are afraid that if they didn't hold on, still as a stone, they might, given the excitation, collapse. Again, instrumental virtuosity proves to be the heads side of the coin whose tails is the monody of deprivation. The singers adopt a trance-like stance, hand cupped to listening ear; the instrumentalists are as motionless as statues. Both hold on through their objectivity, dehumanizing themselves in the interests of survival.

The guitar, fashionable in polite European societies from the middle of the seventeenth century, took longer than the banjo to establish itself in the United States. It is, perhaps, natural that it should belong to a later stage of musical development, as it is a chordal instrument and therefore lends itself to harmonic sophistication. Not surprisingly, the guitar was avidly seized on by black men in their alien land; its ability to speak melodically, with infinite subtlety of nuance, meant that it could join in dialogue with the Negro's voice as he spoke-sung his blues. At the same time the diatonic chords of white march and hymn could be employed in unexpected contexts. Conversely, when white men took over the guitar they used it to deeper, or darker, effect than they had used the banjo or fiddle.

Several parlour pieces for guitar survive in folk tradition, the melody picked on high strings by the index and middle fingers with the thumb supplying a counterpoint or drone in the bass. However, pieces in this manner–such as 'Pearly dew',[26] 'The siege of Sebastopol' and the 'Spanish fandango' referred to previously in its banjo version–are less significant than the semi-improvised numbers that adapt black blues style, the fretted upper strings played slightly off-beat while the ball of the right hand damps the bass strings to produce an ostinato-like pulsation. Hobart Smith,[27] a white musician born in Virginia in

[26] *That's my Rabbit.* [27] *Hobart Smith: The Old Timey Rap.*

1897, was expert on fiddle, banjo and piano as well as guitar, but he turned to the guitar for his most personal and impassioned utterance. Interestingly, he learned banjo from a white labourer, John Greer, who 'went from the thumb string to the bottom, double-notin' and he was the best man I ever heard on the banjo, and I patterned after him'. When Smith was 14 or 15, he met black guitar-playing Blind Lemon Jefferson, who 'came through and stayed with the other coloured fellows. They worked on the railroad there and he'd just play and sing to entertain the men in that work camp. I liked his type of playing. I just watched his fingers and got the music in my head, then I'd thumb around till I found what I was wantin' on the strings.'[28] Black blues was thus directly a formative influence on Hobart Smith's music: though it is significant, in view of his white banjo-picking heritage, that even on guitar he favours fast tempi, despite his black distortions of pitch and his jazzily driving rhythms. The exuberant (real) blues recorded in 1942 is a classic example of fast western barrel-house style, re-created in terms of solo guitar; it has affinities with his fine numbers exploiting the myth of the American railway train. It is interesting, however, that Smith himself regarded as his star number his southern reworking of the old English 'Cuckoo bird', the English lyricism of which blooms in the dusty American landscape.

A similar but even richer fusion of English and American sources can be heard in the playing of Doc Watson,[29] the supreme country guitarist who gives a black musician, Mississippi Fred Hurt, credit for providing his initial impetus. Blind from early childhood, Doc Watson made a living by entertaining the inhabitants of Boone, North Carolina, where he came from and, now internationally celebrated, still lives. Undoubtedly his blindness, like that of innumerable epic bards and blues singers, fostered his dedication to his natural talent. Even when he plays a real country number like 'Muskrat', on jazzily syncopated harmonica as well as guitar, he creates a music that is far from merely eupeptic, let alone amnesiac. This virtuosity is not mindless since the cross-accents (especially the division of rapid

[28] Quotations from the sleeve note to *Hobart Smith: The Old Timey Rap*.
[29] *Doc Watson and Son*.

eights into 3 plus 3 plus 2) are so nervy, the variety of sonority and texture so titillating. Often, as in his version of 'Weary blues', he sings and plays an authentic twelve-bar blues, taking it rather fast maybe, and with a comic ironic undertow, but none the less with potently melancholy blue notes and with quasi-vocal note-bendings and slides: black reality is not effaced by white, apparently throwaway, humour. This is the case because the humour is itself emotionally tough, unlike that of a straight-forward entertainer such as Uncle Dave Macon. Doc Watson's humour is a moral stance; his exuberance is never evasive. His pyrotechnics in an instrumental number like 'Beaumont rag' are perilous and, because here physical well-being thrives on danger, the ear-boggling virtuosity is at once technical and emotional: he keeps going, despite desperate odds. Watson is equally capable of singing an old *Southern Harmony* hymn like 'The faithful soldier' unaccompanied, with an austerely committed simplicity comparable with Almeda Riddle's or even Nimrod Workman's.

Doc Watson was a countryman by birth and upbringing, and he made his music from his world. He is also a distinguished representative of a popular culture and of an industry. The music he makes now suggests that, once country music had become more widely relevant, reality entered it positively, by way of instrumental virtuosity, and negatively, through *cross*-rhythms, *false* relations, *dis*tortions of pitch, all elements relatable to the black blues. In growing to adulthood, white country music had to fuse its negative pole, the monody of deprivation, with its positive pole, the white euphoria; and these poles needed the catalyst of the black blues to spark them off. This is evident in Watson's sequence of blues–black, white and commercially orientated–'Country blues', 'Nashville blues', 'St James's Hospital', 'Deep river blues'.[30] The white–black alchemy is not basically a matter of musical technique. White euphoria could prosper, in conditions of white indigence, only at the expense of the once enslaved and still exploited black man; growing up, embracing reality, meant absorbing the black man's blue music at however unconscious a level.

But the man who in his singing, banjo- and guitar-playing

[30] *Doc Watson.*

most movingly embraces and synthesizes all the strands of the American experience is not the virtuosic Doc Watson, but a man who owes the intensity of his musicianship to his non-professionalism: Roscoe Holcomb,[31] a Kentuckian whose music was born and bred in the mountains. In the sixties and seventies he found himself making a few concert appearances on the circuits and in universities, but he has never and does not intend to become a professional musician. Tall, lean and austere, he works in lumber camps, supports the Baptist Church, and thinks of his music as a service to the community. This service is not, however, mere entertainment: 'You know music, it's spiritual. You can take just a small kid, I've noticed, that can't even sit alone, and you pull the strings on some kind of instrument, fiddle or banjo, you watch how quick it draws the attention of that kid. . . . It draws the attention of the whole human race.'[32] Such commitment informs all the music Holcomb makes. Especially after singing unaccompanied, he is likely to be 'wrung out', physically and spiritually exhausted. His heyday as a performer was during the early sixties and, although the music he created then harked back to earlier days, it was not old-time music since everything he does is re-created. He came from a little town with the pristine name of Daisy, but worked in a place with the allegorically more dangerous name of Hazard where, even in 1959, economic conditions were extremely difficult. His unaccompanied songs are marvellous examples of the monody of deprivation. He sings them loud, high and clear, in his mountain-style tenor, the first notes usually long, protracted, as though calling across the open hills. The manner is not expressive, certainly not 'beautiful': yet the dislocations of rhythm and distonations of pitch give to the lines a heroic poignancy. The more personally involved Holcomb feels, the more marked this is. 'Moonshine', a straightforward song, he presents impersonally, with the long modal line and the sustained initial bleats grandly objectifying the pathos of the illusory panaceas in which we seek refuge. But a song like 'A

[31] *Roscoe Holcomb and Wade Ward; Roscoe Holcomb: The High, Lonesome Sound* and *Mountain Music of Kentucky*.

[32] Quotations from the sleeve notes to *Roscoe Holcomb and Wade Ward, Roscoe Holcomb: The High, Lonesome Sound* and *Mountain Music of Kentucky*.

man of constant sorrow' invites self-identification. Holcomb sings it frequently, each time experiencing it afresh, and achieving by microtonal modifications of pitch or contractions of rhythm minor miracles of expressivity. Still more remarkable is his unaccompanied singing of the Baptist hymns which have been a moral bulwark in his life. 'Wandering boy', for instance, he sings with melismatic roulades that seem to hark back to the darkness of antiquity. The pitch is high and the timbre piercing, but the pulse is so immensely slow, under the weight of feeling, that the line seems about to collapse. The words appeal to Mother and God to save him from sin; the music explains why that is a lot to ask. Most remarkable of all is another hymn from the *Old Baptist Song Book*, 'Little Bessie', recorded at his home in 1962. He supports his voice with guitar, but uses it only as a drone which makes his monodic line sound even more ancient. Time almost stops, so tortoise-like is his pace. The lacerating distonations and the gigantic elongations of syllables are so physically painful that one is more aware of the agony of living than of the potential solace of death. The obliteration of the sense of time may offer release to the small dying girl but no prospect of pie in the sky. Although there is religious conviction in the lyricism which Holcomb wrings out of anguish, his God grants no easy solutions.

Yet there is more in Holcomb's monody than the mere will to survive, such as characterizes the performance of Nimrod Workman. This is obvious when he takes up his banjo, on which his playing is always resilient but never mindless. 'Black-eyed Susie', an old square-dance tune, he takes very fast, using the frailing technique, while preserving in the vocal line an acerbity appropriate to the jittery quality in the man–girl relationship. An old broadside ballad like 'True love' has a comparably nervous equilibrium between wry vocal line and chittering banjo; and some of the simplest traditional tunes–for instance, 'Little birdie'–are subjected to the most devastating contortions of pitch, as in the phrase, 'I *won't* be with you long.' Holcomb's traditional numbers are always re-created; his versions of 'Fair miss in the garden' (an American country rehash of the Ulysses story), 'Willow tree', or 'Across the rocky mountain', are assembled from fragments of several interrelated songs. Holcomb claims that he 'composed' them in that 'that's how you write a song–you take verses from other songs and put them together to make a story'. He does not think of these quasi-traditional songs as different in kind from a narrative song like 'Coombs Hotel burned down' which describes, in archaic modal formulae, a topical and local event.

Sometimes Holcomb substitutes for banjo his guitar which he plays, if not with the technical expertise of Doc Watson, with much of the plangency of blind, black Lemon Jefferson; for whose music he, like Hobart Smith, has confessed an admiration. Jefferson probably influenced his vocal technique as well, for the deprived white intensity of his vocal production is usually modified by a black resonance. An *ad hoc* twelve-bar blues of his own, 'Stingy woman blues', exploits the primitive black technique of the tumbling strain without compromising his habitual pinched whiteness. His version of the traditional black 'Graveyard blues' remains personal while being blue enough to be mistaken for the real thing. Inextricably meshed in whiteness and blackness is his version of the nobly modal 'The rising sun', the origins of which are themselves ambiguously black or white: the displacements of rhythm and of intonation on, for instance, the words 'rising sun', 'listen' and 'youngest brother' have an immediacy that amounts to empirical genius. A single note, suddenly flattened, preserves the reality of the blackness of the holler 'Trouble in mind', but allows it still to sound like white Baptist incantation. Conversely, when Holcomb plays the English ballad 'Barbara Allen' on his mouth harp he imbues it, by slides, wails and fluctuations of pitch, with the dark poignancy of the blues. The lyrical loveliness of this most ubiquitous of British ballads remains; the lonesomeness it acquires is profoundly American.

Holcomb's version of 'In the pines', a number which significantly appears in both black and white traditions, epitomizes his contribution as well as any single song can. In some versions a narrative explanation is given for the girl's vigil in the pines. Holcomb eschews any mention of railway accidents or the like, presenting instead a song which is the quintessence of loneliness. He pitches the line very high without calling on falsetto; the tone sounds as impersonal as the wind itself, yet the 'shiver' the cold wind induces contains *lacrimae rerum*–not just his or the girl's loneliness, but that inherent in the human condition. At the same time the melody is so beautiful and the guitar figuration so serene that the song offers solace rather than despair. We do not think of such music as old time or country, but simply as human. Simultaneously white and black, religious and secular, it needs no justification but its truth–all the more valuable as 'reality' is increasingly absorbed by professionalism and commercialization.

The conventional norm of commercialized country music, as represented during and after the Second World War by Lulla Belle and Scotty Wiseman, does all it can to evade that reality, typified at its finest in the music of Roscoe Holcomb. Whereas Holcomb's songs, balanced between impulses white and black, are pervaded by *false relations* in several senses, Wiseman's commercialized music is unambiguous. Tempo is always *moderate*; leading notes always *lead* and dominants *dominate* in white certitude; metres move squarely together in military formation: concordant triads conform and are comfortable. There is a political dimension to this; during the McCarthy era Wiseman produced anti-Communist numbers to assert that what I have I hold.

Of course, it would be to oversimplify to equate commercialized white country music with political and musical reaction, since the commercial motive, which treats music as a commodity, is to some degree endemic in any evolution from the folk's 'music of necessity' to art. This is evident in the manner in which, from the forties onwards, country string bands succumbed to commercialization. Although this may have been a corruption, it was not all loss. In effect it means that they changed their nature and function in becoming relevant to the modern, urban world.

4

The Liquidation of Tragedy and Guilt

BLUE GRASS MUSIC

Throughout the twentieth century, fiddlers, banjo players, guitarists and mandolinists have collaborated to make music for social and domestic use. The Hometown Boys, the Skillet Lickers and the North Carolina Ramblers started in the twenties as servants of their community, though their influence spread as they were heard, on the radio circuits and on records, by a far more widely spaced and more ethnically varied public. Later groups were made as much by the radio and record industry as by the communities they came from, and as the technique became more professional, so the message changed. The music of the most decisively influential of the blue grass groups, the Monroe Brothers, presents the Old Times not merely as a way of life one relishes and finds supportive, but also as a panacea for the nervous and maybe physical stresses occasioned by big city life. The white euphoria achieves a positive apotheosis. True, the songs of the Monroe Brothers set banal verses covering the conventional themes of (usually frustrated) Love, Home, Mother, Country, God and Disaster. True, the tunes, even when modally inflected, are strongly influenced by evangelical hymnody, the solo line being supported by two or three 'backers' in parallel thirds, in rigid four-bar phrases in common or three-quarter tempo, with a mean diet of three or four rudimentary chords (basically the I, IV, V, I of hymnody). Even when the tunes are old and originally modal, it is only seldom–Wade Mainer's version of 'Little Maggie'[1] is a case in point–that

[1] *Going Down the Valley.*

the modal flat seventh is allowed to affect the harmony or to encourage microtonal embellishments in the fiddle part. More normally–as in the Callahan Brothers' version of 'Katie dear'[2] or Tom Asley's 1931 version of the ubiquitous 'Corinna, Corinna'[3]–the gaps in the scale are filled in by harmony notes, so that no trace of modality survives. Cheeriness is unremitting: Charlie Monroe and his Kentucky Pardners even present a version of that heart-rending ballad of love and murder, 'Down in the willow garden',[4] from which wistfulness, let alone yearning and horror, has been banished by a daft waltz. Although it is good to feel good, one has to admit that one can do so here only by a taboo on tenderness. Such brutal inanity extends to an instrumentally accompanied disaster song, an offshoot of the monodic protest songs of the Kentucky mining areas. Bill Clifton and his Dixie Mountain Boys fashion another idiot waltz out of 'The Springhill mining disaster',[5] in which more than a hundred men lost their lives, telling us that 'We sang through the pain but our prayers were in vain.' Notwithstanding the conventional tribute of a minor instead of a major triad in the refrain, one would hardly expect God to respond to anything so mindlessly and heartlessly vacuous. Here, in the white euphoria, Amnesia Rules.

This is far from the whole story, for, given a certain level of musical distinction, apparently mindless vivacity may represent genuine courage. As early as 1938 the Delmore Brothers recorded in South Carolina a Depression song which hits back at the misery of being 'Fifteen miles from Birmingham' with the blues-infected springiness of their vocal rhythm, the liveliness of their guitar picking, and elastic-rhythmed, sweet-toned fiddling. Later, in the hands of the masters, the blue grass amalgam of traditional ballads, gospel songs and corn-shucking banjo and fiddle dances is remote from the complacent platitudes of a Scotty Wiseman. Why this is so becomes clear as we listen to Bill Monroe's performance of a number by himself and Lester Flatt. Bill Monroe's Blue Grass Boys included Lester Flatt in charge of rapidly liquid guitar figuration. The no less legendary Earl Scruggs played lead on five-string banjo,

[2] Ibid. [3] Ibid. [4] *Bluegrass for Collectors.*
[5] *Hills and Home, 30 Years of Bluegrass.*

adapting the three-finger picking technique previously exploited by Charles Poole and promoting it from an accompanying to a virtuosic solo function. Monroe himself sang the tunes in a high, hard, sometimes falsetto tenor, overriding the momentary shocks and agonies that the tenor of a Roscoe Holcomb is subject to. At the same time he played a very loud 40-year-old mandolin in a driving syncopated idiom influenced by both white breakdown and black blues, while Charlie Wise added flickering descants on folk fiddle. By this time, 1945, country style has been overtly modified by urban jazz, and the jazz element, with the melody lines prancing across the downbeats of Howard Watts's bass and Flatt's heavy, old-fashioned American Martin D-45 guitar, is the heart of the music's vivacity. The words of 'Why did you wander?'[6] deal cornily enough with a broken love relationship and the promise of pie in the sky when the lovers are celestially reunited. The music ironically reverses the words, but does more than that: the breathtaking speed and acrobatic virtuosity act like a jazz break. At this hair-raising lick misfortune is impossible. Faithlessly wandering girls and Death himself are annihilated in the dangerous present, as the pickin' and pluckin' drive onwards in desperate jubilation. Time is effaced in whirling arms and flying feet and heaven is here and now, and nice work if you can get it. The tipsy excitation is wish-fulfilment made momentarily actual–all one can know of a haven in which lover and beloved can seem to be together, as they were in their old mountain home. Musically, the pounding beat never threatens to 'wander'. Home is precisely where they've got to, as bass bounces, banjo chatters, guitar ripples, fiddle twitters and dobro gobbles in an eternally youthful present.

No less exhilarating is Bill Monroe's version of 'Mule skinner blues'[7] a number made famous by Jimmie Rodgers, though it probably had traditional roots. Monroe's voice has a high, strained tension, periodically released in falsetto yells; his mule driver's yodels are a spontaneous extension of the whirligigs of Tommy Magnes's violin and the sharp cross-accents and cutting false relations on mandolin and guitar. There never was a music more rooted in the human body. When Charlie Monroe and his

[6] Ibid. [7] *Bluegrass for Collectors*, and see also *Flatt and Scruggs*.

Kentucky Pardners maintain that 'Mother's not dead, she's only sleeping',[8] the tune may be banal, but the effect is bravely resilient. Too much is going on, musically, for the number to sound cynical, as 'The Springhill mining disaster' did. Death is not made light of, even though the music seems to snigger at it. Given this attitude, it is not surprising that evangelical traditions can be embraced by blue grass euphoria, as in the Stanley Brothers' diatonic but metrically intricate call-and-response patterns in 'Daniel prayed'.[9] This is similar in principle to the antiphony of black gospel music, which in turn relates to the improvised dialogue of jazz. As with solo singers, country music groups grow up when their country manners come to terms with the reality of black jazz–as in Don Reno and the Tennessee Cutups' version of 'Love, please come home',[10] with its disturbing ambivalence between the tonic and the *chord* of the blue flat seventh, and complex cross-rhythms in the final chorus. Still more exciting is Jim and Jesse McReynolds' 'Diesel train',[11] based on the traditional (if now dieselized) railway image. The railway track, a metaphor recurrent in the black man's blues, also pervades the music of the white ramblin' man, carrying him far from his beloved, across the vast American continent on an endless journey to no end. Jazz-orientated country music rides the rails to and through the town. In this limbo hobo black and poor white meet, as near as makes no odds, on equal terms.

COWBOY MUSIC AND WESTERN SWING

Another aspect of the white euphoria, later to fuse country music with urban jazz, can be found in the cowboy music which, sung over the immense plains stretching from Montana in the North to Nevada, Arizona, New Mexico, and Texas in the South, was patently a music about journeys to no discernible end. Cowpunching began in the first two decades after the civil war, but its heyday was brief. During its slow decline from the late nineteenth to the mid-twentieth century, the cowboys, originally called herders, were easy riders with no past and little

[8] Ibid. [9] *Hills and Home, 30 Years of Bluegrass.* [10] Ibid. [11] Ibid.

future. The life was hard, and the cowboys were itinerant and usually young, coming mostly from the southern states. Some were of British, especially Irish, descent; occasionally a Negro found himself among them, bringing with him a repertory of songs which the whites took over without being influenced by black singing styles. Untinged by blackness, the cowboy was an aggressively primitive version of the westward-migrating white loner: in 1875 Laura Winthrop Johnson described them as 'rough men with shaggy hair and wild staring eyes, in butternut trousers stuffed into great rough boots'. Any glamour they possessed came from their superficial accoutrements–Spanish sombreros, Indian beads and elaborately buttoned trousers. Quite a few of them were criminals on the run; all, from the civil war era onwards, had inherited a taste for violence and bloodshed. Their desperado-like nature sprang from the dullness of their lives and the lack of inherited traditions. As so often, violence was counterpoised by an arrant sentimentality. Riding the vast plains, they moonily dreamed of love and brotherhood; the dreams turned into the rowdiness of the drinking and whoring they relished at the end of the trail.

The music they made stemmed from the life they lived.[12] One type of song was amnesiac rather than euphoric, its purpose being to soothe potentially rampant beasts and to while away empty time in empty space. The other main type of music was orgiastic: shanty-town music at the trail's end, for released bodies and footloose feet. The riding songs, which were naturally performed unaccompanied, are more numerous and more interesting. Sometimes they are no more than brief pentatonic hollers of crudely functional intent–as in 'Cowboys getting up holler'–though the raucous vocal timbre of the cowboy, self-exiled on the plains from his own tribe, seems to have lacked the plangency that the Negro, deprived by others of his past and culture, put into his cotton-field hollers. On the comparatively rare occasions on which the cowboy drew on songs of the old tradition, brought from the South or even from the Old Country itself, he sang them in a bastardized form, rendered metrically regular and tonally cosy, as in the most

[12] *The Cowboy: His Songs and Brag-talk* and *Back in the Saddle Again, Cowboy Songs in Two Traditions, Authentic and Commercial.*

famous of all cowboy tunes, 'Git along little dogies'. More usually he founded his songs on reminiscences and permutations of current hits. Diatonic and square-rhythmed, the tunes were music-hall or minstrel-show numbers like 'Sweet Betsy' or 'The gal I left behind me'. Less frequent were gospel hymns like 'Beulah land', de-evangelized into 'Dakotah land', a tough ditty about a rough place; nor is there any hint of religious feeling in the Texan songs adapted from Mormon hymnody. The point lay in their conformity, not in any potential revelation.

As early as the end of the nineteenth century cowboy songs were being commercially exploited. John Steele made up a tune called 'Hell in Texas' which became a financial asset to the proprietor of San Antonio's Buckhorn Saloon when he printed it in 1909, distributing more than 100,000 copies. The tunes are cliché-ridden because their function is to assuage and to dispel threat. This is equally true of tunes disseminated in broadside form or made up empirically in the saddle and handed on to casual cronies in bars and brothels. The verses of Joseph Hanoon are representative; their medley of crude vitality with wistful nostalgia is exactly replicated in the tunes. Usually in 4/4 or 3/4 time, at moderate speed, they favour metrical regularity in order that the song may have a hypnotic effect on man and beast. Slow waltz rhythms are especially popular, and haunting melodies like 'Streets of Laredo' or 'Doney gal', with a lilt reminiscent of old southern society, are sung unaccompanied, in the penetrating nasal timbre typical of genuine country music. 'Doney gal' illustrates the tunes' partiality for the wide interval of the major sixth, which makes for an open resonance appropriate to wide spaces, and encourages breaks from natural voice into falsetto. Such yodelling projections of the voice occur naturally to people who sing in the open air, though it is possible that cowboys were also influenced by the Swiss yodelling groups who, surprisingly, toured the Midwest in the late nineteenth and early twentieth centuries. The same waltzing lilt, the same fondness for sixths both major and minor, characterizes 'A home on the range', perhaps the most widely pervasive of cowboy melodies. This paean to the delights of the open-air life where men range as freely as buffalo, deer and antelope under a preternaturally cloudless sky exists in several versions, some in a swinging 6/8, others in a languorous 3/4. Its popularity dates from Oscar J. Fox's published arrangement of 1910, and in this form it serves either of the basic functions–amnesia or orgasm–of cowboy song. Sung unaccompanied in the saddle, it induces trance; swaying along with eyes half shut, the cowboy might even kid himself that the words are true. But, in the bar-room, sung to the accompaniment of honky-tonk piano or guitar, with the 'deep feeling' Oscar Fox exhorts the performer to, it becomes a song of wish-fulfilment, comparable with the minstrel-show numbers and the Stephen Fosterish parlour songs that are its prototype. It must have been the very obliviousness of cowboy songs that made them so readily exploitable. In the myth of the Wild West simplification achieves an aura of truth.

Cisco Houston was never a cowpuncher himself. He came from Virginia, moved to California at an early age, and lived by travelling the roads as an itinerant singer, often in the company of Woody Guthrie. Houston's performance of 'Mule skinner blues', 'Git along little dogies' or 'Hobo's lullaby'[13] is less raw than that of an authentic singer in the saddle, but the purity of his high tenor line reveals the heart of the matter: the long-sustained tones from which the simple tunes unfurl themselves and the lonesomely floating tone of the falsetto yodels preserve an Edenic illusion, without which the hard life would have been unbearable. When the myth of the Wild West is taken over by Hollywood, something of this sublimation survives: Gene Autry's films glamorize the image presented honestly in his songs. The most famous of his songs, 'I'm headin' for the last roundup',[14] remains oddly potent. The lazily loping tune, combined with the instrumental slides and wails and the wide vibrato of Autry's voice, seems guilelessly exposed to the heavens. Man's pettiness is engulfed in the lonesomeness of empty spaces; and, although the recipe may seem packaged when compared with a lonesome song like Roscoe Holcomb's version of 'In the pines', it is not easily dismissible. If it is an escape, it is far from comfortable.

Much less so, indeed, than the darker-flavoured cowboy music from on or across the border, now known as Tex-Mex

[13] *Cisco Houston.* [14] *Country Music South and West.*

music. There are small, remote communities surviving in New Mexico which make a music in continuity with traditions that hark back to Spain's Middle Ages and beyond. Especially remarkable are the *alabados*[15] or praise songs sung by Spanish Catholic penitents in an ancient, microtonally inflected monody that may even embrace Oriental elements by way of the music of the Spanish Jew or Sephardi. This music is an anachronistic survival, remote from the music to which people dance, all of which is a music of Euphoria, even though its whiteness is coffee-stained. In the Texan–Mexican border country the language is Spanish and there is an infusion of tangoid rhythms into the waltz and two-step common to all cowboy music. This gives a sexy lurch to the *bailes* bands' performance even of North American numbers like 'Turkey in the straw',[16] which Bernardo Roybal rechristens 'El cutilio'. American tunes, Mexican tangos, Latinized versions of the waltz, schottische and polka are all played on folk fiddles with guitars in styles readily relatable to instrumental country musics on the American side of the border. All numbers are moderate to perky in tempo, remorselessly spry and diatonic, and regular in metre except for an occasional added or elided beat due more to carelessness than to craft. This tradition of dance music goes back to the nineteenth century but was still flourishing in the 1970s in the area around Santa Fé. The specifically Texan tradition,[17] centred on San Antonio, was immensely popular on radio and record during the thirties and forties. It still used banjos and guitars as harmony and rhythm instruments but the fiddle was replaced by the accordion, which had been imported into the South-West as well as the East by German workers. The favoured song form is the *corrida*, four-lined rhymed stanzas which tell stories or recount topical events, probably at first improvised and then remembered and written down. The tales–often about tequila smugglers and the like–are usually sung by two voices, in twinned parallel thirds, in a manner that has more to do with nineteenth-century Italian opera than with the medieval *cantus gemellus*. The sonority makes for togetherness, and the music as

15 *Dark and Light in Spanish New Mexico.*
16 Ibid.
17 *Texas Mexican Border Music.*

a whole generates an easy *bonhomie*, modified only by the pungent timbre of the desert air. The aggressive cheerfulness of the diatonic, loping music is surprising in view of the toughness of border life. Perhaps that is the point: if one didn't grin one might growl or grovel.

A far more interesting genre sprang from a fusion of white cowboy music, Tex-Mex music and Negro jazz, and flourished especially in the South-West. A considerable proportion of the music which came to be known as Western Swing remains music of the white euphoria in the familiar evasory sense. 'I wonder if you feel the way I do',[18] performed by Bob Wills and his Texas Playboys, is a verbally melancholy song about a faithless woman; the jogging, blandly diatonic tune is tinged by the wailings of steel guitar with comedy rather than with pain or passion. But as a fiddler, Bob Wills, who flourished from the mid-thirties to the mid-forties, made out of euphoria something at once more positive and more dangerous. Playing a traditional fiddle tune like 'Cotton-eyed Joe'[19] with trumpet, piano, bass and electric guitar as well as the conventional country fiddle and banjo, he created a sonority reminiscent of the contemporary big band. He plays violin rather than folk fiddle, though he favours a fluty tone which makes his virtuosity comparable with that of Eddie South or Stuff Smith rather than with that of the more elegant Joe Venuti. Edgy blue distonations occur even when he fuses jazziness with cowboy corn in numbers like 'Ride on, my little pinto' or 'Little Joe, the wrangler', or with Tex-Mex kitsch in 'Spanish two-step' or 'San Antonio Rose'–the song that made him famous and temporarily fairly rich. Negroid pulse, Mexican–Spanish lilt and cowboy openness meld together in this extrovert music which was the South-West's complement to the South-East's blue grass. Like blue grass, it is a significant phase in the evolution of American popular music, both positively (its body energy is infectious because real) and negatively (the moment of happiness passes even as it is celebrated). White euphoria triumphs in no discreditable sense for the liveliness, even if it has not the more permanent truth of black jazz, is true while it lasts. The music is good to listen to as

[18] *Western Swing: Historic Recordings* and *Bob Wills Anthology*.
[19] *Country Music South and West*.

well as to dance to; its skin-deep pleasure enhances life, rather than induces amnesia. It cannot be accidental that blue grass and Western Swing both reached their apex in the aftermath of the Second World War. The music reasserted man's pride in his body–something worth celebrating in those still-dark days.

The evolution of white country music from its folk origins to its commercialized manifestations in the music industry cannot be rigidly charted. There is no date at which folk music turns into pop music. (Nor of course can folk music be exclusively labelled 'good' and pop music 'bad'.) Archaic and modern styles overlap, as do domestic folk music and the musics of the commercial world. Ernest Pop Stoneman and his Blue Ridge Corn Shuckers[20] began in the twenties as a family group playing for their amusement, but by the forties they were appearing at fiddlers' conventions, on the Grand Ole Opry, on college campuses, TV circuits and in folk festivals. They performed traditional ballads and (diatonicized, metricalized) love songs, evangelical hymns, sentimental parlour songs and novelty numbers without regard to category; and now that Pop Stoneman is dead his large family remains active as much for their own and their friends' satisfaction as for material reward. Similarly, domestic artists with roots in a more archaic folk tradition still perform without reference to a mass audience, even though they are sometimes exposed to one. Ola Belle Reed,[21] for instance, has been living in Maryland for the past forty years, but still regards Carolina as her home. She usually sings in modern style, in that she is accompanied by banjo or guitar, or sometimes by barber-shop vocal harmony provided by her family. Some of her songs, such as 'Going to write me a letter' or 'You led me to the wrong', are patched together from memories of her childhood and are sung in a penetrating, bleak timbre, often with a Negroid tang. Against this the banjo or guitar figurations canter briskly, counteracting if not cancelling the starkness of her voice. Occasionally she sings a hymn unaccompanied–'When I can read my titles clear'–creating a movingly archaic sonority from a nineteenth-century tune; sometimes she inverts this process, re-creating an old ballad like

[20] *Ernest V. Stoneman and the Blue Ridge Corn Shuckers.*
[21] *Ola Belle Reed and Family.*

'The butcher's boy' as a hillbilly song, or singing a cowboy tune like 'The ranger's command' straight. The songs she makes up herself unselfconsciously amalgamate all these manners, also incorporating snatches of ragtime and even–in 'Only the leading role will do'–of Tin Pan Alley. The song she wrote to celebrate her fiftieh birthday is appositely called 'I've endured'. Despite the words, optimistic banjo figuration wins the day, and Reed's voice, though harsh, is resilient.

Although folk music, art music and commercial music coexist without rigid barriers between them, the growth of a mythology of pop music emerges as a new phenomenon. This can be examined by detailed study of a few charismatic figures, beginning with a musical family that is in origin as domestic as Ola Belle Reed's, though their name has become, as the appropriate phrase has it, a household word.

5

The Family, the Loner and the Radio Networks

THE CARTER FAMILY, AND JIMMIE RODGERS, THE LONESOME COWBOY

The Carter Family were and are a family, the most basic of social groups. They are more celebrated than the Reeds or countless other family groups who made communal music in the rural Appalachians because they made the trek from their native Virginia to the radio circuits of the Grand Ole Opry at an early stage and became progenitors of the country music industry. Their importance is attributable not to exceptional talents, which would be inappropriate to representatively common men and women, but rather to the incorruptible integrity with which their songs embody that commonness. They were popularized, even commercialized, but were little changed in the process. Their multitudinous audience could admire in their deep-felt if narrow moral certitudes a steadfastness which modern man had lost. They catered for the instinct for nostalgia, but the old times they invoked were still present in their songs.

The matriarch of the clan, Maybelle Addington Carter, was born in 1909, in Virginia, near the Tennessee border. The Addingtons had migrated from England in the early eighteenth century, settling in the Clinch Mountains of south-west Virginia. The Carters lived on the other side of the mountains. Both families were large, close-knit, deeply religious and musically talented. A. P. Carter, the eldest of eight children, married Maybelle Addington's first cousin in 1915; ten years later A.P.'s younger brother Ezra crossed the mountain to marry Maybelle.

She was already expert on many instruments; A.P. had a vigorous bass voice; and his wife Sara was a deep alto. The launching of the Carter Family as a musical enterprise happened in 1927, when A.P., visiting nearby Bristol in Tennessee, 'happened to run into Ralph S. Peer, who was looking for talent to make some records for Victor. So he came home and told us that he had an appointment for us to make some records, the next day, and that's what we did.'[1] For the next ten years the Carters performed around Virginia, Carolina and Tennessee, but seldom ventured further afield. However, the seal was set on their professionalism when they moved to Texas in 1938, in order to be in contact with the more powerful radio circuits. Although they later returned to the Appalachians, they remained full-time performing and recording artists whose artistry preserved the raw authenticity of their origins. They never became streamlined, and had no need of gimmicks.

The Carters' music[2] is almost aggressively white, unsullied by even a tincture of black 'reality'. Their material consists of genuine old ballads harking back to their eighteenth-century forebears; of gospel hymns; and of parlour songs with a strong bias to the sanctimonious. No more than Granny Riddle or Ola Belle Reed do the Carters differentiate between these genres. The songs are a repository of common experience, handed down through the family and knocked into shape by A. P. Carter, who became the group's leader. He is an arranger rather than a composer, though he is often credited with the creation of tunes that he has merely refashioned. In addition to his job as arranger, A.P. sang bass in the vocal trio; his wife Sara usually sang the lead in her very low, rasping alto. Maybelle Addington Carter was the main instrumentalist, and sang the middle (tenor) part when needed. In purely musical terms Maybelle was undoubtedly the most talented of the group. She played banjo, fiddle, lute, autoharp and guitar, the last in several styles. She was most noted for her 'Carter scratch', playing the melody and scratching a rhythmic accompaniment at the same time, but she was also expert at traditional pickin' style, and had

[1] Quoted in John Atkins, 'The Carter Family', in Malone and McCull, *Stars of Country Music*.

[2] *Famous Country Music-Makers: The Carter Family* and *The Carter Family: Original Recordings*.

a blues technique which she claimed to have learned from a Negro. This didn't add a black flavour to the music, but it probably encouraged a more plangent expressivity.

All the Carters' songs, whatever their origin and whatever their theme, are sung at moderate tempo, in unsullied diatonic major, and with instrumental accompaniment on guitar, banjo or autoharp. Despite the pervasively major melodies–traditional modal tunes are altered to fit the simple instrumental harmonies–the vocal elements in the songs belong to the negative, deprived pole of white folk monody. Enunciation is flat, tone pinched, rhythm pedestrian. This is true whether the tunes are permutations of old songs like 'Waves on the sea', which turns a Child ballad about a horrific disaster at sea into a corny, cosy waltz; a gospel hymn like 'I'm working on a building', which preserves a faint hint of black energy as it damps evangelical fervour into a work-song routine; or a parlour song in barber-shop harmony, such as 'My old cottage home', familiar from Granny Riddle's monophonic version. In all these song types the familial togetherness of close harmony goes some way towards alleviating the dreariness of deprived melodic lines; that's what families are for. Any positive quality beyond fortitude and endurance comes from the instrumental parts: here the Carters are in line with the banjo and guitar picking of the great country players such as Dock Boggs, Doc Watson and Roscoe Holcomb, not to mention the more blatant virility of the blue grass bands. Maybelle Carter's instrumentalism is not virtuosic to that degree; but she does generate a paradoxically numb delight so that the music, despite its homophonic moderation, sounds at once potent and neurotic. It is this residual pain that distinguishes the Carters' music from the streamlined complacencies of a Scotty Wiseman. The Carters' truth is 'the heart of common humanity', to use Charles Ives's phrase; if it is habituating rather than enlivening, that may be a fair comment on the human condition.

The Carters' durability is remarkable. They and their offspring have been singing for more than fifty years and their popularity has scarcely waned. Their keeping up to date is entirely unselfconscious. They feel no need to modify the character of their music when, in a modern gospel number,

'Hello central, give me heaven', they employ a modern convenience to contact the celestial boss; or when, in 'Radio heaven', they relate the wireless's wizardry to God's. But it is not such superficial modernities that account for the appeal of the Carters to a wide and diverse audience. It is due rather to their honesty: although their songs proffer comfort they do not deny tangled nerves and jaded senses. In 1932 the Carters, primal family of old-time rural America, were sundered by a divorce that seemed to strengthen, rather than impair, their musical solidarity. A.P. remained single, faithful to Sara's memory until his death in 1960. Yet although an old-time countryman he was, in his new environment, hardly beyond urban neurosis. In the recording studio he was anything but relaxed, pacing up and down during performance, occasionally seizing a microphone *en passant* to sing a snatch as the spirit took him. It may be this nervosity that gives an edge of reality to even the blandest and most self-righteous of the Carters' songs. There is usually a touch of anguish in their hard lines. This is especially true of the 1963 three-disc set[3] of old songs sung with the Nitty Gritty Band, which includes some of the most famous names in country music, such as Earl Scruggs and Doc Watson. Although the music comes out, in its electrophonic medium, as smarter than the Carters' original homeliness, the new version of their celebrated 'Wildwood flower' preserves the virginal quality of the first version, and sounds the more moving for its paradoxical reliance on technology.

A further stage in the evolution of white country music is represented by the career of Jimmie Rodgers,[4] who was born in Meridian, Mississippi, in 1897. His mother died when he was 4 and, since his father was an itinerant railway worker, Jimmie's childhood was far from comfortable. Travelling the rails with his father, he had virtually no formal education, but acquired a wide experience of life, especially musical life, in the towns and cities of the Deep South and West. He worked as brakeman and flagman during his teens, consorting with both white and black railway hands and picking up musical skills *en route*. This footloose rambling defines his character, but his career as a

[3] *Let the Circle be Unbroken.*
[4] *Famous Country Music-Makers: Jimmie Rodgers.*

professional musician and entertainer owed much to the encouragement first of his sister-in-law, Elsie McWilliams, herself a pianist and song writer, who helped him to work out his own numbers (he never learned to read music); and then to the perspicacity of Ralph Peer, who discovered and launched him as a radio singer in 1927, the same year he promoted the Carters. Success in the music business was opportune, as tuberculosis forced Jimmie to relinquish his hard life on the tracks. The equation between talent and commercial success is a fascinating one. Neither the Carter Family nor Jimmie Rodgers would have achieved celebrity but for the intervention of Ralph Peer; but it was he who spotted their quality. Some such intermediary seems to be necessary for any folk musician launched into the complementary worlds of art and industry.

Rodgers was sometimes called the Texan Cowboy, though he was neither Texan nor a cattle rustler. However, the sobriquet broadly fits the nature of his music, which is lonesome, outdoors, cynical and sentimental. The evangelical strain that dominates the Carters' music is absent from Rodgers's, though his partiality for parlour songs attempts to fulfil the same nostalgic yearning for home and haven. His own 'Dreaming with tears in my eyes',[5] for instance, is a sentimental number sung in his light, insidious tenor, to a silly waltz tune that would seem, were it not for the guileless quality of his vocal production, at variance with the words. The yodelling refrain comes across as religious sensibility *manqué*: dreaming of a love that is true is the equivalent of hoping for pie in the sky. Rodgers, unlike the Carters but like Hobart Smith, Doc Watson, Roscoe Holcomb and others, was deeply, and probably directly, influenced by the black blues, since he worked on the rails with Negroes. His white American experience intuitively admits to the paradox inherent in American industrial society, the affluence of which was dependent on the oppression of a minority. Moreover, during the Depression years in which he was singing, 1927–33, that affluence was itself suspect. His small-town music knew that the heart's truth of the American 'way of life' was threatened by the very mechanistic-commercial techniques that made him famous.

[5] *Country Music South and West.*

'Train whistle blues' is a fine example of the basic Jimmie Rodgers myth. About the railroad, it is pertinent to Rodgers's itinerant life and representative of the American ramblin' man. It is a real blues in twelve-bar form, its opening phrase being a primitive tumbling strain. Despite the lightness of his voice, Rodgers employs vocal techniques that are clearly Negroid. But although he uses modal and pentatonic inflexions foreign to the Carters' deadpan diatonicism, they are compromised by his habitually regular metre and jaunty gait. The suffering waywardness of the black blues is thus discounted: as it is, more obviously, by Jimmie's recurrent breaks into falsetto yelling. This yodelling technique, mentioned earlier with reference to blue grass men and their predecessors, owed its popularity mainly to Rodgers, who acquired it either from indigenous mountain music or, more probably, from cowboys encountered on his Texan travels, who may in turn have picked it up from Swiss visitors. It is from Rodgers's songs that we can best understand the pervasive force of American yodelling: it gives an additional twist to his wry, defensively ironic verses, as it deprives his vestigially blue passion of a measure of its reality. In songs dealing with the traditional blues themes of sexual infidelity, of home or paradise lost, of vagrant alienation, the yodel calls from a *distance,* across empty space, in a *false* (falsetto) voice that induces a forlorn hilarity. This is obvious in any of the sequence of numbers he called 'Blue yodel'. In all these, blue pain and passion are experienced, but seem in the yodelling to be, after all, dismissible. The effect is at once funny and sad, and the sadness is the more potent source of his appeal. This wistful vulnerability is also, less subtly, apparent in a pseudo-autobiographical cowboy song like 'Jimmie the kid', or a black-faced minstrel number like 'Mississippi Delta blues', which is not a blues, though its nostalgia has a period charm. Singing such songs, mildly rakish in his straw hat and light suit, Rodgers was a representative 'little man' keeping a small flag flying even though doomed by tuberculosis. It is not entirely fanciful to see this dis-ease as related to a conflict between ways of life: the small-town rural America he came from and the urban metropolis he briefly encompassed. That he was a brakeman on the railroad also seems emblematic: tied to the past and

1 Sketch of Uncle Sam and the famous American Jazz taken from the songsheet 'Get Out of Mexico', 1866.

2 Sketch of Columbia, Eagle and Miss Liberty from the songsheet 'Peace on Honourable Terms to America', 1815.

3, 4 Waulking women then (18th century) (*above*) and now (*below*) in the Isle of Barra.

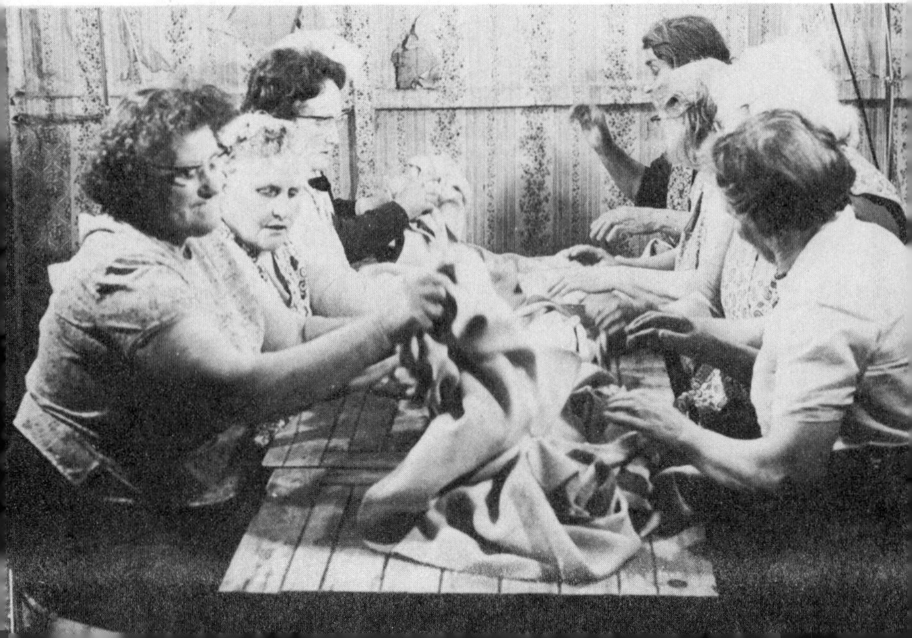

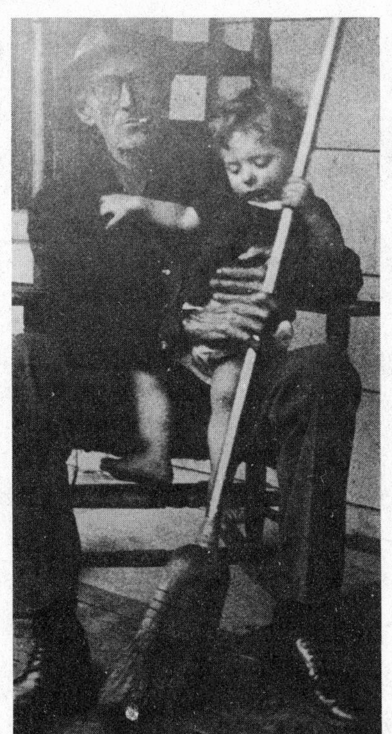

5 (*left*) Nimrod Workman.

6 (*above*) Aunt Molly Jackson in action at New York University.

7 Nimrod and Mollie Workman with mikes at Tennessee Grassroots Days Festival, Nashville, 1978.

8 A Shaker family at Sabbathday Lake, Maine.

9 Fiddlin' John Carson, the first Old Time country musician to be commercially recorded.

10 Dock Boggs the whirligig.

11 Roscoe Holcomb: the real 'High Lonesome Sound', 1963.

12 Jimmie Rodgers the Lonesome Cowboy advertising the 'Jimmie Rodgers Special Model'.

13 The Carter family; A. P., Sara and Maybelle.

14 Mexican cowboys' race on the prairies, wood engraving 1882.

15 Bob Wills, standing centre left with his fiddle, and his Texas Playboys in one of their many musical Westerns, 1945.

undermined by sickness, he couldn't be the easy rider he would have liked to be. Frustration may be the source of his strength.

It was also the source of his appeal; people identified with Jimmie Rodgers because they too felt vulnerable in the face of an encroaching mechanistic civilization, too big if not too efficient to be comprehensible. In musical ability Rodgers was perhaps not superior to successors such as Ernest Tubb and Hank Snow,[6] and was certainly inferior to Merle Travis,[7] whose near-protest songs are as tough as Rodgers's songs are vulnerable, and whose guitar playing had a bluesy plangency and a virtuosity that Rodgers never claimed. Star quality involves a seldom-attained fusion of talent and myth: Jimmie Rodgers spoke for a generation and a society in a way that brilliant Merle Travis failed to. Without Rodgers's talent his myth could not have reached so many thousands of people; without his myth, his talent would probably have sunk without trace. Travis had talent in abundance but little mythic appeal; Roy Acuff, on the other hand, who described himself a 'country tenor without training, performing in Old Harp Style, with a knack to reach the people', achieved some kind of mythic status with his 'Great speckled bird',[8] but did not have enough musical talent to be durable. After Rodgers, country music marked time, awaiting its next truly charismatic figures. They duly appeared in the persons of Hank Williams and Elvis Presley.

HANK WILLIAMS, ELVIS PRESLEY AND THE ROAD TO ROCK

Hank Williams[9] was born twenty-six years later than Jimmie Rodgers, twenty years later than Roy Acuff, and fourteen years later than Ernest Tubb and Hank Snow. By this time country music was well launched on its electrophonic phase. Despite this, and despite the fact that Williams was the most potent seminal force in country music since Rodgers, his rural origins

[6] *Country Music in the Modern Era 1940s–1970s.*
[7] *Country Music South and West, The Best of Merle Travis* and *The Ernest Tubb Story.*
[8] *Roy Acuff's Greatest Hits.*
[9] *The Collector's Hank Williams* and *Hank Williams: Forty Greatest Hits.*

were unambiguous. Born on an Alabama tenant farm, he moved at the age of 5 to Georgiana, Montgomery. His mother was a fanatical fundamentalist; and the choir and organ of the Baptist Church were the first musical influences on him, and remained the strongest, though, since he was taught guitar by a Negro street singer, white hymnody and black blues came together early in his musical education. Williams's religious or hymn-orientated numbers are all, like the Carters', moderate in tempo, diatonic major in tonality, square in rhythm, half-way between chapel and music hall. The difference lies in the fact that their presentation is not morosely deflated. Williams's baritone voice has a rich resonance; the beat, especially when electrophonically amplified, is potent; the minstrel-show harmonies, though related to the clichés of the evangelical hymn, merge into the sophistications of Tin Pan Alley, as in 'Last night I dreamed of Heaven' or 'I saw the light': tunes which may seem too banal to be visionary yet have thrust enough to convince us that something happened to him even if it cannot be accepted as mystical experience. Much the same occurs in many hymnic songs that are not specifically religious. In 'Lost on the river', for instance, he sings of failed love in duet with his then wife, creating close harmony similar to the Carters', but with intenser tone and savager edge.

Jimmie Rodgers wrote most of his words and tunes, and Hank Williams wrote virtually all of his. Occasionally Williams produces a straight number in which virtue resides simply in sincerity, which he said is the only asset essential for a pop singer. The prescription sounds dangerous, but it would seem to be true of the classic among his many lonesome songs, 'I'm so lonesome I could cry'. The verses might almost be called poetry, not for any richness of metaphor or subtlety of rhythm, but because the language is economical, devoid of excrescence. The lilting waltz tune sounds as though it were born with the words and avoids self-pity by being neither melodically flatulent nor harmonically fraudulent. More frequent, however, are the country songs of (usually failed) love in which misery is fortified by an awareness of passion that derives from the black undercurrents to his music, and/or by the melancholy being tempered by irony. Sometimes he creates genuine twelve-bar blues, such as 'Honky-tonk blues', or 'Long gone lonesome blues', in which sexual frustration is salvaged from self-indulgence by the plangency of his voice, by the vigour of the rhythm, and by something not far from fun in the Jimmie Rodgers-style vocal techniques; Williams's yodels may become chortles of triumph, however momentary, over lonesomeness. Although Williams is less black than Jimmie Rodgers, he was clearly off the mark when he sang a number of his producer and mentor, Fred Rose, 'There's no room in my heart for the blues'.

Occasionally Williams's opposition to the slings and arrows of outrageous fortune becomes overtly ironic, as in the brusquely modulating 'Nobody's lonesome for me', or comic, as in 'Moanin' the blues', which is not a blues but employs vocal yodels and wailing steel guitar to dismissive effect. Throughout his secular love songs Williams tends to defuse black passion and pain by an infusion of white country vocal and instrumental techniques. His transitions between blues and country waltz, folk fiddle and electric guitar, owe something to the jazz-orientated country-band style which Bob Wills developed in the thirties and forties. The songs of disappointed love evidently spring from the same death-wish or heaven-aspiration that dominates the devotional songs. Either way he survives by walking a tightrope between commitment and irony.

Only rarely are Williams's defences down, as in a song of lachrymose anger like 'Your cheating heart'; in 'Jambayala (on the bayou)', a number almost as unequivocally happy as a genuine Louisiana Cajun tune; or in 'Ramblin' man', one of his very rare minor-key numbers in which he admits to alienation–he belongs nowhere and rambles because he is rootless, while relating his lost state to an aborted religious impulse–there must be somewhere, 'over the hill', which would be heaven if he could reach it. However, this haunted and haunting song, with its weird mordents and glissandi, its leaps into falsetto register that might be either vision or cheat, is exceptional in Williams's *oeuvre*. Whereas the Carters were glum survivors and Jimmie Rodgers a vulnerable jack-in-the-box, Hank Williams is usually more positive in that he finds zest in the corniness of his sincerity. Rodgers was a contradictory character, veering between over-confidence and hypersensitivity: success overtook him and he was dead before he had realized what was happening. Twenty or more years later, Hank Williams made a success story out of unsuccess on an even more legendary scale, offering a panacea for Everyman's insecurities. Characteristically, in the last year of his life, Williams made one of his most whimsical songs–'I'll never get out of this world alive'–out of his personal predicament and died, not of tuberculosis, for which he could have no personal responsibility, but from his own inability to cope with a world he never made. True, his physical and nervous distresses may have been triggered by the accident he suffered when performing as a bronco-buster in early youth; addiction to drink and drugs began as an attempt to alleviate pain. Perhaps the simple Carter-like virtues he sprang from and might have lived by (as the Carters did and do) could not withstand the pressures his new life put on them. He was destined to be the first of a long line of pop star hero-martyrs: his love life was a shambles, he missed dates, insulted managers, passed out and passed on in his car, on the southern circuit, at the age of 29.

Occasionally the black elements in Williams's songs, reinforced by the mechanized beat, steer him towards early Presley-style rock and roll, as in 'Move it on over'. If the legendary status Hank Williams acquired as hero and martyr is indicated by the fact that twenty thousand people thronged to his funeral, as cult figure he pales into insignificance in comparison with Elvis Presley.[10] Born a decade later than Williams, Presley's background too was southern and smalltown, with strong overtones of religious Nonconformity; his people were fanatical Pentecostals. Williams was nervously introspective, almost exclusively the creator of his own songs, which are about emotional insecurity, broken loves, attempts (usually frustrated) to deal with them, and God's succour when all else fails. As a boy Presley too seems to have been insecure, a pampered mother's darling, an average ordinary guy, unintellectual and not conspicuously sensitive. However, his response to his situation was very different. Williams admitted to his misery and, in creating songs, objectified it, simultaneously triumphing over it and revealing its relevance to his con-

[10] *Elvis's Golden Records.*

temporaries. Perhaps because he was so favoured a mother's boy, Presley narcissistically created his own image, one of overbearing self-confidence. Even before his talents were recognized, he dressed extravagantly, swaggered hopefully. He brought it off because he had ability enough to bolster his charisma. Initially a Jesus freak, he must have been gratified that his fundamentalist talent was indeed God-given: he was endowed with a magnificent voice.

The moving qualities of the Carters' singing do not depend on their vocal abilities; Jimmie Rodgers's voice was pleasantly personal but not in the conventional sense musical–he could hardly have achieved celebrity before the age of the microphone. Hank Williams's voice was more powerful and more skilfully if intuitively exploited; but only with Presley do we find a pop singer whose vocal resources are first rate by any standards. He could and usually did sing with full vocal range, without breaks between chest and head register except when he needed them for some special effect. His confidence in his vocal expertise projected his image: he could do what he wanted, and he wanted at once to conform and to rebel. His musical awakening came, in childhood and adolescence, from the white gospel quartets who streamlined evangelical fervour into close harmony; the Blackwood Brothers were his idols, and there is some evidence that he sang Jesus songs with *ad hoc* groups. The effect of this tradition can certainly be heard in the number which catapulted him to fame in 1956. 'Heartbreak Hotel' was in origin a southern country number, darkened by the black style of the blues shout. Presley sings it lyrically, in ripe romanticism almost resembling that of a concert artist, pitching on the note and eschewing the dirt which a folk singer, black or white, would smear over it. He invites us to take the love experience straight, while rebelliously undermining it by the use of two techniques which Richard Middleton has neatly called boogification and gospelization. The former is a technique of rhythmic displacement deriving from the triplet-drag style of boogie-woogie, whereby verbal stresses in the vocal part get distorted; the latter does to pitch what boogification does to rhythm, breaking the smooth contours of the line in the interests of *ecstasis*. A barrel-house piano player drives instinctively into the unequal notes of boogie-woogie, generating corporeal energy and sexual excitement for a community of dancers; the Pentecostal gospel singers that Presley heard in his childhood yell and ululate off pitch as, in togetherness, they seek communion with God. Presley uses both techniques brilliantly; the difference is that he employs them as part of his performing expertise. Straight romantic lyricism is held in tension with these aspects of reality. The performance stimulates precisely because it is precarious: an act narcissistically boosting self-esteem, his audience's along with his own.

In this context we should remember that the voice came from the Face and the Body. No pop singer before had had such a presence: the hooded eyes, the Apollonian nose, the *almost*-Negroid mouth, the elaborately coiffeured quiff of hair that seemed simultaneously inviting and contemptuous. The gyrations of the body followed the voice and the face, for Presley's *ecstasis* is not spiritual but sexual–as may of course be true of most religious orgiastic dancing. In an early rockabilly number, 'Don't be cruel' (one of his favourites), Presley takes over a number by a black bluesman, Otis Blackwell, and rides the music over ostinato patterns typical of white country music. His dark voice is ripely passionate, while the rhythm is jaunty, almost carefree, so that the song both believes in the love and laughs at it. 'Good rockin' tonight' similarly combines rhythmic charge with vocal vibrancy in such a way as to make it understood that copulation, as well as a rowdy dance-hall, is referred to. In 'I want you, I need you, I love you', it is clear that Presley's love is the consequence of want and need, and not the other way round. Performance, both sexual and musical, is what he is concerned with. It is only a step from here to a number like 'All shook up', written by black Otis Blackwell, but presented in a Fast Western boogie so extravagant that it sounds like self-parody. The whoops and hollers all have their prototypes in real black blues and white country music, but never before were they uttered with such self-conscious panache. The performance is electrifying and does what it promises: we are indeed 'all shook up'. What shakes people up is Elvis in voice and action: he was essentially a performer of other people's songs and not, like Hank Williams, a composer. Of his nature a composer seeks for truth; a performer, on the other hand, is an actor, whose approach to truth is necessarily secondhand. A comparison of Presley's performance of 'Hound Dog' with that of Big Mama Thornton,[11] the black jazz singer who first recorded it in 1952, leads to the conclusion that his truth is, in this instance, partial. While Big Mama treats the hound comically on one level, ending with risible bayings and barkings, the intensity of her edgy pitch and the malleability of her rhythm create a music both tragic and scary. This black sensuality is for real, offering the heights of passion and also the depths of despair. The snuffling outside the door threatens as it excites, and if the hilarious postlude offers a release, there is certainly something to be released from. Presley sings on the beat and on the note, with traditional 'romantic' tone at variance with the doggy lust: what emerges is a game–a lively game, but hardly an invitation to the dangerous unknown. This is why his songs were so prodigiously successful: they brought sexual reality of a sort into the dream worlds of the relatively affluent teenage whites for whom he catered; but although they could make no mistake about what he was offering, the danger they savoured was vicarious.

Presley's performing expertise is the heart of the matter. Even in 'Heartbreak Hotel', where his voice thrillingly exploits black vocal inflexions, the technique is part of the song's self-indulgence–as it isn't in the singing of Little Richard, whom he emulates. In 'All shook up' or 'Baby let's play house', or the later 'Please don't drag that stone around', self-parody substitutes for experience–or rather *becomes* the experience, since making the image is what the songs are about. In numbers like this–which Richard Middleton has termed mannerist–it might even be said that Presley's extraordinary talent was inseparable from his dishonesty: as a performer he was always putting something across. We can relish this when he is blackly boosting our own sexuality along with his own, and we're relieved that the extravagance of the performance evades any hint of the portentous. When, however, he deals with white ballads in the same way, the effect is less easy to accept. In 'Love me tender', for instance, he makes a banal waltz tune sound too good to be true

[11] *Big Mama Thornton.*

by the leery intimacy of his vocal production. 'That's where your heartaches begin' introduces a throatily sobbing speaking voice over organ and twanging steel guitar: either the performance is destroying the credibility of a rather good tune or Presley is sending himself up. It may be good for a laugh, but is it good enough for the young people who took it straight? Bob Dylan, who later parodied the parody brilliantly, clearly thought not. Yet such a defensive reaction to seriousness is by no means peculiar to Presley's whiter songs; it would seem that a performer in his sense–an entertainer as distinct from an artist–can never be quite sure whether he is kidding his audience, or himself, or both.

The conventional account of Presley's career has it that in his early days he exhibited genius in projecting his black-white image, but that he later softened, surrendering to the commercial pressures out of which flowed his string of ballads and sentimental songs. This is far from an adequate account; there is an element of play-acting in all his work, and even his blacker blues were, as Greil Marcus put it, 'a set of musical adventures, and as a blues-singing swashbuckler, his style owed as much to Errol Flynn as it did to Arthur Crudup'.[12] It therefore 'made sense to make movies of it'–which is what happened after he had been drafted into the forces at the instigation of his tyrannical manager and emerged in 1960 with a new image, that of a well-groomed film star. John Lennon said that Elvis died when he entered the forces and one can see what he meant. But Lennon's point of view was not that of Presley, who as a boy accepted his mother's belief in home and duty, patriotism and God, and preached godly and homey homilies at the very time his sexuality appeared most rampant. Perhaps there was always an element of what is now called deconstruction in the extravagance of Elvis's sexuality, which embraced the passively feminine along with the aggressively masculine. Certainly the last years of his life were a personal deconstruction of a peculiarly painful kind.

His vintage years stretched only from 1954 to 1960, when he sang out of his simultaneous instincts for conformity and rebellion, imaging the cosy dream worlds where little boys are

[12] Greil Marcus, *Mystery Train*, New York, 1975.

safe, and at the same time flirting with danger–the irrational, the dark or the black–which, although to be feared, is necessary for self-gratification. In those years, howling, hollering and writhing in 'Heartbreak Hotel', 'Mystery train' or 'Milk cow boogie blues',[13] he changed the lives of thousands of young people, uncovering immemorially ancient impulses in the liberation of teenage libido, linking country with city strains, white with black, brothel with chapel. Yet when the performance was finished, he too was spent, as he had no inner resources. During his stint in abysmal films he produced one fine song, 'Jailhouse rock'–among his blackest creations. In the sixties there was a powerful Fast Western number, 'Guitar man', and an interesting sophistication of country music in the form of a talkin' ballad, 'In the ghetto'. By 1970 he had lapsed into silence, the retreat into his mausoleum mansion being also a regression to the womb. Degenerating into a mountain of fat, he slowly succumbed to drink, drugs and near-infantilism, while still bolstering Mum, God and the American Way of Life. In a sense his end, so much direr than the early deaths of Jimmie Rodgers and Hank Williams, was implicit in his beginning, since the performance was pretence. Perhaps his film career should have been triumph, instead of disaster. He ought to have been a good actor, not a zombie, but failed because he couldn't believe in his roles enough. In the last resort neither the white dream maker nor the black rebel escaped from routine.

Among his contemporaries and immediate successors[14] there was no one to challenge Presley's supremacy except perhaps Jerry Lee Lewis,[15] a white country or rockabilly singer born in Louisiana in 1935. He admitted to a debt to Jimmie Rodgers and Hank Williams, as well as–for his talents as showbiz man–to Al Jolson. In performance Lewis vocally emulates the black gospel shouter, while executing gyrations on and around his brilliantly played barrel-house piano hardly less extravagant than Presley's gyrations with his guitar. His performance of Hank Williams's 'Honky-tonk blues' is much blacker than the original, and he sings 'Someday' with a savagery rivalling that of

[13] *Country Music in the Modern Era 1940s–1970s.*

[14] *Kings of Country Music.*

[15] *Shake, Rattle and Roll: Rock and Roll in the 1950s* and *Chuck Berry's Golden Decade.*

Little Richard himself. 'Good golly Miss Molly' (1962) rocks with devastating precision, its drive only enhanced by the intermittent rhythmic hiatuses.

Charlie Rich,[16] also an able pianist as well as country singer, does not attempt such ferocity but in his more relaxed way can–in his 'Time and again' and 'Ain't it a shame', for instance–merge white country song into fully-fledged, black urban jazz. The Texan Buddy Holly died too young (at the age of 22, in an air crash) to prove whether the white adolescent ingenuousness of his quivery, even hiccuping, voice–charming in his first success, 'That'll be the day', and in the Mexican-tinged 'Tell me how'–could combine with his snappy rhythmic sense to produce music of substance. Jim Reeves[17] in his country manner, creating lonesome train or feckless gambling numbers, relies too passively on the amiability of his voice, which euphorically defines potentially dangerous experience. Johnny Cash, who came from a clan of indigent Arkansas share-croppers, has turned a disordered life into a success story and a happy marriage with June Carter, daughter of A.P., while his songs have continued to moan indulgently of loss and failure. There is little reality in his blatant rhythms and harmonic complacencies–though the appeal of his deep-brown voice seems to many irresistible. His sinister, solemn visual image is similarly potent, though, when compared with Hank Williams's mythology of failure, it would seem to be at several removes from truth.

In attaining maturity, American pop music needed to synthesize white euphoria with black reality–and not merely in the racial sense. Such a synthesis occurs intuitively in the music of a few old-timers, such as Dock Boggs, Doc Watson and Roscoe Holcomb; among folk musicians who crossed over into art and commerce, the Carters minimally and Jimmie Rodgers and Hank Williams more enthusiastically grope towards it, while Elvis Presley stages it as a quasi-theatrical performance. When history comes to be written it may seem that their significance is as precursors of Bob Dylan, the first white American poet-

[16] *Charlie Rich: I'll do my Swingin' at Home.*
[17] *The Country Side of Jim Reeves.*

composer-singer whose genius is both creative and interpretative. History may well regard black blues as evidence of twentieth-century man's radical strength, and white country music as evidence of his all too human frailty. Dylan is a pop artist who, unlike Presley, has grown up. In his work frailty and strength meet in an adult recognition of modern man's predicament–which is probably much the same as it has always been, if more so.

PART II

BOB DYLAN

Freedom, Belief and Responsibility

The common opinion is that we cannot be responsible until we are free. This is an illusion. We become free by accepting that we are responsible.

John Austin Baker: *The Foolishness of God*, 1973

For my part, I doubt whether man can support complete religious independence and entire political liberty at the same time. I am led to think that if he has no faith he must obey, and if he is free he must believe.

Alexis de Tocqueville: *Democracy in America*, 1848

I desire not to sleepe in security & dreame of a nest which no hand can reach. I cannot
but expect changes . . . .
(there is so much sound and noise of purchase and purchasers) . . . .
Having sought Truth deare, we must not sell it cheape.

Roger Williams: quoted by Paul Metcalf in *Apalache*

1

Grass Roots

Born in Minnesota on 21 May 1941, Bob Dylan spent his childhood in Hibbing, a small, derelict mining town near the Canadian border. As a child he was quiet and secretive, a loner. Growing to adolescence he was an inveterate story teller, fabricating myths about himself so vividly that he hardly knew whether he spoke truth or falsehood. Central among these myths was his pretence that he was an orphan. This, and his repudiation of his Jewish ancestry, may have been a rebellion against the small-town business world his father represented; like many sensitive youths, he loved his mother but disliked what he thought his father stood for. Furthering his rebellion he became a 'greaser' or motor-cycle maniac, pursuing the James Dean legend. Yet he belonged no more to a jet set than he had done to the kids he'd consorted with as a child. His true identity he sought, from the age of 10, through poetry and music. He changed his Jewish family name of Zimmerman to Dylan, probably in emulation of Dylan Thomas, bardic Welsh poet and another congenital outsider. Desultorily, he attended the University of Minnesota, but spent more time singing and playing (reportedly rather badly) in coffee bars than at lectures and seminars. His mind was as sharp as his senses, but his attitude to his teachers, who were *ipso facto* part of the Establishment, seems to have been mildly contemptuous.

The legend that in his early teens Dylan hoboed across the great American continent, equipped only with harmonica and guitar, seems to have been one of the tales he told. But the story, untrue in physical fact, was apposite to his mental state: just as his opting out of college after six months was not merely a negative rejection of the American Way of Life but also a positive return to an older, more basic American culture. To deflate a civilization that seemed to the young moribund was not a destructive act but an assertion of human rights. It is in this sense that we may call Dylan a folk singer: his words and music are of, about, and for people. There is an apocryphal story that when the great Louis Armstrong was asked by a radio interviewer whether he considered the music he made to be folk music he replied, 'Wal, yeah, I guess so; leastways, I never heard of no horse making it.' Dylan–who dislikes being termed a folk singer in the sense relevant to the folk 'movement'–would surely accept Satchmo's prescription: like Louis Armstrong he used folk techniques and in his early days derived much of his material from folk sources; and when his material was his own he dealt, like a true folk artist, in rock-bottom reality. True, Dylan's words and music, unlike those of real folk song and dance, are written down; what is notated is, however, no more than an approximation to the sounds heard, which are created empirically for each performance. To a degree this applies also to the rock heroes–Elvis Presley, Bill Haley, Buddy Holly and, most fervently and significantly, black Little Richard–on whose music Dylan was hooked during his boyhood.

While Dylan's originality is his strength, his art has roots, and these are a strength also. In the early days the words were paramount, and the significance of the young Dylan is inseparable from his articulateness. His basic verbal source is the traditional folk ballad, both in its British origins and in its American permutations. Closely allied to the ballad are children's rhymes and runes, again both British and American; Negro blues poetry; the Bible, the mythology of which permeates the American Midwest; Bunyan's *Pilgrim's Progress*, scarcely less pervasive in the Bible belts than the Good Book itself; and a few more sophisticated poets, especially William Blake, who sang his Songs of Innocence and Experience to his own improvised, and presumably folk-like, tunes. Dylan seems to have read American beat poets like Allen Ginsberg, Frank O'Hara and perhaps Kenneth Patchen. Very sophisticated poets like T. S. Eliot and W. H. Auden, sometimes listed among his sources, seem to me to have little affinity with him: he is an aural poet, for whom words must always be the impetus to a tune. To these more or less indigenous literary influences must be added two foreign ones. The first is Bertolt Brecht, whose trenchant, politically motivated early verses were often declaimed to a rudimentarily strummed guitar, and were later set to tunes by Kurt Weill, Hanns Eisler and Paul Dessau which, though stemming from an alien tradition, have a Dylanesque pungency. The second is Arthur Rimbaud, a poet who haunted Dylan's early years as he did those of many exceptionally aware adolescents. They empathized with the French boy's self-imposed exile and found in his surrealistic imagery a release from the computerized routines of industrial technology. Protesting Dylan recognized in Brecht a soulmate, a singing poet belonging to a very different culture; and found in Rimbaud's discontinuous metaphors a technique that might–especially in Dylan's psychedelic phase–be exploited by a poet in a totally distinct tradition.

Such were Dylan's verbal roots. In his early days he operated with his voice–untrained, natural, veering between speech and song–and his acoustic guitar and harmonica. The gradual sophistication of his resources in one sense represents a growth towards conscious awareness; in another sense, however, electrophonic presentation, with Dylan as with other folk artists, implies a merging of individual into communal consciousness. (How does one assess the relationship between composer, arranger(s) and technicians?) A singer such as Dylan becomes a shaman for the global village's tribe: in which respect his songs are ritual as well as art.

Dylan's musical sources are, predictably, both white and black. Most fundamental is the American transmutation of British balladry, whether in northern (Yankee) or in southern (Appalachian) style. In the hard-bitten world of the Poor White American the grand modal themes of the ancient British heritage survive, though vocal line becomes tighter and rhythm more cabined and confined by the metres of hymnody: as noted in Part I, the vocal production of singers from the southern mining areas, such as Aunt Molly Jackson, Sarah Ogan Gunning and Nimrod Workman, has become both pinched and lacerating. The resilience of the Poor White found an outlet not in singing, but in instrumental playing: on banjo, guitar, fiddle or autoharp a Hobart Smith, a Dock Boggs or a Doc Watson could create a music sometimes unsubtle in line–the old modal flexibilities are often banished in favour of harmonically centred diatonicism–yet virtuosic in command of instrumental resource. The jollity is eupeptic, but may also be euphoric, for the shutting out of pain–the liquidation of tragedy and guilt–may involve a wilful deadening of sensibility. This insensitivity is more crudely apparent in another of Dylan's white sources, cowboy songs, the blatancy of which, we suggested, may be connected with the fact that cowboys, despite their rural isolation, tended to be itinerant townsmen who could not draw on traditions which Appalachian agrarians had built up through several centuries. The contrast between this music, especially in its instrumentally accompanied form, and black folk music is extreme. Although Dylan is white, in his music white and black sources can be no more disentangled than they can in the singing of a real folk artist like Roscoe Holcomb. In this respect Dylan is much closer to grass roots than are Jimmie Rodgers, Hank Williams and Elvis Presley. In Dylan's world the melding of white and black into a darker shade of pale attains maturation: so it is essential to examine the nature of his black roots in greater detail.

The precise derivations of black jazz from African sources are a matter of enquiry and dispute. What is inescapable, however, is that African tribal musics were and are even further removed from the post-Renaissance, European notion of music as personal communication than are the British folk musics discussed in Part I, chapter 1. The African's musical techniques explore identification, a process of self-loss, rather than identity, an act of self-discovery. Forms tend to be circular rather than linear, reiterative, habituating, incremental; African musics are music of necessity in that they effect magical acts of worship or work or play, of praise or dispraise. The music creates its world while it lasts; we live in it until the sounds stop. In so far as it momentarily creates a way of life, it is a communal act, based orgiastically on the movements of the human body. When solo voices sing or play they are seeking to lose, rather than to affirm, personal identity. The singer is a mouthpiece for his people's culture and history. If he sings of himself or of topical and local events it is positively to assert his oneness with the tribe, or to assuage his distress at having defected from it.

In his new, white American world the black African inevitably used the musical techniques he had been reared on. He danced to express solidarity with his however oppressed fellows; alone he hollered to the empty fields, of isolation, of hope, and of despair. His monophonic ululations, in the fields, in labour camps, in prisons, were virtually unchanged from those he had uttered at home, but for the sharper edge oppression gave to the traditional distonations of pitch and disruptions of rhythm. This can be heard in the voice of J. B. Smith,[1] a lifer in a Texan prison, recorded as late as the mid-sixties. Unaccompanied, he sings to himself, in an act of therapy, of his personal predicament which is also the human condition: 'O Lawd, I got too long for the crime I done.' The crime is Adam's *mea culpa,* the 'too long' an apprehension of the apparently irremediable burden of human suffering. So although the Afro-American is, as outcast, no longer singing a tribal song, at least he still sees himself as belonging to the downcast tribe of mankind. In so doing he calls on immemorially ancient vocal formulae of roulade and tumbling strain, and on his traditional vocal techniques, modified only by the fact that he sings in the American, rather than in a more heavily inflected African, language.

The black man's African heritage was to suffer, in his white world, an even more radical sea-change: inevitably it came into contact, and then conflict, with the musical manifestations of its new world. The white hymn offered a harmonic substratum of Western tonic, dominant and subdominant harmony, while the march provided the four-square beat of military discipline. When the American Negro responded to this music and adopted and adapted the white man's guitar–relatable to a large variety of strummed and plucked instruments in his own country–the blues was born, and with it the heart of jazz. There is no decisive moment at which the folk holler turns into the

[1] *J. B. Smith: Ever Since I have been a Man Full Grown.*

blues. Pete Williams,[2] for instance, another black man in a southern prison, uses guitar to accompany himself in what he calls 'Prisoner's talkin' blues' and 'Levee camp blues', but these are still basically hollers in which speech is translated into pentatonic tumbling strains, with the guitar providing an ostinato accompaniment, with no sense of harmonic progression. 'Levee camp blues', as a labour song, is more metrical in rhythm and less primitive in melody (Aeolian rather than pentatonic), but the guitar still plays mainly a tonic chord, with fleeting touches of dominant and subdominant. The poetic theme is the traditional one of the faithless woman: no human relationship, not even the fundamental one of sex, can alleviate the loner's lonesomeness. This music is still personal therapy rather than art. It makes little difference whether the black man instinctively recalls melodic and rhythmic conventions from his African past or whether he directly adapts the white man's evangelical hymnody. Blind Willie Johnson,[3] a very primitive country bluesman, sings the hymn 'Mother's children' in a blackly African, guttural, growling timbre, reducing the tune to pentatonic ululations incrementally repeated. Another hymn, 'Dark was the night', he croaks with shamanistic intensity, allowing himself in this case vestigial touches of white harmony on his guitar, and achieving plangent nuance in its solo lines.

Although Blind Willie Johnson is not here singing blues, in 'Dark was the night' he uses his voice in duologue with the guitar–a melody instrument that can sing with much of the nuanced sensitivity of the human voice and can also strum harmonically those basic chords of Europe's, and in particular white America's, hymnic convention. Formally, the (usually but not always) twelve-bar blues was created as white hymn and march became a prison against which the black singer or instrumental soloist beat. If he sometimes beat desperately, he did not do so in vain, for from strife is generated ebullience. Against the square metre of the eupeptically military march the sinuously flexible rhythms of the black body dance and prance–and lock in a stance, as the rigidity of military metre induces

[2] *Angola Prisoners' Blues* and *Angola Prison Spirituals.*

[3] *Blind Willie Johnson, His Story Told, Annotated and Documented by Samuel B. Charteris.*

tension. This dichotomy between two conceptions of rhythm is complemented by a dichotomy between black melody and white harmony, which interact in a pain that simultaneously disturbs and heals. This is evident when Robert Johnson sings a blues with the pertinent title of 'At the crossroads'.[4] Johnson was a highly neurotic black man, addicted to wine and women no less than to song; he was murdered in 1937, at the age of 21. Both the harsh timbre of his voice and the pentatonic contours of his melody are profoundly African: launching the phrases on a high, pinched note, he descends in a tumbling strain, while the chittering of his guitar, fretted with a bottle neck, brokenly attempts to affirm a march-like beat and to delineate the tonic, dominant and subdominant bases of white tonality. Unlike the examples previously mentioned, this is a real twelve-bar blues, affecting a compromise between black melody and rhythm and white (I–IV–V–I) harmony and metre. But the compromise is an agony; vocal and instrumental elements cannot cosily fit–not surprisingly, since he yells, 'Ain't nobody seem to know me, everybody pass me by.' Yet the desperate reiterations of the phrases still have some therapeutic efficacy: fortitude, even power, is generated from violence and contradiction.

The alienation of the blues–the basic conflict between black and white sources–is epitomized in the phenomenon of 'blue' notes, often referred to in the white music previously discussed. Repeatedly the natural thirds and sevenths of pentatonic and modal melody collide with the sharpened sevenths and leading notes demanded by Western dominant–tonic harmony, the more so because the natural thirds and sevenths can only approximate to harmonically tempered intervals. The phenomenon of blue notes repeats a process that had happened, in a wider and more complex context, in Europe, when the mystically orientated theocracy of the Middle Ages was engulfed by the Renaissance and by the humanistically and scientifically centred modern world. Then too the new post-Renaissance harmony called for sharpened thirds and sevenths to define cadence and mark temporal progression; while music-makers nurtured on folk monody and on liturgical polyphony instinctively favoured the natural, flatter intervals.

[4] *Classic Jazz Masters: Robert Johnson 1936–7.*

Simultaneous or near-simultaneous clashes of minor and major thirds occurred, at first intuitively, then with conscious artifice in ecclesiastical association with painful experience like crucifixion or, more commonly, in secular association with the anguish of love despised or the ecstasy of love fulfilled. In the European fifteenth and sixteenth centuries this device was known as false relation. Blue notes in Afro-American jazz are a technique exactly comparable, likewise springing from a clash between two views of the world. They are indeed false relations which, in the context of history, may prove to be symptomatic of a change no less crucial than that between the Middle Ages and the modern world. It might even be valid to suggest that the evolution of temperament, especially equal temperament, in European music was a Fall from Eden, from grace to disgrace, without which the splendours and miseries of modern Faustian man would have been musically inconceivable. That melodic line in the blues–and in the songs of Dylan and other folk-affiliated pop artists–is relatively free and natural in intonation cannot be fortuitous. It is natural because it seeks, though it may not find, an Edenic state, the Eternal Return which is the basic motive of the music: the affinity of Dylan with black bluesmen goes much deeper than race. He often sounds very like Robert Johnson, and he too is 'at the crossroads'. He has also admitted a debt to Leadbelly, Blind Lemon Jefferson, Big Bill Broonzy, Mance Lipscombe, Big Joe Williams, Muddy Waters, Victoria Spivey, and, more surprisingly, to both the singing and playing of Jelly Roll Morton.

But the immediate impetus to Dylan's songs was a white man whom he recognized as his master. Born in Oklahoma in 1912, Woody Guthrie[5] was a poor white ramblin' man who, in the *Grapes of Wrath* era and area, wandered deprived, rootless and disordered, differing from hundreds of similar hobo types only in the possession of sharp intelligence, verbal facility and an acute musical ear. He picked up verses and tunes wherever he found them, refashioned them, created others of his own so true to type that it is difficult to extrapolate what is new from what is traditional. Singing a number such as 'It was sad when that great ship went down' he creates a topical news sheet out of

[5] *Woody Guthrie: Library of Congress Recordings.*

fragmented white ballad, Negro blues, evangelical hymn, country-western banjo, fiddle and harmonica music, circus tune and music-hall ditty. What appealed so powerfully to the young Dylan was clearly not so much Guthrie's art–as poor white minstrel he is notably inferior to Doc Watson and Roscoe Holcomb–but his immediate relevance to and in Dylan's world. He made verses and music from firsthand experience, whether he adapts a traditional number like the 'Boll weevil song', makes a memorable tune to catchy verses as in 'So long, it's been good to know you', or merely talks, to a rudimentary accompaniment, of events as they happen, as in the series of Dust Bowl Blues, which are blue in mood though not in form. Guthrie's own numbers stem from the monody of deprivation in their flat, deadpan vocal production and in the self-enclosed, usually stepwise moving tunes or mumbles; but from the white euphoria in their chattering, major diatonic banjo or guitar accompaniments, and in the use of harmonica or fiddle as a blissful evocation of Eden. 'Talkin' Columbia' is musically irreproachable, though the near-spoken words are socially critical; 'New found land' is comparable, though sung to a jaunty tune suggestive of minstrel-show music. 'Oregon trail' calls directly on cowboy music; 'Pastures of plenty' is a dust-bowl trudge, melodically deprived but rhythmically and tonally euphoric, offering escape and pie in the sky by and by. The famous 'Goin' down the road feelin' bad' ballasts the deprivation of the badlands with the comradeship of one's cronies, in parallel thirds, as well as the conventionally unremitting rhythm. In vocal production Dylan is closer to Nimrod Workman or Aunt Molly Jackson (whom he had listened to avidly), or still more to Roscoe Holcomb, than he is to Woody Guthrie. None the less it was Guthrie who decisively awoke the young Dylan to the verities of an America alienated, persecuted and dispossessed: first through the moving simplicity of his autobiography which told of his impending destruction by the industrial disease known as Huntington's chorea; then and more importantly through the laconicism of his words and tunes, which related his own fate to the destiny of 'poor white' Americans in general. For a while Dylan came near to identifying himself with Guthrie, having no ambition but to continue his work. If it seems odd that much of the music of today's relatively affluent young should stem from similar roots, the development of Dylan's art may provide both explanation and justification.

2

Protest and Affirmation

Dylan's main sources we have seen to be North American (Yankee) transformations of British ballads, southern Poor White (Appalachian) metamorphoses of them, cowboy or hill-billy songs, Negro hollers and blues, and gospel music both black and white. But it is important to recognize that influences with Dylan are never more than skin deep: they mean no more than that he was alive in a world where other things happen. Everything is re-created in his performance, which is also composition; and in his composition, which is also performance. What matters is what Dylan does, not what he absorbs; and this is true even of his initial album, issued under the basic title of *Bob Dylan* in 1962, when he was a lank stripling of 20. By that time he was living penuriously in New York, singing at folk clubs in the Village, mostly at Mike Porco's on West Fourth Street. He told New Yorkers that he was an orphan from New Mexico!

Hardly any of the music on this first, 1962 disc is original Dylan. Significantly, he finds his material impartially in models white and black. 'Pretty Peggy O' is based on a traditional Scots folk song, 'The bonnie lass o'Pyvie' though–despite the Scots hoots that Dylan farcically injects into his Texan country version–that would be difficult to realize. He almost certainly picked it up not in its original form but in a modification sung by Joan Baez and published in a song book. He turns it into a white American march, whitely euphoric in its bouncing beat, tipsily chattering in its virtuosic harmonica interludes–which are funny, yet on tenterhooks. The raspy voice–especially on 'died'–provides a disturbing edge to the guitar's and harmonica's low comedy. 'Man of constant sorrow', on the other hand, is unambiguously sorrowful, as it is when this southern American mountain song is sung by real folk singers like Sarah Ogan Gunning or by a modern revivalist like Judy Collins. Dylan takes over from traditional mountain style the bleatingly sustained tones that echo across the valleys, the painful elongation of vowel sounds, and the quavery melismata on words like 'troubled', complementing these vocal features with the spluttering gasps and the lonesome train hoots of his harmonica.

Still more remarkable are the numbers adapted from black singers. 'You're no good' he picked up from Jesse Fuller, the itinerant West Coast bluesman. He barks it huskily, fast and fierce, but tempers savagery with a minstrel-show style hint of the ludicrous. His harmonica playing, perhaps influenced by Sonny Terry whom he deeply admires, is very drunk: high, perhaps, because he had 'no food to eat'. Two death songs, however, balance this by being as primitive as black field or gospel hollers. 'Fixin' to die', adapted from Bukka White, has no tune but hollers in repeated notes and falling minor thirds, the rhythm distraught, the vocal timbre strangled. 'In my time of dyin'' has a rudimentary ostinato on guitar and a shouted incantation for voice as savage as a black tumbling strain. Dylan cannot remember when he first heard the song but makes no claim to have invented it–nor need he, since its shapes are so basic that they are common property. Another holler, this time in gospel vein, is his deeply moving version of Blind Lemon Jefferson's death-haunted 'See that my grave is kept clean'. This is a real blues, though often the guitar is content to substitute a throbbing drone for the conventional blues chord sequence. Whatever he may have learned from Jefferson, Dylan's control of line in relation to verbal meaning is here already *sui generis*; his extraordinary, instantly recognizable voice whispers, chuckles, grunts, growls and howls without impairing the line's musical contour. This is still more evident in 'House of the risin' sun', a semi-folk tune so haunting that it has been adapted by generations of folk, pop and even jazz singers. Dylan sings the number, originally the protest of a New Orleans prostitute, in her persona; in introverted intimacy, yet with disturbing immediacy, as the pain-induced words provoke a tremor, even a soft snarl, in the rather noble melody. The wildly melismatic expansion of the tune in the middle stanzas and its graduated decline at the end show a remarkable, spontaneous maturity for so young a man. Although the song is not his own, there is enough re-creation to suggest that Dylan will soon emerge as a creator in his own right.

Other people's experience is personalized: singing 'Gospel plow', a spiritual that may be white or black, Dylan crowingly pleads for God's help in hanging on to the plough's handle. It is no longer merely a plough, but also any prop that the rudderless young might grasp at. Twenty years later Dylan is to grip that plough with a difference, but there can be no doubt of the intensity of this potential commitment in early youth. Desperation is not, however, an exclusive or even the main note of this album. Much of it is sheer fun, and some of it is comic to the verge of parody. He treats 'Freight train blues', a railway number garnered from Roy Acuff, in guitar-strumming white country abandon, blurting into Jimmie Rodgers-like yodels in emulation of the hooting train. Dylan makes himself laugh as much as his listeners. Caricature, benign rather than savage, balances his protesting anger, in a manner essential to his evolution as an independent song writer.

Such an equilibrium is embryonic in the only two originals on this disc, though neither is of much musical consequence. 'Talkin' New York', the first of Dylan's talkin' numbers, makes no pretence to musical substance. The words, jotted down–according to the record sleeve–on a hitch-hiking trip west as he abandoned a disillusioning New York, manage to be both acidly acute and funny. The incanted inflexions, over a thrummed ostinato, give vestigial musical pith and point to them, already indicating that Dylan's music will always be in some degree 'performed literature'. 'Song to Woody', the other original, is precisely what it says: a lonesome hobo song, with a tune that, like 'Three blind mice', is memorable if not distinguished, and with words addressed to, and in the manner of, his folk hero–with passing references to other legendary figures. Talkin' and Woody Guthrie were sparking points for Dylan's art. The song is both a homage and a farewell. Though he is to leave Guthrie far behind as he gives the heritage presented on this first disc radical and wondrous transformations, he might legitimately claim that 'in my end is my beginning', as well as vice versa.

Dylan's development, both as man and as artist, was rapid and remarkable during the first three years of the sixties. By now he was concentrating mainly on originals in which the story-telling he had indulged in in boyhood takes on a deeper, more archetypal import, with resonances relevant to everyone. His musical techniques grew, through sedulous imitation and a hard process of self-discovery, in consort with his poetic flowering; his voice acquired its characteristic twang, his guitar and harmonica playing became potent enough for him to teach himself all he needed to know, at this stage, about composition. Like a real folk singer, he never had a formal music lesson and never needed one. His 1962–3 disc is pertinently called *The Freewheelin' Bob Dylan,* followed in 1964 by *The Times They are A-changin',* another title apposite in both private and public terms. These discs present numbers which are either originals or are made from traditional material so transformed that the re-fashioning has become a creative act. The songs may be grouped into four basic conventions.

The first is the narrative and/or preaching number in which the words are crucial because they tell a tale and deliver a message, to which the music is ancillary but supportive. Dylan's master, Woody Guthrie, though remarkable for the direct immediacy of his songs, was a complex, neurotic man whose obsession with radical politics was intellectually potent; he read widely and deeply, and knew what he was talking about. Dylan's politics, absorbed at second hand or from the air around him, were emotive and instinctual. In his teens older women mothered him and young women adored him for his waif-like vulnerability and boyish charm; many detected in him a comic pathos recalling Charlie Chaplin, whose films he had never seen. This image changed as he discovered his poetic and musical voice; but although, growing up to confront the painful realities of the world, he acquired a tart astringency, he was animated by gut reactions–by social conscience rather than by political intent. This is true even of 'Talkin' World War III blues' which, like 'Talkin' New York', has no tune and therefore no lyricism. The words, spoken against a rudimentary blues sequence on guitar, are bitterly sophisticated in their comment on the plight of modern man, and the number seems to differ from a Woody Guthrie talkin' blues only in that Dylan's voice is more cunningly inflected. Even so, the tone is different; the words' fantasticality has a poetic rather than a social-political dimension.

This is more evident in a slightly more musical narrative number, 'The ballad of Hollis Brown'. The verses tell a true story of a farmer in South Dakota who, maddened by penury, shoots himself and his family. The motivation is political, but what Dylan responds to is the basic, pitiful human situation. He uses a straightforward linear technique to tell the tale, yet the literary form turns out, as with 'Talkin' New York', to be circular. Past and present tenses are confused; flashes of poetic metaphor and folk-like magical references–for instance to the number seven–enliven the flat language, while the music, consisting of a pre-pentatonic incantation supported by an unchanging ostinato of tonic and dominant chords on acoustic guitar, could hardly be more deprived. Dylan sings the mostly four-note incantation in middle register, in rasping sonority, with painful elongation of vowels. He sounds remarkably like Roscoe Holcomb or Nimrod Workman (whom he is unlikely to have heard), with a black tinge from, perhaps, Fred Macdowell. Musically, nothing happens within the song, except for a slight agitation of the guitar figuration in the penultimate stanza, yet the numbing vocal line, the nagging instrumental ostinato, the inexorable continuity, serve an imaginative purpose: it is possible to *go on*, at whatever rock-bottom level of fortitude. If seven people are dead on a South Dakota farm, somewhere seven new people are born. Dylan's deadpan, throwaway delivery of this statement leaves it open to the listener to interpret it as optimism or defeat.

Dylan's singing technique here testifies to the sense in which his identity as poet is, even in these early days, inseparable from his identity as composer. Although his numbers are notated, as a real folk singer's are not, the pitches and rhythms he sings are not those on the printed page: microtonal distortions of pitch and flexibilities of nuance determine both musical and verbal expression. In this song, for instance, the potent metaphor of the grass 'turning black' in the sixth stanza, the 'cold coyote' that howls in the wilderness of stanza seven, and the 'seven breezes a-blowin' all around the cabin door' after the murder and suicide, introduce linear arabesques and hesitancies of rhythm that are the heart of the musical experience, not a decorative addition to it. The relationship between words and music is as intimate as it is in medieval and non-Western cantillation, and considerably more so than it is in the Elizabethan ayre with lute.

Similar in technique to 'Hollis Brown' is an explicit preaching song, 'Masters of war', one of the few numbers which Dylan admits to being motivated by hate. The words are satirically trenchant and cumulative, the music a pre-pentatonic incantation close to that of 'Hollis Brown' over the same oscillating tonics and dominants. However, the song is the obverse of 'Hollis Brown' in that the words are highly charged and rhetorically pointed, safeguarded from hysteria by the music's non-developing reiterations. In 'Hollis Brown' the music's inexorability reinforces the flat telling of the tale, incrementally inducing panic which explodes in murder and suicide, before placing the 'tragedy' (in the newspapers' sense) in the context of history. The language of 'Hollis Brown' is poetic because the words invite sympathy for, though not identification with, the protagonists. The words of 'Masters of war', on the other hand, are plain, apart from the 'pale afternoon' on which, in the last stanza, the funeral of the mass murderers takes place. In those two simple words, the dire machinations of the war-lords are revealed to have human consequences. The afternoon is anthropomorphically pale: it is drained of our blood. In the penultimate verse there is an early reference to Jesus, though he belies his nature in that even he would 'never forgive' what the war-lords do.

Sometimes these incantatory songs are narrative and preaching at the same time. 'Who killed Davy Moore?', a number which Dylan has not recorded commercially,[1] deals in primitive intonation – the last six bars merely alternate between two tones – with a specific human situation. In the tersely vernacular

[1] Pete Seeger's rather melodramatic version is available on *Pete Seeger: We Shall Overcome.*

verses everyone–boxer, referee, promoter, manager, journalist, crowd–in turn disclaims responsibility for a ringside disaster, and the music universalizes this by floating, in pentatonic spontaneity, to the surface of the mind. It is as archetypal as the 'Cock Robin' rhyme it transmutes, and this must be why the effect of the song is more musically impressive than its minimal notation would lead one to expect. The 'Cock Robin' phrase has wide and deep mythological references, and a tale told in the squalid context of the boxing world proves to be a confrontation with, not a liquidation of, universal guilt.

Such an exploitation of old and powerfully reverberative sources leads to the second type of song typical of Dylan's early years. In this category interest centres not in declamation but in a tune. None the less, the impact of these melodies is inseparable from the way in which the words would be spoken: particularized tenderness, grace or vivacity; or anger, disgust or malice. Sometimes, though infrequently in the early period, these lyrical numbers are love songs, and are in both verbal and musical formulae closely related to or directly derived from real rural melodies. 'Girl from the north country', for instance, is a rehash of 'Scarborough Fair'; the singer conveys, in traditional folk style, a message to his girl by way of a third party, and in the process nostalgically identifies person and place. The tune's obsession with a tonic major triad is reflected in the simplest triadic harmony, yet so sensitively does Dylan vary pitch and rhythm that the melody lilts across the beat, emulating the 'snowflakes and howlin' winds' making the girl's hair 'flow and roll all down her breast'. 'Boots of Spanish leather' is a comparably tender, original love song. The poetry has something of the radiance of real folk verse:

> O but if I had the stars from the darkest night
> And the diamonds from the deepest ocean,
> I'd forsake them all for your sweet kiss,
> For that's all I'm wishin' to be ownin'.

Even the wryly defensive last stanza, in which he suggests that if she is going to leave him he may as well get a pair of Spanish boots as compensation, is not without parallel in folk sources. The tune is clearly diatonic and again tends to be triadic; none the less it floats across the triple beat and hints, since the III–IV–I harmony evades the dominant, at a folk-like modality. The guitar figuration is continuous, but gently enveloping, rather than mindlessly merry. Such a song belongs to a young man of the second half of the twentieth century, while incorporating elements that spring from a remote rural past–as does his version of a genuine country song, 'Corinna, Corinna', which he sings with an open-eyed and open-eared tenderness safeguarded from sentimentality by the tranquillizing, jogging 6/8 metre, and an occasional falsetto lift.

The two most characteristic love songs on these two discs are, if not anti-love songs, at least dismissive in tone. 'Down the highway' is a farewell to a girl the singer has obviously been fond of but has become disillusioned with. Although the number is credited to Dylan as an original composition, its manner is so basic to black blues idiom that it can be thought of as part of an old and primitive tradition. The verse structure is that of the blues; the falling pitches are as rudimentary as a field holler; the vocal distonations and colorations are worthy of Big Joe Williams to whom, in this context, Dylan pays homage. He is also justified in claiming that, like a real black bluesman, he is here using the blues authentically–as a means of getting outside personal distress, instead of wallowing in it–as is implicit in the tremolando guitar interludes.

The same therapeutic function is served by another song, this time in white country idiom. It is not really surprising that 'Don't think twice, it's all right' has remained one of the most potent of Dylan's early songs, for it does far more than wave a cheery goodbye to a girl who has proved inadequate. When the rooster crows, he is 'travelling on', not because the woman was particularly 'unkind', but because she 'could have done better', and 'kinda wasted my time'. He wanted a relationship which didn't waste time because it was rooted in the truth of feeling, with which, Dylan has said, all his songs are concerned. Having failed to find such a relationship, he does not feel vindictive, but knows he must have the confidence to move on, even to be lonesome a while, if need be. This necessity to be himself is what he learned from Woody Guthrie, and in this song it is the music that offers an affirmation. The tune rocks between minor and major thirds over the vivacious beat, balancing its dominant by a subdominant modulation, and effecting release by a chromatic twist in the return to the tonic. It comes across as a song about dawn and the rooster rather than as a song of farewell. Its re-creativity is inherent in the immediacy of Dylan's vocal inflexions–for instance the open caws on 'break' (of dawn) and on 'all' in contrast with the decline of pitch and discoloration of tone on 'stay'. 'Don't think twice' is a love song because it is infectiously pro-life.

Songs in Dylan's lyrical category are not necessarily love songs. 'North country blues', for instance, is not a blues but a mining town song in the form of a waltz. The Aeolian tune, enclosed within fourths and fifths, is as austere as a real Kentucky mining melody. The tale is told, again in authentic folk spirit, without rhetoric, though the self-enclosed identity of the melody assuages pain in a way that the declamatory technique of 'Hollis Brown' does not. Occasionally a lyrical song may be also satirical and covertly or overtly political. 'With God on our side' retells American military history with savage verbal humour, to a swinging hillbilly waltz tune. On any count this melody–with its cowboyish upward-arching sixth and slow declension–is memorable, and Odetta's very slow and very beautiful performance proves that it can be deeply affecting. This is not Dylan's intention: the total impact of *his* performance depends on an equilibrium between the bitterness of the words:

The cavalries charged,
The Indians died,
O the country was young
With God on its side;

their grotesque horror:

Though they murdered six million
In the ovens they fried,
The Germans now too
Have God on their side;

and the annealment the lyrical tune offers. The tune comforts, even delights, yet at the same time is recurrently modified by

Dylan's response to specific words and phrases. With Dylan melody is never an absolute.

In this song the harmonica sometimes sounds Edenic, but sometimes emulates–ironically in the context–a chapel organ. This fits with the Christian gloss given to the penultimate stanza, which ought to be the end of the number, since the moralizing last stanza is tautological. Though the point of the words:

> But I can't think for you,
> you'll have to decide
> Whether Judas Iscariot
> Had God on his side.

remains political or at least sociological, Dylan is later to give an explicitly religious answer to his hitherto unanswered question. The same is true of other songs of the period which are usually construed as political. The folk technique of question and answer in antiphony, allied to the positive, unmodulating, resolutely diatonic country tune, gives 'Blowin' in the wind' a dimension indicative of a change of heart as well as of political organization, reminding us that an answer to the question:

> How many deaths will it take till he knows
> That too many people have died?

cannot be given in merely material terms. A political panacea, though necessary, is not enough; nor was it even Dylan's ostensible theme, for he remarked in an interview for *Sing Out*! that, 'There ain't too much I can say about this song except that the answer is blowing in the wind. It ain't in no book or movie or TV show or discussion group. Man, hip people are telling me where the answer is but oh *I won't believe that*. I still say it's in the wind and just like a restless piece of paper it's got to come down some time . . . But the only trouble is that no one picks up the answer.'

In his notorious speech to the Civil Liberties Committee which had awarded him the Tom Paine medal for his services to civil rights Dylan came near to biting the hand that fed him. 'I'm trying to go up without thinking of anything trivial, such as politics,' said he. 'That has got nothing to do with it. I'm thinking about the general people, and when they get hurt.' Even when he is writing positively of political issues, his approach tends to be as much religious as sociological. 'When the ship comes in' sounds like a revolutionary song and John Herdman may be right in suggesting that it was prompted by Brecht's 'Pirate Jenny'. Yet the basic provenance of this ship is messianically biblical, and its vision of the 'dreadful day' (of Judgement) is no less theologically traditional for being comic. Whether the words are taken politically or apocalyptically, and both are valid, the song comes across as neither bitter nor even satirical, but as merrily affirmative. The mainly stepwise-moving, unambiguously diatonic tune bounces out of the wittily lilting words:

> Oh the fishes will laugh
> As they swim out of the path
> And the seagulls they'll be smiling.

And the very symmetry of the tune, which thrusts forward but does not modulate, demonstrates how

> The sun will respect
> Every face on the deck,
> The hour when the ship comes in.

Here Dylan has imbued the euphoria of the white American march with recharged electrical energy. The song does not merely encourage its audience to keep going by being vacuously cheerful in the face of desperate odds; rather it achieves a resilience in its metrical rhythm and an elasticity and drive in the repeated notes in the marching melody that effect a creative awakening, even a new birth. The benign glee with which Dylan announces that even 'foes', jerked from their beds, will

> . . . pinch themselves and squeal
> And know that it's for real,
> The hour when the ship comes in.

clearly involves more than social metamorphosis. Words and music have an equal and complementary liveliness. Although tune and beat seem to carry all before them, Dylan's response to individual words and phrases is continually renewing: consider his treatment of the long note, originally a 'breaking', at the end of the stanzas, and the effervescent rhythms, half rhymes and internal assonances that prompt one to laugh out loud. Such technical skill should not be underestimated because it is largely instinctual.

Such a song crosses the border into the fourth category which we may call apocalyptic. In these songs words and tune are often a permutation of real folk sources. 'A hard rain's a-gonna fall', for instance, is a refashioning of the ballad of Lord Randal. The sinister story is remade in universal terms:

> O what did you see, my blue-eyed son?
> . . . I saw a newborn baby with wild wolves all round it,
> I saw a highway of diamonds with nobody on it,
> I saw a black branch with blood that kept dripping . . .
> I saw a white ladder all covered with water.

Such poetic imagery has an affinity with runic folk verse such as the magnificent 'Nottamin Town' in which a country boy, marooned in a city, sits himself down

> . . . on a hard, hot, cold frozen stone,
> Ten thousand around me, yet I was alone;
> Took my hat in my hands for to keep my head warm,
> Ten thousand got drownded that never were born.

There are parallels too with the visionary writing of Bunyan and Blake. But although Dylan preserves the incremental treatment of the original tune, he damps down its wildness, transforming its modality into a halting seven-bar phrased hillbilly waltz, and singing it flatly, even monotonously. The song is often related to the Cuban missile crisis, with the hard rain being atomic fall-out. Dylan denied this, with some point since the first version of the number predates that event. Associations with the Bomb inevitably intrude, though there are no specific references to it in the text and the 'pellets of poison' are virulent enough in representing 'all the lies that people are told on their radios and in the newspapers, trying to take people's brains away'. The text functions by way of ironic parallels between the private crime of Lord Randal's murder in olden times and the public holocaust faced by the modern world. The scenes evoked in the poetic imagery are indeed archetypal; and the attitude of the narrator–both Dylan himself and an anonymous representative of our beleagured race–varies from stanza to stanza, being now hopeful, now despairing, now savage, now sad. The reference to the young girl's rainbow in the last stanza has Christian overtones which grow stronger in Dylan's later work. But the Christian hope is present merely among many, often contradictory, possibilities. The ambiguity mirrors that of the world we live in, and is feasible only in an aural poetry which may be modified in the moment of utterance. Even in his protest days Dylan was seldom a didactic artist.

Prophetic songs like 'When the ship comes in' and visionary songs like 'A hard rain' set the stage for Dylan's second period which is broached, though not conclusively entered, in his fourth album, appropriately titled *Another Side of Bob Dylan* (1964). Links with his earlier songs are obvious enough: 'I shall be free No. 10' is a talkin' number with a political burden, while 'Chimes of freedom' might be described as the last of the protest songs, with an apocalyptic undertow. There is, however, a difference: the 'victims' who are involved and prayed for are not merely casualties of an unjust economic system but rather the 'countless confused, accused, misused, strung-out ones an' worse'. There is therefore a connection between such public appeals for freedom and the more personal songs in which Dylan seeks escape from any human relationship that threatens his personal integrity. These songs are not really cruel, because he is asking the other person not to fear self-knowledge. Sometimes the effect is comic, as in 'All I really want to do', a rudimentary country waltz with a verse that simply flops down the scale and is then perked up by a yodelling refrain in Jimmie Rodgers style. Both the internal rhymes and half rhymes and the bouncing phrases are irresistible, defining positives by listing the negative qualities his girl would be better without.

'Black crow blues', a mean, low-down honky-tonk number, seems more desolately negative, yet generates energy from its meanness, so that it comes across as a kind of affirmation. 'It ain't me, babe', also dismissive in that he refuses to allow the girl's self-regarding love to engulf him, disarms through its lyricism and chuckles through its internal rhymes. Here Dylan's irony laughs rather than blisters, and laughter can be a great healer. Something similar is true of 'To Ramona' and 'Spanish Harlem incident', which move closer towards Dylan's second phase–perhaps because the young women in these songs are exotic. Ramona's Tex-Mex waltz slides through a ninth on to a firm tonic, as Dylan tries to dispel her dreams and make her face herself as well as him. 'Spanish Harlem incident' concerns a 'gypsy gal' whose 'temperature's too hot for taming'. This time it is the singer who learns self-knowledge: 'Will I be touching you/So I can tell if I'm really real?' The tune is not as insidious as Ramona's, but it gets the words across–which in this case is the point.

If such songs are regarded as transitional, Dylan's second period proper can be said to begin in the following year, 1965, with *Bringing It All Back Home*. Whereas his first phase had been a kind of anti-litany, exorcizing the devil in an incantory, even at times unmusical, cawing style, raucous and rancid, the evolution from protest to ambiguous acceptance is also a move towards lyricism and music. 'It's all right, ma (I'm only bleeding)' is a turning-point. Basically it is a talkin' number in which the words, building incrementally with complex internal rhymes, devastatingly comment on the hypocrisies of (especially modern) civilization. There is a mixture of narration and preaching but both, perhaps continuing from the apocalyptic numbers, have a somewhat hallucinatory quality. The analysis of social ills is no longer merely from the outside:

> My eyes collide head on with stuffed graveyards,
> False gods, I scuff
> At pettiness which plays so rough
> Walk upside down inside handcuffs
> Kick my legs to crash it off.

But when Dylan reaches the refrain and tells his mother and us that he can make it, the music breaks into a pentatonic roulade that is at least more lyrical than the previous talk. Over a rudimentary guitar ostinato the pentatonic falling third is augmented on 'It's all right, ma'. The effect of this unchanging refrain grows stronger through the slowly exfoliating stanzas, getting the better of both the nagging and the talk. The music amplifies the words: despite the horrors abroad, the bleeding and sighing and dying, it *is* all right, and the mother figure can be addressed comically yet without contempt.

There are more Negroid elements in this song than in most of the others so far discussed. Out of black rhythmic flexibility and ambiguous blue thirds comes the hint of a new world, embracing a reality within as well as without the mind. Given that white had to absorb black in order to attain to adulthood and that blacks are popularly supposed to be closer to instinctual sources than ego- and intellect-bound whites, it is not surprising that the merging of white with black idiom in Dylan's songs should initiate his exploration of the inner life of dream and nightmare. Certainly it would be on the mark, in comparing 'Subterranean homesick blues' with the first period's 'Talkin' World War III blues', to point out not only that the music is much blacker in its barrel-house beat and false relations, but also that the words are more potent but less logically explicit, with their derisive internal rhymes:

> Ah get born, keep warm,
> Short pants, romance, learn to dance,
> Get dressed, get blessed,
> Try to be a success. . . .
> Don't wanna be a bum,
> You better chew gum,
> The pump don't work
> 'Cause the vandals took the handles.

That last clause is not only funny but also–since handles are used to control things–exact in encapsulating the demise of industrial technocracy. 'Outlaw blues' has a similar comic ferocity. It is a genuine twelve-bar blues in fast barrel-house style, in which Dylan uses his voice like blackly neurotic Robert Johnson. Even white country numbers have acquired something of this interior electricity. 'Maggie's farm', for instance, is a half-speaking, half-singing, narrative ballad with social implications in that Dylan dismisses Maggie's brothers, Ma and Pa as the predators and slave drivers they seem to be. Yet at the same time he invests his comments–especially by way of his varied distortions of the interval of the fifth–with a blue-black edge that is both passionate and hilarious. It follows that his denunciation is not totally negative. Ma and Pa are vividly realized, and for Ma there is even a hint of compassion: although she is an old bag who 'talks to all the servants about Man and God and Law', she is vulnerable–after all, she is 68, though she says she is 54.

Even 'Love minus Zero/no limit', though a country song with no obvious black features, has a new interior intensity in its displaced, slightly hallucinatory chords. It hints at an ideal(ized) love relationship with a woman who, Zen-affiliated, is beyond the evasions and insincerities that afflict most social intercourse: she 'winks, she does not bother,/She knows too much to argue or to judge'. There may be an anticipation of the surreal imagery of Dylan's psychedelic phase; and the revelatory moments seem to be precipitated out of the admission of harsh and abrasive realities:

> The bridge at midnight trembles
> The country doctor rambles
> Bankers' nieces seek perfection
> Expecting all the gifts that wise men bring.
> The wind howls like a hammer
> The night blows cold and rainy
> My love she's like some raven
> At my window with a broken wing.

The imagery startles in its unexpectedness. Herdman suggests that it owes its evocativeness to a probably unconscious reference to Edgar Allan Poe's 'Nevermore'-cawing raven; and since kafka means raven in Czech, there may be a reference to Franz Kafka's story *The Country Doctor*. Certainly Dylan's obliquities about events and motivations are often Kafkaesque, and the ghostly presence of Kafka's country doctor may have some bearing on his verse's mysteriousness: as does the airy melody which, floating waveringly over plain diatonic concords, mostly I, V, IV and III, seems at once real and illusory. This is one of the first Dylan songs to explore the cinematic technique of mutable images which he is to develop in much of his later work. It is both verbally and musically potent.

As Dylan's art embraces more layers of experience, it equivocates more between appearance and reality, dream and nightmare. 'Mr Tambourine Man' is the first and remains one of the greatest of his dream songs, with a melody the more haunting because it is impossible to categorize. Although it has something in common with Celtic folk song and American country music, its quality cannot be defined in terms of them, and it has no connection with the Negro blues. Far from being socially committed, 'Mr Tambourine Man' looks as though it might be an escape song: and may be so, if there is any basis to the suggestion that a tambourine man is a pedlar of pot. But the hallucinatory imagery need not have narcotic origins: Dylan specifically says that he is 'not sleepy', though there 'ain't no place' he's going to. The heart of the matter is that his Pied-Piper myth encourages us to follow the unconscious wherever it may spontaneously lead us–ecstatically into the sky where there are 'no fences' to confine 'the skippin' reels of rhyme', but also into vaguely minatory regions 'down the foggy ruins of time, far past the frozen leaves,/The haunted, frightened trees, out to the windy beaches'. Poetically, Dylan wings to lyrical heights, in a manner that is inherently aural rather than visual in its patterned internal rhymes, assonances and alliterations. Musically the refrain wavers irregularly, like the smoke rings, which are imitated by the circularity of the repeated clauses, sidling down through an octave, then unfurling.

The verbal and metrical equivocations are also reflected in the ambiguous tonality: although the song is notated as though it were in D major, the tune behaves melodically, and is harmonized, as though it were in a Lydian G major–D major's subdominant with sharpened fourth. It can be only fortuitous, though happily so, that the Lydian mode was traditionally associated with healing. Here it is the tonal ambiguity that makes the melody float so dreamily, so that when a D major cadence is reached at the end of the stanza, it has little finality and the music, like the words, seems ready to take off again. So, as the rings of the melody unfold, we are liberated; and the song turns out to be about recharging our spiritual batteries today in order to find life again tomorrow. The song is unexpectedly disturbing because its mythology plumbs unexpectedly deep. What Dylan is dealing in here, on behalf of the spiritually if not materially deprived young of the sixties, is musical therapy with its origins in real folk art. He is a shaman who effects psychological fulfilment.

This bears on the fact that Dylan's harmonica playing in this song is extraordinarily poignant. He ends with a fade-out through a long da capo of the tune on his harmonica which, being a primitive country instrument, invented about 1820, evokes the pristine world of the American New Adam. The harmonica, like the voice, has to find its own pitch, and owes its pathos to its failure quite to do so. Its quavery tones sound young and hopeful, yet at the same time frail. It longs for Eden, where pitch could be perfect, and its lonesome sound–especially as Dylan expressively plays it–contains both promise and regret. It cannot be an accident that the next song in the sequence is called 'Gates of Eden'. The Blakean poem is again richly allusive, and if the tune is less memorable it creates, within the compass of a seventh in the Mixolydian mode, an appropriate naval-gazing hypnosis. Again the song concerns the state of Eden as a condition to be won and from which to be reborn:

> At dawn my lover comes to me and tells me of her dreams
> With no attempt to shovel the glimpse
> Into the ditch of what each one means.
> At times I think there are no words
> But these to tell what's true,
> And there are no truths outside the gates of Eden.

None the less these truths are being outmoded, and *Bringing It All Back Home* marks, for Dylan, the end of an era. Significantly, the album concludes with 'It's all over now, Baby Blue', a number which seems to be a rejection of the blue-eyed folk music within which Dylan had been nurtured. Songs like 'Baby Blue', 'Mr Tambourine Man' and 'Gates of Eden' mark an end to Dylan's interest in the folk 'movement' or in overt protest. It was about this time he made one of his most revealing pronouncements, dismissing protest songs as

> vulgar–the idea that somebody has to say what they want to say in a message type song. It's a stagnation kind of thing . . . worse than being a pregnant dog.

He dismissed folk song also, but only in its conventional stereotypes:

> Most of the people who are down on me because of folk music just don't know what they're talking about. They always say folk music should be simple so people can understand. *People*! That's insulting somebody, calling them people. But the truth is there are weird folk songs that have come down through the ages, based on nothing, or based on legend, Bible, plague, religion, just based on mysticism. Those old songs weren't simple at all.[2]

Indeed they weren't; and it's possible that Dylan was helped towards this realization by the stunning impact made on him by the songs of the Beatles' middle phase. Henceforth his songs will veer between reality and dream which may be nightmare; and this is true even although the first song on the next disc, *Highway 61 Revisited*, (1965), seems to dismiss dreams as mere illusion.

[2] Quoted in Scaduto, *Bob Dylan*.

3

Between Vision and Nightmare

'Like a rolling stone' is about a girl whom Dylan calls Miss Lonely because that is what–though she has 'been to the finest school'–she is. He strips her of both her possessions and of her self-deceits:

> You shouldn't let other people
> Get your kicks for you.
> You used to ride on the chrome horse with your diplomat
> Who carried on his shoulder a Siamese cat
> Ain't it hard when you discover that
> He really wasn't where it's at
> After he took from you everything he could steal.

Although the words are dismissive, the music–with its jaunty repeated notes and eyebrow-arching rising thirds, its fragmented phrases that leave one agog for what's coming next–is positive in total effect. Stripped to a rolling stone the girl, like Dylan himself, has a chance of starting again. The sheer exuberance of the rocking instrumentals imparts to Dylan's broken crowing a heady glee. He is putting down a girl who may have wanted to gobble him up like a lollypop, but music so affirmative cannot be finally destructive. Although the tune is so potent, it is restricted to very few pitches. Its affirmation depends largely on its irregularly rhythmed repeated notes, and on an opposition between rising third and falling fourth, changed to rising fourth and falling major third during the refrain. From its simplicity springs its universality. Dylan seems to have been aware of this, since it was about the songs of this period, and this one in particular, that he confessed that in saying 'he', 'she', 'it' or 'they', 'I was really talking about me. I hadn't really known before that I was writing about myself in all these songs.'[1] So in a sense Dylan is here putting himself down, as well as the girl, and finds strength in self-knowledge. 'Like a rolling stone' became an anthem for youth in the sixties, and is still susceptible to varied transformations, some of which will be discussed later. In all versions the song, though it is about rejection, comes across as positive, for the denial of secrecy and pretence leaves Dylan free.

This song, and *Highway 61 Revisited* as a whole, represent a new start, the basis of which is freedom. But freedom, though exhilarating, is also dangerous, for it means accepting everything that the mind contains, the rough with the smooth, the black with the white. Dylan's resort to the drug experience was not an escape but rather an attempt to face up to whatever darker depths, as well as whatever lighter heights, were waiting to be revealed. It cannot be an accident that this evolution coincides with Dylan's rejection of folk tradition and his adoption of electrophonic technology. Whereas 'Mr Tambourine Man', although a drug song, is folky and countrified, with acoustic guitar and Edenic harmonica, 'Ballad of a thin man', a key number on the new album, is in city blues style, late Chicago vintage, with driving rock beat and electric amplification. When he first turned from folk guitar to the pop groups' electrophonic media Dylan was branded as a traitor by folk purists, even though he had never been, strictly speaking, a folk singer. Their objection was frivolous. A folk-pop artist, communicating with thousands, has no choice but to use the media his environment offers him, and may do so the more potently when these media may be used to turn the tables. The fine modal tune of 'Ballad of a thin man' can embrace both the subtlest harmonic ellipsis and the spooky electrophonic gibberings, so that although Mr Jones is witheringly demolished, the melody's breadth preserves something like compassion. There have been many specific identifications of Mr Jones and none of them matters. We need recognize only that he's the (fairly) respectable man in the street, and possibly you or I. He might

[1] Interview in *Rolling Stone*, 1969.

even be Dylan himself, for the singer is no longer outside his victim:

You raise up your head
And you ask, 'Is this where it is?'
And somebody points to you and says 'It's his'
And you say 'What's mine?'
And somebody else says 'Where what is?'
And you say, 'Oh my God, am I here all alone?'

The nightmare is both without and within, and the song asks questions about identity and, indeed, about existence itself: 'What *is*?' The dark threat inherent in melody, harmony and driving pulse is poles removed from the self-righteous arrogance of some of the early protest songs. The same could be said of 'Desolation row' in comparison with an early monologue like 'Talkin' World War III blues'. In a sense it is a political piece, cataloguing at some length the ills of modern civilization, its hypocrisies and self-deceits. But these ills cannot be righted by a particular course of action. We are all involved in them, as we are all to some degree the Mr Jones whom Dylan's deeper voice seems momentarily to threaten. Our involvement is the more anguished because the desolation that faces us is not merely our failings and perversities but also the nuclear holocaust that may bring a Day of Judgement in its wake. From this man-made horror the moon and stars are not merely hidden because dust-shrouded, but are themselves cowering, 'beginning to hide'. The 'fortune-telling lady' has packed up shop because no individual human creature has a life or fortune left to tell; only 'Cain and Abel and the Hunchback of Notre-Dame' find some perverse gratification in the situation. Ophelia has a fleeting glimpse of Noah's rainbow, but the rest of the world is mindlessly making love or, in several senses, 'expecting rain'. 'Praise be to Nero's Neptune, the *Titanic* sails at dawn,' caws Dylan with grim jubilation, encapsulating in this brilliant image the possibility that only through disaster, as Nero fiddles while New York-London-wherever burns, can there be any hope for mankind redeemed, even though individual men and women may have been obliterated. The bass is animatedly melodic, even perky.

On this disc there is a comparable deepening and opening out in lyrical as well as in talkin' numbers. 'Never say goodbye' is beautifully economical in setting its wintry scene of silent twilight on the frozen lake, and in balancing dubiety about a relationship with someone else with self-doubt; his 'iron and steel' dreams reach after a 'big bouquet of red roses' hanging from the heavens, and he reaches for the girl's hand as the 'crashing waves' threaten to engulf him. Musically it is a slow loping blues in barrel-house style, played on a honky-tonk piano, with harmonica making wailing train noises. Its synthesis of toughness and tenderness is strangely moving.

Some such fusion of poetic with musical depths becomes the heart of the work of Dylan's mid-sixties phase, and especially of the next (double) album, *Blonde on Blonde* (1966). Here apparent opposites have become almost indistinguishable, as Dylan gets deeper into drugs, especially LSD, hopefully to aid his search for inner identity. In later years Dylan has been cagey about his drug use which has, of course, a negative aspect in so far as it was an attempt to deal with the paranoic, near-psychotic state induced in him by conflict between the personal integrity and social honesty his songs dealt in and the nightmare life of a superstar, which he yearned for yet hated. What matters is not the nature or extent of his recourse to drugs, if any, but the intensity of his songs' equivocation between reality and dream. Quasi-surrealistic imagery has become pervasive, yet the verse is not automatic writing by free association. The openness of the words functions in the same way as oral poetry, and although meanings may be multifarious and sometimes contradictory, they do exist, and are ultimately apparent in what the music, in any given performance, does to them. Dylan has retained a special affection for *Blonde on Blonde* as the album in which he first uncompromisingly explored his inner resources. Speaking of the disc he said:

> It's the sound and the words. Words don't interfere with it. They punctuate it. You know, they give it purpose. And all the ideas for my songs come out of that. . . . I'm not doing it to see how good I can sound, or how perfect the melody can be, or how intricate the details can be woven or how perfectly

written something can be. . . . I symbolically hear that sound wherever I am . . . the sound of the street with the sunrays. The closest I ever got to that sound I hear in my mind was on individual bands in the *Blonde on Blonde* album. It's that thin, that wild mercury sound. It's metallic and bright gold. . . . I haven't been able to succeed in getting it all the time.[2]

The electrophonic sophistication of Dylan's resources is clearly an aspect of that search; and although Dylan's use of electrophonics must owe much to his experienced associates, notably Robbie Robertson, the above quotation would seem to indicate that Dylan provided the imaginative initiative. He knew the sound he wanted in a given context; the technical gadgetry was a means towards the heart's truth. In later work Dylan sometimes builds on it and sometimes, as in *John Wesley Harding,* bypasses it. But the metamorphosis remains radical. That thin, wild mercury sound is pertinent to most of Dylan's later music.

Characteristically, *Blonde on Blonde* is introduced by a number which consists simply of variations on a pun. 'Rainy day women ♯ 12 & 35' is musically corny: a parody of a New Orleans marching or Yankee Revivalist band, with a tune that is a crude chromatic descent over a lolloping, Sousa-style 6/8 beat. The electrophonic scoring, with crowd noises offstage, is brilliant. The words pun playfully upon two meanings of 'stoned': the honest man or woman, an outsider because of his or her freedom from conventional values, will have stones hurled at him or her by the conformists, even when 'tryin' to be so good'; he or she will also get stoned on whatever it might be, partly as a consequence of this outlawism, partly in an attempt to discover truer values through the Blakean Doors of Perception. The words are mostly comic, though their serious portent surfaces in the later stanzas:

They'll stone you and then say you are brave,
They'll stone you when you are set down in your grave,
But I would not feel so all alone,
Everybody must get stoned.

[2] Interview, *Rolling Stone*, 1969.

Dylan's voice rasps subtle changes, through the tritely trotting tune, emphasizing different words–now 'would not', now 'alone', now 'everybody', now 'must'. Although it is a joke number, musically insignificant, the joke itself may have profound implications–as is perhaps evident when Dylan follows 'Rainy day women' with 'Pledging my time', a very black blues in a slow-lilting boogie rhythm that reflects back on the perfunctory jogging of the previous march. In this number Dylan's distonations of pitch are authentically Negroid; the blue thirds and fifths are always painfully indeterminate–which fits the words, teetering between negative emotions of disgust and betrayal and positive emotions of hope and trust, as he pledges his time to her, *in potentia*.

These two quite brief numbers are preludial to 'Visions of Johanna', one of Dylan's longest and most complex songs, and poetically among the finest. The words are usually considered to be psychedelically obscure, though they are intelligible enough if one grants that Dylan is using a cinematic rather than a chronologically linear technique. The scene is set with maximum economy, without resort to overt description: in a nocturnal urban tenement room, 'lights flicker from the opposite loft', 'the heat-pipes just cough' and 'the country music station plays soft'. Dylan or the poet-speaker is there, apparently in bed with a girl called Louise, though her physical presence gets confused with the ghostly identity of an absent girl, Johanna, whose image is far more potent. (She has sometimes been identified as Joan Baez, though that is needlessly and destructively to limit the poem's reverberations.) That the pronoun veers between 'I' and 'he' is not only in folk tradition, but also psychologically apposite in that Dylan is aware of a dual identity: a self that is here with 'delicate' Louise, who is like a mirror (of himself) and makes it 'all too concise and too clear'; and an *alter ego* that lives and breathes, in this room, with Johanna's ghost. In the third stanza Dylan is outside both identities, seeing himself as a lost little boy who fails to relate either to the present or to the past. The blurring of time and consciousness is marvellously realized; particularized present moments–the all-night girls whispering, the nightwatchman clicking his flashlight–give sudden definition to the haze of sensations and memories, even during the later stanzas when Johanna becomes a mythic *femme fatale* as well as a real woman, floating in and out of the 'museums where infinity goes on trial'.

In the context of history and myth she becomes a countess who 'pretends to care' for a pedlar; a madonna; the mysterious Mona Lisa. The last stanza ties up the fluctuating images in an encapsulated recapitulation, ending with the 'skeleton keys' the all-night girls had played with, and the elusive 'rain' that Louise had pathetically tried to hold in her hand; it is of course heroin or cocaine, though it can be visualized as real rain too, trickling refreshingly yet hopelessly through the fingers. At the end visions of Johanna are *all* that remain; the music enacts this since throughout the song the dotted rhythm is potent but the vocal line is waveringly undefined. That the tune itself should be unmemorable is the point, for it is borne along on the tide of dream and memory. The magical words resonate in the mind because Dylan declaims or incants them with maximum malleability of both rhythm and pitch.

Side I ends more lyrically with one of Dylan's songs of apparent rejection. 'One of us must know' is about a love gone wrong, ending with the blunt words:

> You weren't really from the farm
> An' I told you as you clawed out my eyes,
> That I never really meant to do you any harm.

None the less rejection turns out to be once more a kind of affirmation, partly because the tune soars upward in triadic form, and turns into a forceful tumbling strain in the refrain. The beat is sturdy, the same as that of 'Johanna' but faster; the tonality is a clear diatonic major, with no blue notes. At the same time the music attests that he is sad to have caused pain, that he really did 'try to get close to you'. Dylan's singing of words like 'personal', 'understood', and 'believed' particularizes a generalized emotion; in the faster-moving rhythms of the middle eight song turns into highly inflected speech.

The next number, the famous 'I want you' is unequivocally positive. It too is in an unsullied major, with a briskly unremitting beat. The timbre generates an overwhelming erotic compulsion from what on paper is no more than a series of oscillations between two tones. The immediacy of the cry of desire in the refrain comes as climax to the highly charged verses, in which the singer's regular woman and the girl's other man hint at the hallucinatory landscape of 'Visions of Johanna' in being described respectively as the Queen of Spades and as a 'dancing child with his Chinese suit'. Here is further evidence of the interdependence in Dylan's songs of everyday reality and myth. A brilliant example of this is provided by 'Stuck inside of Mobile with the Memphis blues again', a long strophic song which presents Dylan *im*mobilized in dreary Mobile confronted by a ragman, a senator, a preacher and a rainman (some twentieth-century shamanistic quack?), who purvey their sundry deceits but suggest no 'end' to the minor hell of Mobile. A man called Shakespeare and a woman called Mona (Lisa?) also appear among the personnel. They are an everyday guy and girl–he chats with 'some French girl' and she consorts with railroad men–but at the same time they are given mythic overtones by their names and by the fact that he wears 'pointed shoes and bells' like a fool, and she warns Dylan that the railroad men will 'drink up your blood like wine'. Not all the characters who pass by or flit through Dylan's consciousness come from the other side of the fence: Grandpa, though dead, makes a farcical appearance, while a warm-hearted hooker called Ruth may be justified in remarking that though his 'debutante' knows what he needs, she knows what he wants and can give it to him. Despite the hallucinatory threats and the boredom, the song as Dylan sings it, lyrically, with a ruthful wonder, comes across as almost benign. The tingling sonority, the lilting tune and the energetic beat–especially the dotted-rhythmed declining scale at the end of the refrain–alleviate any sense of non-communication between stranded Dylan and the beings who float in and out of his consciousness.

The delightful 'Leopard-skin pill-box hat' is another song that defuses negative emotions with humour. The girl is laughed at in a frisky boogie rhythm, with plangent blue notes so rapid that they sound more like chortles than sighs. The tale of infidelity, ignominiously revealed in a glimpse through an unclosed garage door, is ludicrous enough to seem phantasmagoric, especially in the pungent, 'wild mercury' sound of the scoring.

The number has been construed, even dismissed, as a satire on Carl Perkins's 'Blue suede shoes', which is not only to limit its range of reference, but also to ignore its good humour. Attempts to turn 'Just like a woman' into a homosexual number seem to me equally misguided, not because it is inconceivable that Dylan should create a homosexual song, but because there is nothing in the words or music or manner of performance to hint that this song does not mean what it says. The tune arches through big leaps and declines gently, again in an unsullied F major, which seems to be the positive key on this album. The words carry an ironic sting in reference to women as a class as well as to this particular member of the species; yet both lyricism and rhythm are healing rather than aggressive, and when she 'breaks just like a little girl' Dylan's arabesques are compassionate as well as critical.

'Most likely you go your way' is another rejection song that is really about freedom. In a bouncy boogie beat, it is gleeful, almost jolly, the 'mercury' sonority glinting and gleaming. 'Temporary like Achilles', also in G major, also carries us into a low barrel-house, but gently, the blue notes pathetic as Dylan atypically appeals to the woman to take notice of him. But the boogie lilt gathers energy as the stanzas unfold until the other man, Achilles(!), is discovered lurking in the alleyway. Dylan turns the tables in presenting him as a judge who

> . . . holds a grudge.
> He's gonna call on you
> But he's badly built
> And he walks on stilts
> Watch out he don't fall on you.

The farcical words contrast piquantly with the quietly seductive tune.

'Absolutely sweet Marie' is an ironic title. Again there is a precarious balance between negative emotions (the girl is absent, has probably let him down) and positive emotions (she is, or was, sweet, as can be heard in the fast tingling rhythm and the open tune, with its leaping fourth and falling sixth). The middle section modulates nervously to the submediant; and there are verbal equivocations too in Dylan's masterly handling of conversational half rhymes: 'Well, anybody can be like me, obviously,/But then, now again, not too many can be like you, fortunately.' Though these are speech rhythms, they effect the song's lyricism, coolly throwing away the cadential arpeggio. 'Fourth time around' is an anti-woman song alleviated by its plangent broken chord sonority, again in a diatonic F major. It may have some parodistic reference to the Beatles' 'Norwegian wood'; but in context serves mainly as respite before 'Obviously five believers', a powerful rock song in driving beat, prickling with black blue notes. He yells for his girl to come home, his black dog barks, the girl's mama moans; but in the fifth stanza:

> Fifteen jugglers and five believers
> All dressed like men
> Tell yo' mama not to worry because
> They're just my friends.

It is not clear what the point of these mythical intruders is unless he is recognizing that they are substitutes for the woman's flesh and blood. He seems to be saying that there are three times as many jugglers (charlatans?) in him as there are true believers; but when in the last stanza he cries for her to come back 'early in the morning' he sounds as earthily honest as a black bluesman. It will be sad, and surprising, if she fails to come.

The final song, which covers the whole of the fourth side, is the most mysterious of all, reminiscent of 'Visions of Johanna' in that the poem is in more than one sense highly evocative. It is less tethered to the reality of present moments through which dreams swim, but directly explores 'the savage and beautiful country' below or beyond the waking mind. This may be why, whereas 'Johanna' has a vocal line that stems from speech, 'Sad-eyed lady of the lowlands' has a melody almost as memorably self-subsistent as 'Mr Tambourine Man', the classic dream song from the earlier period. Like much genuine folk verse, the complex poem functions allusively as well as elusively. The sad-eyed lady has been identified with Dylan's then wife, Sara, as well as with America and with the Statue of Liberty. To be specific is, as usual, to miss the point; the lady is a maternal goddess because imagery, rhythm and most of all music make her so. The song is basic to Dylan's work because it hymns the female divinity he seeks from the heart of the patriarchal dominance that made him. This motif is endemic in much of the art, especially the pop art, of our time, but nowhere is it more richly incarnated than in this song. The sad-eyed lady is presented in religious and magical imagery that makes her at once madonna and harpy. Because she is 'beyond good and evil', Dylan offers her his gift of his 'warehouse eyes' and 'Arabian drums' more insistently in each stanza. ('Warehouse' because he haunts the periphery of cities, without stable roots, 'Arabian' because she offers him magical dreams and exotic horizons?) Like an ancient earth goddess the Lady releases him from moral choice and commits him to Being, here and now, embracing within the verbal assonances and alliterations the harsh with the hilarious, the grim with the grotesque.

The scene and story are not presented in linear sequence but in a swinging, circular 6/8 tune that contains, in Dylan's elongations of line and darkenings of tone, both fulfilment and regret. Oddities of vocal production are here peculiarly extravagant: the ululating permutations of 'lowlands' for instance, are strange to the point of risibility yet also induce a sense of awe. The music makes the words function in mythological rather than chronological time. Although the song's temporal duration approaches twelve minutes, it enters a once-upon-a-time where the clock–unlike the hypnotic percussion beat–has ceased to tick. The regularity of the beat and the enveloping organ sonority underline this womb-regressive, pre-conscious quality, which may or may not be inherent in the (drug-induced?) imagery. Dylan is left playing his Edenic harmonica in a long postlude which is perhaps even more poignant than the one that ends 'Mr Tambourine Man'. 'Ends' is, however, too strong a word: the fade-out in Dylan's music–as in much pop music and in jazz–is one manifestation of the yearning for release from Western temporal progression. Both the lack of linear sequence in the narrative and its endless circularity recall the incantations of those waulking women in the outer Hebrides. The fade-out on the harmonica insists that Eden ought to be for ever; the melancholy springs from the fact that it isn't.

Much of the power of *Blonde on Blonde*, especially in hard

blues numbers like 'Obviously five believers', derives from the talents of the instrumentalists: Charlie McCoy, Kenneth Buttrey, Wayne Moss, Hargus Robbins, Jeremy Kennedy, Joe South, Bill Aikins, Henry Strzelecki and the brilliant Al Kooper and Robbie Robertson. The increased range and enriched timbre of Dylan's voice may have been stimulated by this backing. Yet although *Blonde on Blonde* is now accepted as a, perhaps the, high in its 'high' genre, 1966 was a traumatic year for Dylan. On gruelling tours he was booed offstage by folk fanatics who objected to his electronic gadgetry and to what they considered his political betrayal. Physical and nervous strain may have led to increased reliance on drugs, and certainly lends edge to the Albert Hall bootleg tapes issued in 1966 under the title of *In 1966 There Was*, and to the patchier but intermittently brilliant *Basement Tapes* issued in 1967. For although with the backing of The Band–the rock group whose own recordings, from *Music from Big Pink* onwards, have so vividly evoked an era and an American landscape–Dylan sometimes relaxes into relatively easy-going numbers that foreshadow the country manners of *Nashville Skyline*, he also, in songs like 'Tears of rage' and 'Wheels of fire', achieves a fierce intensity that is as unafraid as it is uninhibited. These two poles of experience complement one another: the emotional commitment is safeguarded, by the relaxation, from self-indulgence, while the relaxation is toughened by the passion. In the light of this we can understand why, when Dylan 'legally' released another disc, he had made a radical change of front; and had created a new sound.

This phase climaxed in the motorcycle accident in which Dylan, breaking his neck, came near to eliminating himself. This may or may not have some connection with drug usage but it certainly has, like Beethoven's deafness(!), allegorical overtones: Dylan's next album, *John Wesley Harding*, issued in 1968, represents a new start. Here he relinquishes the heavy instrumental backing of *Blonde on Blonde* and relies as support for his own voice, guitar and piano on only his two trusted Nashville sessions men, Charlie McCoy on bass and Kenney Buttrey on drums, with a brief appearance of Pete Drake's steel guitar in the two love songs, 'Down along the cove' and 'I'll be your baby tonight'. Yet although the verses use comparatively plain language, with biblical overtones, and although the music returns more starkly to his poor white country manner, the introversion of the psychedelic period is not bypassed. Rather the public and the private manners become one, as the social commitment of the early years is refashioned in the light and (especially) dark of the middle years' dreams and nightmares. Although the words have gained undertones from Dylan's retreat within the psyche, they are usually intelligible, if not unambiguously so; and the songs deal in moral issues without the crudity sometimes occasioned, in an early number such as 'Masters of war', by Dylan's assumption that he is always right, 'they' wrong. As the words have grown up, so the music complementarily matures in its interrelations of line, rhythm and harmony, and no less in manner of performance. Dylan's post-accident voice is riper, richer, more varied in timbre.

The title song, 'John Wesley Harding', is lightweight and is placed first, Dylan says, because he could not decide where to put it. It is about an outlaw, presented with characteristic ambiguity. For Dylan, the outlaw is a hero, in the sense that he was one himself when he spurned the Establishment and rejected the superficies of the American Way of Life. He lights on a fetching tune, in straight, white diatonic country style, to embody Harding's strength and resilience. Yet, like much white country music, this tune is slightly crass in its cockiness; and dubiety is latent in the words too, for while this outlaw seems noble in that he was 'a friend to the poor' and 'was never known to hurt an honest man', the last stanza praises him for more suspect reasons. 'No charge against him could they prove . . ./ He was never known to make a foolish move' may mean no more than that he was crafty and ruthless; and looked at retrospectively the first lines of the song–'John Wesley was a friend to the poor,/He travelled with a gun in every hand'–turn out to encapsulate an archetypal American paradox: the freedom that promotes courageous independence may also lead to violence. The comic irony in the phrase 'a gun in every hand' has a sting in its tail, especially in Dylan's intonation. Not surprisingly, a tinge of irony can be detected in the Edenic harmonica interludes too. There seems little doubt that this is intentional, for the real John Wesley Hardin was an anarchic murderer, without recorded empathy for the poor and outcast. Perhaps Dylan added a 'g' to his name to indicate a hardening process in his legendary version of the genuine outlaw.

The second song, 'As I went out one morning', is still more equivocal. The lovely tune, airily balancing rising fifth against falling fourth in a mainly pentatonic contour, is as archaically folky as the verbal cliché the song opens with. But the 'fairest damsel' he meets with in the bright morning is certainly not the traditional maid of folk song; or if she is, she is also a siren of foreboding, and seems to be also the material lures of America, with her technological pseudo-panaceas–which may be why the rhythm, beneath the old-world tune, beats in jazzy jitteriness. Libertarian Tom Paine, a hero who celebrated the American Revolution, comes 'running from across the field' to make the girl/America 'let go her grip' on Dylan. He succeeds, and the siren gives up her attempted seduction with a crooked look and words muttered 'from the corners of her mouth'. But Tom Paine no longer has any political solution to offer, and contents himself with a lame 'I'm sorry, sir.' He is sorry, presumably, because 'America' has betrayed her original ideals of liberty, equality and fraternity. Both as a woman and as America the 'damsel' is the sad-eyed lady goddess whom Dylan had to embrace if he were to grow to maturity. Once he has done so he can recognize that he and she have now to come to terms with the social moralities of his early youth.

This process begins in the third song, 'I dreamed I saw St Augustine', which is very freely based on an earlier political song, 'Joe Hill', but relates the political dimension to the Calvinist religious responsibilities of Dylan's Yankee heritage. Religious conscience plumbs deeper than political duty, and the haunting country tune, beginning with a simple spread triad, lyrically blooms even as it teeters microtonally between major and minor third, never quite making either. Augustine was a saint who knew more about guilt than most, and Dylan gives him an oblique reference to his own autobiography, for he too has come through dissipation, sexual confusion and drugs and is waiting for–though he does not at this point find–a redeemer. The Augustine who tears 'through these quarters/In the utmost misery' is also Dylan, searching for souls who have 'already been sold'. Presumably this means sold in the modern colloquial sense of being betrayed and sold down the river; and the point of the second stanza is that guilt-ridden Augustine-Dylan tells these 'gifted kings and queens' (social, political and ecclesiastical VIPs–'gifted' with wealth as well as talents?) that he is in the same boat ('Know you're not alone'). But in the third and last stanza there is a further turn of the screw: Augustine, in his guilt snorting like the dragon 'with fiery breath' from the Book of Revelation, is 'put out to death' by Dylan himself. Technically speaking Augustine was not a martyr except in the sense that he believed he was slaughtered by his own sins. In this sense Dylan identifies with him, and with a final twist cries

> Oh, I awoke in anger,
> So alone and terrified,
> I put my fingers against the glass,
> And bowed my head and cried.

He too is 'angry' because he recognizes in himself that 'tearing' fiery dragon; but is also 'terrified' because he admits to his responsibility and cannot see where he is to find the absolution that Augustine, after his anguish, won through to. The glass is a mirror in which Dylan sees himself, and the fingers pressed against it exactly convey the agony of self-knowledge. This is the more affecting because the tune's pentatonic innocence belies its intermittent, very tentative blue notes, and has no need of the electrophonic distortions Dylan had so brilliantly exploited.

The protests of Dylan's early songs did not necessarily imply a Christian interpretation, though they often had a biblical background. In this mysterious song Christian eschatology is powerfully evident, though in awareness of its fearfulness rather than of its remedial potential. So it is no surprise when 'All along the watchtower', the finest song in the cycle, heroically confronts, in grandly swinging Aeolian melody, deeply oscillating bass and thrusting rhythm, the chaos of fallen man. The biblical reference is to Isaiah:

> Watch in the watchtower, eat, drink: arise, ye princes, and anoint the shield. For thus hath the Lord said unto me, Go, set

> a watchman, let him declare what he seeth. And he saw a chariot with a couple of horsemen, a chariot of asses, and a chariot of camels; and he hearkened diligently with much heed: And he cried, A lion: My lord, I stand continually upon the watchtower. . . . And, behold, here cometh a chariot of men, with a couple of horsemen.[3]

Dylan transfers the biblical references into the arid landscape of the Wild West, in which Isaiah's mysterious riders are at home, while at the same time evoking the apocalyptic horsemen; Isaiah's lion becomes a desert wildcat. The two human creatures who are threatened by this unknown and perhaps unknowable doom are allegorically described as the joker and the thief. The equation between the modern life of 'business men and plowmen' who have no notion of 'what any of it is worth' and the biblical world of 'princes, women and barefoot servants' is delineated with masterly economy. The joker and the thief, stripped of the pretences of civilization, can at least confront confusion, even though 'the hour is getting late'. 'Outside in the distance a wildcat did growl'–the 'did' imbues him with sinister intention–'Two riders were approaching, the wind began to howl.' The menace is almost overwhelming; but not quite, for the threat is not exterior to the tune which remains, in its noble arches over its gravely descending bass, unruffled. Dylan sings it firmly, but without rhetoric; the wildcat is the more venomous because Dylan makes no attempt to dramatize his growl. As in Isaiah, the watchtower the tune and bass represent is surely conscience and self-responsibility which, jokers and thieves though we're reduced to being in this naughty world, enable us to face fear.

Although this great song confronts doomsday with fortitude it offers no redemption. The long narrative 'Ballad of Frankie Lee and Judas Priest', placed at the centre of the cycle, may explain why. The musical fulfilment of 'Watchtower' is abandoned for an unremitting talkin' style, and the words spoken, for all their biblical references, could hardly be more confusedly bleak. The landscape is again that of the American West, and Frankie Lee may be a fusion of the outlaw hero of

[3] Isaiah 21.

'Frankie and Johnny' with Robert E. Lee. Judas Priest is presumably the Established Church gone rotten: a priest who is a judas, a judas who is a priest. Honest stupid Frankie Lee capitulates to the wiles of Judas and his dollar bills, and enters a paradise of illusion, a brothel where he dies, apparently of sexual excess, in Judas Priest's arms. Church and state are identified with the bordello in which Judas claims yet another victim. At the end a 'little neighbour boy' carries dead Frankie to some kind of 'rest'. It is significant that he is a child as well as a neighbour, recalling the biblical injunction: 'except . . . ye become as little children'. Even so, the solace he can offer is not great:

> And he just walked along, alone,
> His guilt so well concealed,
> And muttered underneath his breath,
> Nothing is revealed.

The little boy's guilt, although latent, already exists and will presumably one day become patent. No revelation is at hand; Dylan speaks the words flatly and inexorably.

'Nothing is revealed' in the rest of the cycle. 'Dear Landlord' is a slowish 12/8 number in countrified barrel-house style, and is about the equivocation of its title. Although all landlords must be wicked, belonging to the category that the young Dylan had dismissed as 'them', the verses function on levels beyond their political and social implications. Indeed in a sense the landlord appears to be God, owning the whole show and renting it to humankind; Dylan is trying to establish a relationship with him that combines respect with an awareness of his own dignity. The adjective 'dear' is double-faced. The tune, lingering almost caressingly on the word, combines toughness with an upward-aspiring hopefulness; the sudden shift, at the top of the phrase, from the tonic major triad to the upper mediant with flat seventh, opens our ears in tragi-comic wonder as well as dismay at the discovery that Dylan and landlord, human creature and creator, might have mutual responsibilities. There is a similar, more extravagant effect at the wild modulation to the *flat* upper mediant on 'I'm gonna give you all that I gotta give.' The melismata induce surprise, yet carry conviction, and Dylan's variety of timbre, from sonorous confidence to raucous bleat, has never been more impressive. The final line–'If you don't underestimate me, I won't underestimate you'–carries contradictory if complementary meanings. Dylan, as a human being, is willing to respect authority but not to cower or to grovel. The little chortling crow on the E flat run-up to the quoted phrase is a tribute to human fortitude, even bravado; and the song stops, unresolved, *on* rather than *in* the dominant.

Three of the songs, not surprisingly, are about rebels. In 'Drifter's escape' the outlaw is accused by the Establishment of indeterminate crimes for which he offers no apology. Ironically, he escapes from authoritarian law and order that have little to do with the heart's truth by an arbitrary act of God in the form of a bolt of lightning. This may be cynical, but more probably it implies that he deserves to escape, having faced up to the true law of his own conscience. Musically, the song sounds cheery, over an unchanging tonic pedal, but at the same time it is blackly sprinkled with blue notes and metrical contradictions. Even blacker is 'I am a lonesome hobo', and in this case the drifter is presented negatively as blackmailer and thief; here the continuous tonic pedal fails to stabilize him. Although once 'rather prosperous', he falls through lack of trust in his 'brother', all that remains of friends, comrades or relatives. The moralistic coda is not Christian, but appeals only to individual conscience: one should live by 'no man's code' but 'hold your judgement for yourself,/Lest you wind up on this road'. Still bleaker and more morally ambiguous is 'The wicked messenger', a stern song in the Dorian mode, again liberally peppered with blue notes. The messenger, like Judas Priest, would seem to be a devil disguised as an angel, who cannot speak truth but only flattery. The people advise him, in biblically flavoured language, 'If you cannot bring good news, then don't bring any.' At one level this seems an unnecessary admonition to a flatterer, though at another level, spelling the Good News with capitals, one gets the point. Clearly he won't bring any and they know he won't; once more, there is no revelation.

A climax to these confusions and ambiguities is offered in 'I pity the poor immigrant' in which there is a gross and grotesque disparity between the whitely euphoric F major country waltz which is the music and the frightening words. These describe the immigrant to the new-found land as a fallen Adam totally evil in impulse, cheating with his fingers, lying with every breath. He comes 'passionately to hate his life and fear his death'; any visions he may have cherished 'shatter like the glass'. The immigrant who has succumbed to the wiles of Judas Priest and the Wicked Messenger may be Tom, Dick or Harry–or Dylan himself. The savagely ironic dichotomy between words and music is somewhat alleviated by Dylan's delivery which, singing often against the waltz beat, through variations of pitch, contortions of vowel sounds and weird elongations of time values, transforms the messenger's flattering voice into a strong but forlorn melancholy. All the fortitude of Dylan's watchtower is necessary to navigate these quicksands.

In the remaining two songs Dylan relinquishes his confrontation with doom. He changes the instrumentation, bringing in a steel guitar suggestive of the pop music industry rather than the aridities of the Wild West; and produces two apparently slight, even light, songs of heterosexual love. The moment of revelation–what Dylan is later to call the Changing of the Guards–has not arrived, but what remains to offset fear and horror is sexual love, which may offer its momentary truth. In 'Down along the cove' the experience is as yet hardly for real. The verses are almost coy:

> Down along the cove
> I spied my little bundle of joy.
> She said 'Lord have mercy, honey,
> I'm so glad you're my boy.'

Dylan sings the artless phrases in a rarefied, airy timbre, as though he is looking wonderingly at rather than entering into the experience. Yet though the melody bounces in delight, the song is no escape into hedonism: it starts on a tingling blue note, never acquires a sharp third in the tune, and is rhythmically precarious as well as vivacious. Formally, the number is a blues, and the young woman may speak more truly than she realizes in asking the Lord to have mercy. The love is blessed, if not sanctified.

That certainly applies to the final number, 'I'll be your baby tonight'. Although apparently slight, it turns out to carry enough weight to justify its placing at the end of this often harrowing cycle of songs. The significance of this totally if momentarily committed love song is that Dylan is no longer concerned with himself in opposition to the world, nor with the mazes of his dreams and nightmares, nor with open questions about guilt and responsibility, nor even with his personal destiny, released by dreams and nightmares. He is simply concerned with himself in relation to another human being. This is real, though he makes no claims he might be unable to fulfil; he'll be her baby tonight, but nothing is said about tomorrow. Sufficient unto the night is the good thereof. Superficially, Dylan is psychologically regressing in becoming, in something more than the colloquial sense, her 'baby'. But going back to the womb may bring about a rebirth; and in that case what matters is what is reborn. Here the creation is a minor miracle.

Listened to casually as background noise, the music may seem corny, ragtimey, in the manner of Hank Williams, while the quietly humorous words–'That big fat moon is gonna shine like a spoon,/But we're gonna let it, /You won't regret it'–forestall emotional indulgence. In total effect, however, the tune, lyrically extended in the silence of the night, is so beautiful that the song, far from being comfortable, almost stills the breath. The comicalities in Dylan's performance–the upward glide on 'sail away', or the hazardously deep glissando on 'bring that bo[tt]le over here'–underlines rather than undermines the loveliness of the tune. The music *demonstrates* that 'You don't have to be afraid': all the doom, the bleeding and dying and the minatory Thin Men, are banished from this silent room and warm bed. The melody's climax, rising from dominant to tonic and then leaping an octave, liberates; while at the same time the 'squeezed' notes, edging upwards, make us aware that love's joy, even in this impermanent moment, is inseparable from its pain. The harmonica postlude emphasizes this: the whining country instrument carries us 'out of this world' to the room of love, which is haven and heaven. Yet there's a hint of *lacrimae rerum* in its wailing. The song leaves us warmly at peace, yet also vulnerable, and it is not extravagant to describe its simplicity as Blakean. Indeed it provides a precise gloss on Blake's marvellous fragment:

> He who bends to himself a Joy
> Doth the winged life destroy;
> But he who kisses the Joy as it flies
> Lives in Eternity's sun rise.

With Doomsday in the offing, that is all one can hope for; and it is much: so although it seems homelier, and in a sense that is the point, 'I'll be your baby tonight' is no less magically mysterious than Dylan's other great lyrical songs, 'Mr Tambourine Man' and 'Sad-eyed lady of the lowlands'.

16 'A wild wolf in the canyons of New York': the young Woody Guthrie, 1928.

17 Elvis Presley in action.

18 Hank Williams on the circuit.

19 The adolescent Dylan performing.

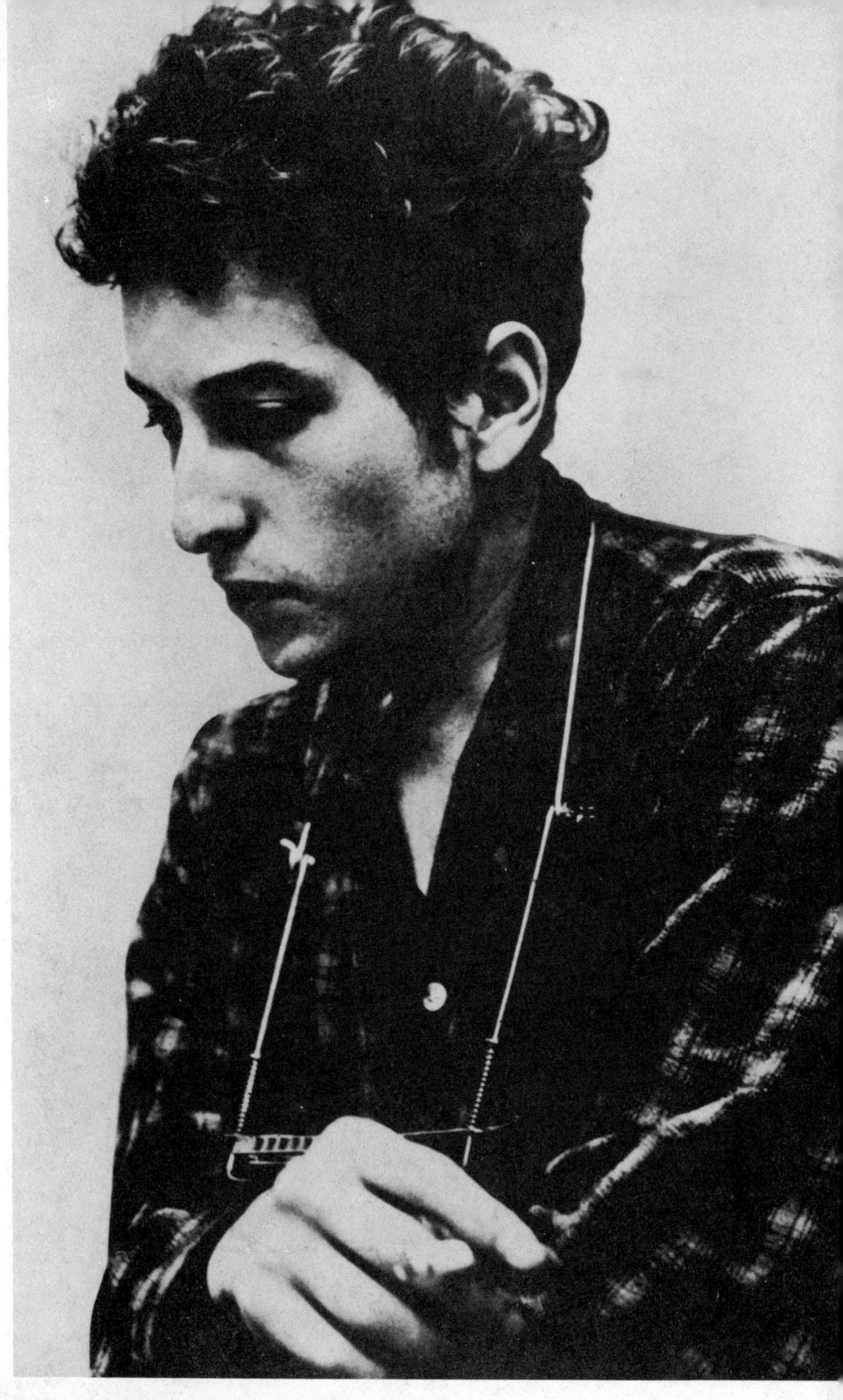

20 The young Dylan in pensive mood.

21, 22 Dylan in the Wild West from the MGM film *Pat Garrett and Billy the Kid*.

23 The cover of the album, 'John Wesley Harding', showing Dylan as Outlaw among Indians in front of the tree that is supposed to incorporate the four heads of the Beatles.

24 Dylan, in leathers, performing with the Band.

25 Portrait of Dylan, 1970.

26 Gypsy Dylan.

4

The Country Dream: The Private and the Public Life

John Wesley Harding is the crucial album in Dylan's evolution in that here he directly confronts an awareness of evil in the world and in himself. He hints at an eschatological Christian answer but cannot provide it. He explicitly said that *John Wesley Harding* was 'a fearless album–just dealing with fear, but dealing with the devil in a fearful way, almost. All I wanted to do was to get the words right. It was courageous to do it, because I could have *not* done it, too.'[1] In view of Dylan's later development the reference to the devil is not to be taken lightly: so it is not surprising that Dylan should have been left spiritually, if not emotionally, exhausted. Although the love song, 'I'll be your baby tonight', with which he ends *John Wesley Harding* is far from being merely an escape from the sense of doom, it *could* suggest a path of relaxation; and for some years Dylan does not return to his basic theme of freedom, guilt and responsibility, but instead creates his own unconventional version of the conventions of commercial country music. Indeed, his next disc is called *Nashville Skyline* and on it he can even be found duetting with Johnny Cash.

Not surprisingly, Dylan opens *Nashville Skyline* with a rehash of one of his earliest country songs, 'Girl from the north country', which is in turn based on a real British folk song. The music is not substantially changed, though the presentation–especially in the 'coat so warm' phrase and in the passage about her long hair–is more sensuous. Perhaps Dylan can now enjoy his and her sensuality with less inhibition because, as a lover, he

[1] Interview, *Rolling Stone*, 1969.

is both more affirmative and more aware: consider his delayed rhythm on 'one who lives there', low in register, or the microtonal distortion on 'true'. To tune with this more positive experience Dylan's voice has developed resonance. His explanation was that he had given up smoking: not necessarily a frivolous comment since it might mean that, accepting love, he had less need of adventitious props. The new voice suggests that the duetting with Johnny Cash, in the final stanza, is meant to be taken at its face value. This isn't easy, as their off-pitch, off-beat hesitancies teeter on the edge of farce. But this song at least has the advantage of preparing the way for the palpable ironies of a country song like 'One more night', a Hank Williamsish number which, with its unsullied diatonicism, steady beat and cheeky coda, might approach the 'white euphoria', were it not for the unexpected expansion of the tune's range, and its intrusive chromatics, in the final refrain. More subtly, cliché is used to demolish cliché in 'Tell me that it isn't true', which is simultaneously passionately committed in its leaping sixths, fragmented rhythms and wailing blue notes, and self-defensive in its presentation of the rival as 'tall, dark and handsome'. The quavery melismata on 'counting on you' suggest that he isn't, much.

The best songs in *Nashville Skyline* are those in which irony is fun, or passion unalloyed. 'Country pie' is a comic song which is far from being a mere take-off of country music: the blue notes and rhythmic hiatuses have such electrical agility that mirth outweighs satirical dismissiveness. Similarly 'Peggy Day' puns delightedly on day and night in a boogie number in which again blue notes and metrical dislocations become sheer ebullience. The tune is irresistible, like the girl: by the time the barrel-house or minstrel-show coda in half-time is reached, the parody of rockabilly music–perhaps of Presley himself–has become a thrilling release of energy and love. There is thus a link between this quasi-satirical song and the directly passionate numbers. Sometimes they are songs of loss, like 'I threw it all away', with its powerful approach to the initial tonic by way of the supertonic, its painfully crushed blue notes on 'But I was cruel', and its desperately straying melismata on 'I must have been mad'. More often they are songs of fulfilment, like 'Tonight I'll be staying here with you', a variation on the theme of 'I'll be your baby tonight', less moving because it lacks the earlier song's precarious lyrical innocence, but impressive in its contrast beween the repeated tonics that, at the end of the refrain, affirm his staying power, and the disturbing subdominants and mediants of the middle eight. Clearly she does not succeed in making him forget–though in another song, 'Tell me that it isn't true', he asks her to–'all of those awful things that I have heard'–things out of which had sprung the testament of *John Wesley Harding*.

Most striking of all is the sexiest song, 'Lay, lady, lay', which has a refrain in descending chromatics (harmonized in triads of A major, C sharp minor, G major and B minor) which effectively lays the girl *down* on the 'big brass bed', but balances this descent with the upward fourth of the vocal line's invocation. This is affirmative enough to suggest that she *wants* to 'stay until the break of day'. If in the middle eight there is a hint of debunking irony ('You can have your cake and eat it too'), this does not compromise the positive effect of the song in which the refrain returns, unaltered harmonically though not melodically, in hypnotic obsession. The peroration of the I–II–III–IV–I rise of the instrumental coda has been melodically, and experientially, justified. In this fine song Dylan's voice is as sexy as Presley's, though the down-to-earth rather than rhetorical music suggests that, even in bed, he has more to offer. At this point of fulfilment Dylan paused, partly to take stock. His return, initiating his third period, was problematical.

If the tender love songs at the end of *John Wesley Harding* and the powerfully erotic love songs in *Nashville Skyline* can and I think should be construed as a triumph for the personal life, they can also, from a stance of social commitment and political militancy, be seen as an opting out. Although to take them in that way betrays a damaging imperviousness to the qualities of Dylan's verse and music, this seldom worries the socially and politically committed; and one has to admit that the double album that followed in 1970, under the initially perplexing title of *Self Portrait*, provided ammunition for Dylan's critics. Many of the songs cosily celebrate country life, wifie and the kids, with glossy pictures as a bonus. Some of the songs are not by

Dylan and seem improbable choices for him to have made. All are presented not just by Dylan's voice with acoustic or even electric guitar, but with streamlined opulence, in elaborate arrangements involving not only the Band but a total of more than fifty performers. One might be forgiven for thinking that Dylan had been listening to his sycophantic Wicked Messenger. If so, in what sense can he call this double album *Self Portrait*?

Such a reaction takes account of only a part of the truth. Although *Self Portrait* is a minor achievement, it is not dishonest: the partly ironic self-portrait is surely the image Dylan is unashamed to present, not to the youthful drop-outs for whom he had been high priest, but to the vast audience he had discovered through the media. It's significant that he opens the album with an affirmation of innocence derived from a children's rune. It is sung by girls, not by Dylan himself, though one waits expectantly for him. The words, disclaiming 'work' and purpose, simply repeat 'All the tired horses in the sun,/ How'm I s'posed to get any ridin' done' to a slender, pentatonic near-monody. Innocence is not betrayed by the dreamily soaring violin obbligato and the tune, in the fade-out, remains as wistful and as endless as childhood illusorily seems to be while we're in it. If this dream seems false compared with the harshness of the early protest songs, Dylan has already proved, through the sequence of *John Wesley Harding* and *Nashville Skyline,* that that is not the case; and does so again when in this album he sings an innocent song with a difference. 'Belle isle' is freely adapted from a traditional song–though Dylan credits himself with 'new music', and justifiably so, since the number comes across as a modern rural folk song as convincingly constructed as an art song, and is among the loveliest and tenderest of his creations. Lyrically smiling in open sixths, the tune evades any hint of sentimentality, while the stilted, archaic language is tinged with a Dylanesque humour ('Young lady I wish not to banter'). The graceful melody shivers with a tremor of fear when the *minor* of the subdominant clouds the words 'more than my heart can endure'. Even the 'beautiful' scoring and the highly polished performance of the instrumentalists is germane to the effect, for although the dream is more perfect than life can be expected to be, it is real while it lasts, and ought to be valued.

'Belle isle' is Dylan's version of a wish-fulfilment number like Richard Rodgers's 'Blue moon', and it may be to the point that Dylan's wish-fulfilment has roots in genuine folk tradition. He includes 'Blue moon' in this album, and sings it sensitively and straight–unless the screechy pentatonic postlude must count as derisive. If so, the irony is no harsher than that of Jimmie Rodgers's yodels, for Dylan is admitting to the truth inherent in the dreams of common humanity. Such newly won humility is evident too in 'Wigwam', a wordless vocalise–pentatonic with microtonal arabesques–celebrating the red American Indian whom white American technology has destroyed. Here Dylan walks a tightrope between tragedy and farce, and just brings it off. *Self Portrait* also includes a number of traditional or composed country songs re-created. 'Days of '49' and 'Copper kettle' are far from being Edenic dreams like 'Belle isle', but the bummers who made them up and sang them were looking for the days of old which were days of gold, both literally and metaphorically. The words, with their comic internal rhymes, are reflected in the jazzy syncopations and blue notes with which he peppers the pentatonic-cum-Aeolian tunes.

Once more, these black intrusions make nostalgia immediate: as is more extravagantly evident in the explicit bluesy numbers, such as 'In search of little Sadie', a number recorded several times by Johnny Cash. Dylan's version is wild, with howling, false-related melismata in the vocal line, and chaotically unrelated triads in the instrumental line. A second version of the song, called simply 'Little Sadie', is more equable–presumably because she's been found. Another number, based on a traditional blues, 'It hurts me too', hurts in the same way: savage vocal roulades, juxtapositions of unrelated chords and keys. 'Livin' the blues', an original that sounds more like a free adaptation of traditional material, is no less uncompromising in its telescoped false relations and rhythmic contractions. Clearly the blue-black songs in *Self Portrait* have little truck with cosiness, and just as the magic dream of 'Belle isle' affects the way in which we listen to Dylan's version of 'Blue moon' or of Gordon Lightfoot's 'Early mornin' rain', so his re-creation of the bluesy numbers influences our response to a Hank Williams-like number such as Cecil Null's 'I forgot more than you'll ever know'. Occasionally the transmutations of country songs are brilliant. 'Gotta travel on'–a basic Dylan motif–is as tough as leather boots, the vocal line squeezing microtonally between the minor and major third, and thereby conflicting with the harmonic oscillations between tonic and flattened upper mediant. Similarly the 'chilly wind' gives the melodic line a frisson, both in pitch and rhythm, while the jerky rhythm of the 'lonesome freight at six o' eight' brings the pang of lonesomeness home.

Somewhat the odd man out in this company is 'The mighty Quinn', who seems to be a god figure of dubious import. The number is sung harshly and raggedly, in nervously irregular syncopation; the words are often inaudible, probably because the number was recorded live, at the Isle of Wight concert. The world is full of people busily doing their own thing (building boats or monuments, jotting down notes), yet all are 'in despair', waiting for some kind of redeemer:

> Everybody's out there feedin' pigeons out on a limb,
> But when Quinn the Eskimo gets here
> All the pigeons gonna run to him.

It might be a rehearsal for the gospel songs, were not Quinn a farcical monster and were not the music scary in its jaggedness. The last stanza hints, perhaps, that he might be a dope-pedlar–Eskimos know a lot about snow–and that that is the alleviation the people are waiting for. 'Now, nobody can get any sleep,' but when he gets here, 'Everybody's gonna wanna doze.' These alternative meanings are not mutually exclusive. Either way, the number is discomforting, and seems the more so in the basically benign context of *Self Portrait*, for which it was intended.

Apart from 'Belle isle' and 'The mighty Quinn' this double album cannot be said to amount to much more than a scrapbook of bits of music that had played a part in Dylan's evolution, elaborately packaged, and surrendering reality in that packaging. None the less his re-creative ability survives, however dubious the material. Looked at positively, the widening range of the songs justifies the picture on the sleeve, which presents

Dylan in sunlit woods, gazing up at the heavens. And the next disc is called *New Morning* (1970), but turns out, despite the promise of the title, to be no easy option. True, the first (title) song is a simple statement: the voice prances across the beat, with an uplifting pentatonic crow for the rooster and a long-swelling note on 'new'. Although false-related G naturals in the declining bass and, more potently, in the middle section, hint at unease, it is only enough to give conviction to the buoyancy. Even more positive is the country song, 'If not for you', which links new-morning mirth to a specific person, presumably Sara Dylan. She is evoked in an upward-floating arpeggio, balanced by a glissandoed falling fourth on 'blue'. The song is in Edenic E major, and tends to modulate sharpwards. Pentatonics flower on 'winter would have no spring'.

These are the only two country songs on this album that are unequivocally happy. 'Time passes slowly' looks like a homey country waltz, but the tonality, beginning with flattened seventh, wobbles vaguely between tonic and subdominant, and the rhythm is consistently lopsided. The vocal line too limps across and all around the beat, hazy and lazy, wanting love perhaps, but not finding it. The music mirrors the words, which 'ain't got no reason to go anywhere'. The red rose of summer fades like and with time. The weird postlude establishes no centre, for there is no dominant nor even a clearly defined plagal cadence; the piece stutters out on repeated triads. The song is not intrinsically very impressive, but honestly faces up to Dylan's bemusement: he has to admit to being lost before he can regather his energies. This is equally true of 'Sign on the window', sung and originally notated in the flatness of G flat major. There seems to be a fly in the country love-nest's ointment in the form of another man, whom Dylan treats with amused contempt: 'Looks like a-nothing but rain. . . . Hope that it don't sleet.' The last stanza reintroduces the country 'cabin in Utah' and the 'bunch of kids that call me Pa', adding (twice) that 'that must be what it's all about'. The music seems doubtful: the intermittent metrical affirmations of a IV–I cadence in 2/4 time are no answer to the wandering wondering instability of the bulk of the song, which was notated originally without bar lines and tonally strays from its G flat major bass to triads of C flat and

E double flat! The voice's final utterance is a wilting, half comic, 'oo'. Even 'Winterlude', a straight country waltz, has elements of ironic exaggeration in its affirmation, being funny in a way the genuine article would not be: 'You're the one I adore,/Come over here and give me more'–to rapidly insistent repeated notes.

The deflating of Dylan's country dream occurs most potently, as might be expected, in black-tinged numbers such as 'One more weekend', a raw, swinging barrel-house blues, very black in false relations and in rhythmic displacements, and in context rather frenzied, 'like a weasel on the run'. Its reality would seem to be difficult and impermanent: a weekend stolen from domestic unbliss, attained only by leaving the kids at home. This may also be the theme of 'The man in me', in which, having attempted to justify his country dream on the grounds that he 'doesn't want to turn into some machine', he discredits it with an inane la–la–la refrain. This undermines the sexuality of his address to the woman, as though he recognizes that the dream is a cheat. Blackest of all these numbers is 'If dogs run free', in which Dylan speaks flatly against ecstatic blues piano, superbly played by Al Kooper, haloed by the loonily scatting voice of Maretha Stewart, whose role veers from loon to bitch to woman. The spoken words are, for the first time for a considerable period, once again overtly about freedom and responsibility. If dogs run free, why shouldn't we, doing our own thing regardless? Most of the time Dylan's inflexions encourage us to take the words ironically, knowing they are not true: consider the way he articulates 'sym–phony' and 'tap–es–try' in reference to his music and verses. Yet at the same time the last stanza asserts the positive aspect of doggy freedom, which can 'cure the soul' and 'make it whole'. The jazzy liberation of the music sounds, if crazy, also jubilant. This is a basic Dylan number in that it defines the Janus-faced relationship between freedom and responsibility without oversimplification. This equilibrium parallels that between security and vulnerability in 'I'll be your baby tonight'.

The remaining songs, however, though turning from the country dream, tend to end in limbo, hinting at, but not finding, some kind of religious salvation. The longest, most interesting, and most ambiguous is 'Went to see the gypsy', a fortune-teller who, as an agent of the supernatural, seems phoney: a modern-style shaman who has got rich (he is staying in 'a big hotel') on false prognostications. Dylan approaches him in a spirit of mistrust: 'How are you? he said to me,/I said it back to him' – with snarlingly distorted pitch. A 'pretty dancing girl' advises him to take the gypsy seriously, for he can 'move you from the rear,/Drive you from your fear,/Bring you through the mirror' so that you are not afraid to confront yourself. He 'did it in Las Vegas, and he can do it here,' says the girl. Since Las Vegas is a city of gamblers, it is not surprising that when Dylan, taking her advice, returns to the gypsy's room he has vanished, and so has she. Dylan's frustration is heard first in a nagging oscillation between two tones, then in a pentatonic tumbling strain infuriatingly reiterated. Throughout, the rhythm is dislocated. He is left in 'that little Minnesota town', watching the sun rise: a force of nature, which does go on, independent of bogus prophecies.

Companion to this song is 'Day of the locusts'. Receiving an academic accolade from a world he never made and does not want to enter, Dylan is at odds with the Establishment, in summer heat, standing next to a man whose 'head was exploding'. Bizarrely he is 'prayin' the pieces wouldn't fall on me'. In the refrain the locusts chitter in the distance, making a pentatonically 'sweet melody', the significance of which is, however, dubious. He looks into a 'chamber where the judges were talking,/Darkness was everywhere, it smelled like a tomb'; as the locusts sing, light illuminates the gloom, and Dylan drives off, with his girl, into the hills. If that makes the insects a force for good, the last stanza complicates matters, for the hills they drive into are 'black' and the locusts' 'sweet melody' gives him 'a chill'. It would seem that they are at once liberation and threat: melodious locusts ravage the earth.

The two remaining numbers bring in an overtly religious note. 'Three angels', who turn out to be Christmas decorations, belie their spiritual implications since 'dogs and pigeons', 'a man with a badge', 'fellas crawlin' on their way back to work', cannot hear the music they utter. It may not be worth hearing, since the words are spoken and the accompaniment consists of trite Muzak-like arpeggios shifting up unrelated major triads; but 'does anyone even try?' The final invocation of the godhead, 'Father of night', offers cold comfort, significantly putting night and negation before day and affirmation. If this fast, brusque, rigid four-note incantation over a declining bass is compared with the first song, 'If not for you', it would seem that any dawn we might hope for from this New Morning depends on the love within us. Dylan has admitted that other possibilities exist, but has not been able to encompass them. These songs, unlike those in *Self Portrait*, cannot possibly be accused of escapism; such tenuous hope as they offer is befuddled.

New Morning is, then, a transitional and problematical album which, despite its title, contains only two straightforwardly happy songs; includes several that concern disillusion with the country dream; and ends with a sequence of numbers about the thwarting of religious impulse. The gypsy's magic is suspect; the promise of the chanting locusts is uncertain; the three angels are satirically debunked; the godhead whom in the final song we 'solemnly praise' (in the Aeolian or Phrygian mode) is made of cold stone, and probably has feet of clay. Yet again it is typical of Dylan that this apparent denial does not totally invalidate the newness of the morning; indeed since the music is as resilient as Dylan's new voice, his acceptance of reality–of what life is really like as against evasion and prevarication–can anticipate rebirth. This happens in the sequence of the next three albums. *Planet Waves* marks out the trail (the original title was *Love Songs*); *Blood on the Tracks* brings in (as the title suggests) the negative emotions, most of the songs concerning failed loves; *Desire*, subtitled *Songs of Redemption*, continues the sequence. The process is completed in the four remaining albums. *Street-Legal* is transitional; with *Slow Train Coming*, *Saved* and *Shot of Love* Dylan embraces the gospel message, and the idiom of gospel musics, white and black.

5

Love and Loss, Redemption and the Myth of the Wild West

The progression towards a new birth is not immediate. After the question mark of *New Morning* Dylan pauses again in a three-year silence, interrupted only by his music for Sam Peckinpah's film, *Pat Garrett and Billy the Kid*, and by a curiously anonymous disc, mostly of other people's songs, issued under the minimal title of *Dylan 1973*. The movie score is interesting, intelligent and imaginative, and in carrying him into the Wild West it frees him from the countrified nostalgia of *Nashville Skyline* and *Self Portrait*. The mythology of the western movie had long been implicit in many of Dylan's themes, and in this film it becomes overt. The story concerns the complex relationship between law and outlaw; 'Billy', a swinging Tex-Mex tango harshly scored and raucously delivered, says what there is to be said on both sides. Dylan's sections of incidental music are vividly evocative with minimal means: consider the 'Cantina theme' ('Workin' for the Law'), which consists merely of a severe, declining ostinato in rigid rhythm, yet does all that is necessary as aural background to visual images in motion. Similarly the 'Bunkhouse theme', a lonesome cowboy waltz in plangent Tex-Mex scoring, is the complete musical complement to the outlaw alone, with the law threatening. 'Knockin' on Heaven's door' is no less trenchant as accompaniment to the law itself disillusioned: Dylan sings a mournful yet assertive declining phrase over a rolling bass, as Sheriff Baker asks basic questions about responsibility and authority.

The three more extended instrumental sections all function effectively. 'Turkey chase' is a set piece in blue grass idiom, well composed and brilliantly executed by Jolly Roger on banjo, Byron Barline on folk fiddle, Booker T. Jones on bass and Bruce Longhorne on guitar. Like the finest examples of real blue grass the music balances a burbling euphoria against a bluely distonated sense of the danger inherent in its virtuosity. The 'Main title theme' presents plangent Tex-Mex guitar over a fast, quiet, regular beat, with intermittent melodic intrusions from electric bass; the music, though not especially interesting in itself, does what it has to do, providing a neutral background for action. The Wild West is opened up unobtrusively. After the tale has wound to its stark conclusion the 'Final theme' relates back both to the preludial music and, more directly, to 'Knockin' on Heaven's door', and is more musically developed than either. From its dour premises it creates, as a flute solo wafts pentatonically aloft, a sense of spaciousness, almost of grandeur, which stems not merely from the visual images of open country, but also from the movie's exploration of the theme of law and outlaw. Dylan is reported to have been unhappy about the film, which was heavily cut. His score none the less shows remarkable aptitude, and this may have some bearing on the closer affiliation between much of his later work and cinematic techniques.

The 1973 album *Dylan* was released by Columbia without Dylan's knowledge. It consists of out-takes from *Self Portrait* and *New Morning*, originally just warm-ups, not intended for public issue. Since the vocal production is somewhat unprojected and unfocused and Columbia's remixing makes the back-up girls much more obtrusive, it has been suggested that the company acted with malice intended, as a riposte to Dylan's flirting with a rival firm. This seems a little melodramatic; and the disc is by no means a dead loss, even though it contains no Dylan original. Two slight country songs named after girls, 'Sarah Jane' and 'Mary Ann' are delightfully arranged by Dylan, the former in fast hoedown, the latter in slowish hillbilly style; they are presented at their charming face value, in a New England with 'dew on the grass', and clearly belong to the world of *Self Portrait*. Other numbers relate to the Wild West images of the movie, and prophesy things to come, especially on the 'cinematic' album *Desire*. Dylan's rehash of Jerry Jeff Walker's famous 'Bojangles' poises speech-rhythmed song excitingly and rather grandly over the swinging pulse, and uses a girlie chorus in a vein we'll hear much of later. This song, and the version of 'Lily of the West', may count as harbingers of the great 'Señor (Tales of Yankee Power)' in the way they carry modal tunes, abrasively scored in Tex-Mex sonorities, through an irresistible beat, with antiphonal choric refrains. 'Spanish is the loving tongue' is another re-creation that anticipates the late 'desert' songs, with barber-shop vocal harmony at the beginning, and with Tex-Mex mandolin, bar-parlour piano and flamenco-style cantillation. The slow, hesitant opening would be touching if it weren't comic; it is farcically debunked by the lurching Tex-Mex tango. The parodistic vein sounds uneasy, though it is a try-out for manners that will bear rich dividends later.

On the whole this disc is relatively benign compared with *New Morning*, let alone Dylan's earlier vein of protest. The satire in 'Spanish is the loving tongue' is almost whimsical; his version of Joni Mitchell's 'Big yellow taxi' is much less nervous, more kittenish, than the original; while he turns the sentimental standard 'Can't help falling in love with you' into a love song almost as vulnerable as 'I'll be your baby tonight' from *John Wesley Harding*. But if some of his admirers deprecated this as a namby-pamby evasion of responsibility, they were in for a rude, but no doubt welcome, shock: Dylan answered criticism in his usual forthright way, by producing, in 1974, his most statistically successful American tour thus far, plus a new disc which, if less authoritative than *John Wesley Harding*, similarly fused passion and pathos. Significantly, the songs in *Planet Waves* are all love songs, which two words were, indeed, the original title of the album.

So Dylan returns to the point where *John Wesley Harding* had ended, and the first of the new songs, 'On a night like this', deals with a situation similar to that celebrated in the last of the *Harding* songs, 'I'll be your baby tonight'. But this is no simple sexual heaven or haven; here love tries to forestall pain in a music relatively vigorous and astringent: as it needs to be, since the wind outside is minatory, making the bounding upward arpeggio that opens the song nervous as well as expectant. It is poised in precarious equilibrium with the declining arpeggio at the ends of the phrases–'heat up some coffee grounds'; 'you'll never go away to stay'–and with moans through a glissandoed fourth.

Particularities–the frisson on the 'cold outside' phrase, the permutations on 'it sure feels right'–ensure that love, however openly erotic, is not oversimplified. Much the same is true about 'Going, going, gone', about opting out, and not merely from a love relationship. The urgency of the inner distress is implicit in the tonality, which shilly-shallies around modalities irresolutely centred on D. There is one real, and unexpected, modulation to C when Grandma advises him to follow his heart, discovering and staying with his 'own true' love; but this doesn't happen, and the song is disconcerting and disconsolate. The delayed resolution of the harmony on 'gone', the elongation of 'before', and Robbie Robertson's brilliant guitar solo are half comic, half scary. The song manages to live 'on the edge', but does so with mirth–in the medieval as well as the modern sense.

The reason for this becomes clearer in 'Tough mama', a bluesy heavy rock number with driving beat. It would seem from the haunting poem that the woman celebrated in these love songs is both a real girl and also the mythical Sad-eyed Lady, the moon-goddess-harpy who had been, in the psychedelic days of *Blonde on Blonde,* Dylan's muse. Having a (dangerous) love affair is equated with rediscovering that sweet goddess and dark beauty. The song ends with the words, 'Meet me at the *border, late* tonight.' He is at the crossroads, but does not find her in this song: no distinctive tune emerges from the jagged, musically confused phrases. None the less that he should seek her is further evidence that his country dream is spent. This applies also to 'Hazel', a real girl deglamorized by her 'dirty blonde hair', yet also unattainable, much needed yet never really 'there'. Musically the song depends on a conflict between the wandering melismata of the vocal line, which cover a considerable range and mount unusually high, and a repeated harmonic progression–B flat with sharp seventh–dominant seventh in C, tonic F major, dominant seventh in D minor–which recurs obsessively. The obsession is in part the source of the music's eroticism, since it is richly chromatic; but at the same time it checks the erotically soaring vocal line. Such equilibrium between attraction and repulsion is no doubt the heart of any honest relationship, but in this song it is difficult to know which is which. Is love the winging vocal line or the enclosing instrumental harmony? Is the vocal part escaping from the harmonic obsession, or does the reiterated harmony give cohesion to the erring line?

The girl in 'Something there is about you' is again both a real woman and a mythical lady, reminding him of 'something that used to be . . . from another century'. And again Dylan comes close to defining the indefinable, the unknowable mystery in any act of love. The lilting phrase, balanced between tonic and subdominant, is expanded as 'the spirit in me sings', knowing he has discovered 'a long-forgotten truth'; melismata tenderly evoke her free-flowing hair (always a key image in Dylan's as in folk poetry) and 'sweet easy breath'. The inversion of the opening phrase in the last stanza makes us laugh out loud–not because it is funny but because it is a blessed release tempered by the intricate patterning of the instrumental parts. Similarly, 'Never say goodbye' opposes the hope or maybe dream of an ideal love to the frozen lake and nipping wind, in a poem of haunting economy. Although the visionary love appears in the relaxed subdominant, the vocal line is wild, even distraught, and is toughened by a bass line both melodically and rhythmically animated, over which Robbie Robertson's picked melody whines wintrily. Musically the number never quite establishes an identity, but this may be the point–in that the beloved doesn't either.

There is another kind of duality in the two versions of the simplest song on the album, 'Forever young'. The first version is as guileless as a white country hymn, with a few gentle false relations that give immediacy to the melismata on 'young'. Dylan calls on no defensive irony in delivering this little moral homily, nor would one expect him to, as the song is supposed to have been written for his children. At the same time the reverberation of his voice at the ends of the stanzas and his unexpected speaking of the phrase about the surrounding light demonstrate that he knows that the Shaker song's 'gift to be simple', to 'grow up to be righteous and true', is limitlessly demanding. The song is oddly moving in its unpretentiousness; and although the second version, in fastish rockabilly style, banishes the countrified hymnic vein, it does not discredit it. The false relation on the phrase about growing up to be true is as affecting as it is in the first version.

The two long numbers in the cycle are similarly complementary. 'Dirge' justifies the lyric's statement that although Dylan knows about loneliness, he does not 'worship' it; having paid 'the price of solitude', he is 'out of debt'. As an anti-love song this is mysteriously compassionate: seeing through 'that foolish game we played' has been a road to self-discovery. Dylan's caw here generates deep resonance, especially to 'I'm glad the curtain fell' in the first stanza and the weeping martyrs and sinning angels at the second verse's end. The melisma for the angels is painfully extended in subsequent stanzas, on 'I'm out of debt', 'it's a dirty rotten shame', and 'what difference would it make'. The song climaxes in the woman's celebration of 'progress' to the Doom Machine in opposition to 'the naked truth'.

> Can't recall a useful thing you ever did for me
> 'Cept pat me on the back one time
> When I was on my knees

is putting it hard. (What, is the inevitable rejoinder, did he ever do for her?) Even so Dylan's attitude is too ambivalent to make this a hate song, and the laconic final couplet is open to more than one interpretation: 'I hate myself for lovin' you/But I should get over that' hinges on whether 'should' means 'ought to' or 'may naturally be expected to'. It could mean both, and the confusion amounts to a personal pain, deepened by the *im*personally chugging piano chords and by Robbie Robertson's guitar line, wailing and whimpering through and across the piano's thuds. It is as expressive as the black blues, yet unmistakably part of Dylan's rawly white world.

'Wedding song' is the opposite, positive pole. It purports to be a celebration of lasting love, yet the conventional hyperbole, even the hysterical reiteration of the words, is in part belied by the tonal ambiguity of the tune which, though harmonized in diatonic concords, cannot decide between the Aeolian or the Mixolydian mode. This makes the devotional simplicity of the words seem convincing. Clichés of amorous verse, remote from the complexities of Dylan's psychedelic period, become a yearning for truth, if not truth itself. Much depends, of course, on the way Dylan sings them, investing even words like 'soul' with unexpectedly edgy heartbreak, within the folk-like yet tonally rootless melody. The song just deserves its Edenic harmonica postlude because it has won through to it. Perhaps the ease it achieves would be unacceptable without the dis-ease of 'Dirge'. None the less the two songs in sequence demonstrate how much more difficult an ideal is marriage than revolution; and who, having grown up, could doubt that?

On *Planet Waves* Dylan is again backed by The Band, the rock group who accompanied him on the triumphant 1974 tour. Between them Robbie Robertson, superb on electric guitar, Garth Hudson and Richard Manuel on keyboards and drums, Levon Helm on drums and Rick Danco on bass brilliantly encapsulate the spirit of the seventies. They helped Dylan not to forget his country roots, but to replant them in the concrete of the big city. The Band's own, Dylanless, performances owe their profoundly American flavour to the fact that their idiom springs from the small-town, even rural, America exemplified in blue grass tradition. The idiom is metamorphosed into big city music by being in more than one sense electrified, both in its precision and in its nervous intensity. The one-time country sonorities clang with the hardness of steel, as the tingling music offers promise that the real old America might be mechanistically reborn. The Band's importance for Dylan can be heard on the tracks taped from the 1974 tour and issued as a double album under the pertinent title of *Before the Flood*. Songs from various periods of Dylan's career are re-created with a positive, forward-looking, forward-thrusting drive liberated by The Band. 'It ain't me, babe' becomes not merely a cheeky woman-rejecting number, but a positive celebration of freedom, chortling in cock-a-hoop abandon. Taken considerably faster than the original, in high register, with The Band's sonorities sizzling and fizzling, 'Ballad of a thin man' creates a gleeful malice, the 'Mr Jo–ho–hones' refrains rendering the enemy too ludicrous to be taken seriously. 'Lay, lady, lay' on the other hand, though no less sexually potent than the original on *Nashville Skyline*, is much more nervous. Again it is taken faster, and the scintillating solo roulades from The Band make the sex seem no less satisfying, but more dangerous. 'Rainy day women ♯ 12 & 35' also acquires a deeper unease, with purple-shaded instrumental distonations. Only the magnificent 'All along the watchtower' suffers from The Band-instigated metamorphosis: at this fast tempo and in this jangling sonority it surrenders the slow momentum which is its heart. However, the climactic versions of 'Highway 61 revisited' and of 'Like a rolling stone' are superb, converting the rolling-stone state into breathtaking as well as limb-shaking anthems to spiritual, not merely (or at all) political, freedom. When, as encore, Dylan appends his very early protest anthem 'Blowin' in the wind' he can accept its pristine simplicity more or less at the original tempo and can, abetted by The Band, create from it a paean in which innocence is vindicated, even in the heart of the city.

On the third side of *Before the Flood* Dylan accompanies himself in three numbers merely with his guitar and harmonica. None the less his performances are affected by his collaboration with The Band, for they all speed up the original tempo and give the numbers a cockier resilience. 'Don't think twice, it's all right' is taken very fast, in high, strained register. The vocal line is on edge and the harmonica whirs as Dylan makes his gleeful rejection. 'Just like a woman' is also mirthful in rejection, both in the comically distonated harmonica and in the uproarious 'little gur–hur–hurl' refrains. 'It's all right, ma (I'm only bleeding)', very fast and nervous, becomes a crow of perky triumph, though inevitably it surrenders the hint of pathos in the original refrain.

The complementary numbers 'Wedding song' and 'Dirge' on *Planet Waves* were probably prompted by the inner tensions in Dylan's own failing marriage. If so, the electrical surge of power in *Before the Flood* may have sprung from an attempt to gird his nervous energies, and for the most part the attempt was successful. Certainly his domestic situation is a backdrop to his next disc, *Blood on the Tracks* (1975), in which Dylan presents himself as the easy rider travelling to no destination but doesn't, in accepting rootlessness, abrogate responsibility. Although most of the love relationships in these songs fail, or succeed only transiently, loss of love is borne without rancour, while its uneasy discovery is accepted without indulgence. Together, Dylan's words and music have an immediacy compared with which a Kerouac or a Ginsberg seem merely to write 'about' a generation, not to be it.

The cycle begins with 'Tangled up in blue', a narrative song which is a fine example of the way in which Dylan's semi-speech itself becomes music: listen to his varied treatments of the 'tangled up in blue' refrain itself and its rhyme words–avenue, grew, flew, etc. The story, or its implications, are even more than usually difficult to unravel. John Herdman is probably right in suggesting that the women referred to in stanzas 1, 2, 4, 5 and possibly 6 are different, all except the first one being casual loves encountered on his travels. In the last stanza 'he', an easy rider who has covered the States in his search for the first girl, is on his way back to this true love–though if Herdman's suggestion that there is a parallel with the Scots ballad, 'The demon lover', is correct, he is in for a further disappointment. The talkin' style, with the voice moving in narrow compass, is stoical rather than desperate. Although musical as distinct from verbal development is minimal, the musical is no less subtle than the poetic effect: the line wanders, like the uneasy easy rider; the harmony tends to oscillate between triads of E and G major; and the texture, with piquant pickin' style guitar, is tangled and jangled, as he is.

'Simple twist of fate' is another narrative song about a casual encounter. The man and woman walk in a park,

> . . . by the old canal,
> A little confused I remember well
> And stopped into a strange hotel.

This particularity is universalized in authentic ballad style and by the same technical means, such as confusion over tenses. The 'he' of the story finds more meaning in the chance screw than the 'she' does, but he does not resort to self-pity when, waking up, he finds she has gone. The tune is at first restricted in compass, in ballad style, yet it acquires intensity from its fragmentation, which is controlled by a chromatically declining bass. When the stanza unexpectedly climaxes in an arpeggiated leap through an octave on 'and wished that he'd gone straight', Dylan's voice acquires an explosive frenzy–only to be stifled, with throwaway effect.

The harmonica interlude in 'Simple twist of fate' is nostalgic, as it is in Dylan's early work. In 'You're a big girl now' the harmonica is, if choked, more vigorous since, although the lovers are separated and she is apparently promiscuous, he wouldn't mind having her back. This is the most lyrical song so far, with tessitura in tenor range, high and strained. Strain spills into 'Idiot wind', a complex story song dealing with guilt and retribution, and the only number that might be called angry. 'They'–scandalmongers and newspapers–say that 'he'–Dylan or an anonymous hero or anti-hero–murdered a drab Mr Gray and seduced his wife in sunny Italy, coming into a million bucks in the process. But crime doesn't pay as 'he' can't be happy. One of Dylan's ubiquitous fortune-tellers hints at ambiguous nastiness; the hero seems unable to decide whether he is a smart guy or a Christ-like scapegoat, 'a lone soldier on a cross'. The woman he is now living with on his ill-gotten gains (if he *is* guilty), is now more harpy than goddess, an object of hatred and even terror, haunting him with her idiot grimace. As hate and disgust take over Dylan is not entirely immune to the self-pity that disfigured some of his early songs: how does he know that she will 'never know the hurt I suffered nor the pain I rose above'? Still, he does add that he will never know her pain either; and the music is strong enough to ballast the insecurity of the words. Beginning quietly, in talkin' style, and off key on the dark minor of the subdominant, it surmounts the cumulating frenzy of Dylan's wails through glissandoed fourths and fifths, to arrive at a characteristic recognition that he too, as well as the woman, cannot be exempt from blame: '*We're* idiots, babe, it's a wonder we can even feed ourselves.'

It has been suggested that this angry song is Dylan's response to criticism levelled against him for what was taken to be submission to his country dream: the idiots are his public, personified in this chump of a woman. Allegorically, this would make the Mr Gray he may have murdered his real self, and the wife with the million bucks commercial success on the Nashville skyline. Even if the allegory fitted the rest of the story adequately–it doesn't–it is difficult to believe that Dylan would have called his real self Mr *Gray*. It is possible that an element of pique triggered off the number's fury, but to take that as the main theme is damagingly to demean the song. The reverberant poetry and the strong music have wider and deeper implications; by the instrumental coda where the flattened subdominant harmony of the opening grows sourly oppressive, it is clear that the song concerns catastrophe simultaneously private and public. Although this is not a political number, it is a song of the Watergate era; values are confused, *Macbeth*-like reversals are current:

> Now everything's a little upside down,
> As a matter of fact the wheels have stopped
> What's good is bad, what's bad is good
> You'll find out when you reach the top
> You're on the bottom.

Yet it is characteristic of Dylan at this stage of his evolution that he ends side 1 of a disc of usually frustrated love songs with an intimate statement. 'You're gonna make me lonesome when you go' initiates a change of direction. Although still about loss it seems probable that this love was the real thing on both sides. The music starts as a childlike permutation of country-western style, where the harmonica again has no need of nostalgia. Even so, the fetching tune is too irregular to be euphorically goofy, both in its balance between declining bass and uplifting melody, and in details like the touching shift from D to E major that opens the horizon on to the 'blue river'. Verbally too, lyricism is tinged with a gentle irony, even an ironic gentility–as in Dylan's playfully plaintive confession that he'll 'give myself a good talkin' to'. This is one, pretty effective, way of dealing with personal distress.

Meeting rather than missing is the burden of the first song on side 2, as is evident from the title, 'Meet me in the morning'. It is typical of Dylan, however, that the possibility of meeting provokes not a happy number but the most distraught song in the sequence. This is no white ballad, but a strict, very black twelve-bar blues, with strangled vocal production and a plethora of distonated false relations–the F sharps and F naturals at the top of the D major and dominant seventh of C chords are never quite either one or the other; the picked guitar ejaculates painfully, in dialogue with the voice. Both vocal and instrumental style soberly recall neurotic Robert Johnson, so it is not surprising that the song gives little promise of a hopeful resolution: 'Look at the sun, sinking like a ship' (all hands on board); 'ain't that just like my heart, babe, when you kissed my lips.' Presumably the girl won't turn up. On the other hand 'If you see her, say hello', though a song about separation, is the most positive number in the album. In five quite short stanzas the tale is revealed rather than told. It seems that the girl left him and is now in Tangier; it is clear that he wishes her well, and probable that he would like to have her back. Telling the story to a third party, in folk ballad style, enables him to get outside his grief; while at the same time the lovely tune, springing through a seventh and an octave, sends his love winging across land and sea. The bass too sings supportively and the rhythm is sustained: so the chill of the recurrent flat seventh chords is counteracted by a generosity of spirit, a dignity comparable with that of a real folk ballad. The music really does 'say for me that I'm all right'. Dylan's vocal inflexions give human truth to verbal cliché.

'Lily, Rosemary and the Jack of Hearts' is somewhat out of place in this cycle, anticipating the next album, *Desire,* in being a story song based on the mythology of the Western movie. It presents the traditional stereotypes–the bank-robbing outlaw-hero-villain, Big Jim with his diamond mine and bodyguard, Rosemary his dark, misused wife, Lily his 'fair-skinned moll', the hangin' judge–in obscure narrative sequence though with some psychological acumen. Dylan was interested, it seems, in the story behind the story of Wild West movie mythology, and at one time considered making a short film out of the ballad. It works as a story song in sixteen spacious stanzas–one is omitted in the released version–so long as one doesn't worry about precisely what happens to whom, when. I *think* Big Jim, the shanty-town capitalist, tries to shoot Jack of Hearts, the outlaw hero whom Jim's women, like most women, are crazy over. He fails, probably because the revolver has been unloaded by his 'wife' Rosemary, who finally stabs Jim with the balladeer's conventional 'penknife', and is hanged for it. That Lil, the peroxide moll, ends by undyeing her hair and perhaps abjuring her wanton life to return to her father, brings in the theme of purgation as well as retribution. But if this is hinted at in the words it is not evident in the minimal music, in which the scoring of the jaunty diatonic tune brilliantly simulates the bar-room calliope.

'Shelter from the storm' takes up the theme of woman as goddess and siren, so movingly explored in 'Sad-eyed lady of the lowlands'. But here the narrator and/or Dylan–the two are not necessarily identified–is acting in his traditional role as would-be heroic male predator; he is an outlaw who is personified as warrior, highwayman, authoritarian, and ultimately as Christ. The song, like 'Sad-eyed lady', evades temporal sequence, presenting the hero in flashes, now as a traveller on the road before he meets the woman, now with her in her room, now after the event. In each stanza she offers him 'shelter from the storm', a refuge where 'it's always safe and warm', as the refrain floats over a regular beat and stable I, V, IV harmonies. Melismata garland the 'silver bracelets on her wrists and flowers in her hair'; but Dylan cannot capitulate to her as he did to the sad-eyed lady. Trapped by his patriarchal heritage, he can envisage submission only 'in another lifetime'. He ungrammatically admits that he cannot 'turn back the clock to when [a pre-Christian] God and her were born'; identifying himself with the Christ, a (modern) man in whom God became incarnate, he wants back the crown of thorns which he had allowed the woman to relieve him of. Such an admission gives the end of the song a strange resonance:

> I've heard new-born babies wailin'
> Like a mornin' dove
> And old men with broken teeth
> Stranded without love.

He seems to be suggesting that in accepting the shelter of the goddess-harpy, as she now seems, he was abrogating responsibility. Taking 'too much for granted', he had 'got his signals crossed'. There is a hint, prophetic of later developments, that the only valid way of redemption is Christ's.

'Shelter from the storm' is the climax to the cycle, but the final number, 'Buckets of rain', despite its apparent slightness, justifies its position as coda. There is a virginal quality in the lifting tune, balanced by level repeated tonics, and in the sonority of the country-style guitar. Yet the pain in the false relations stains the innocence, making the tune simultaneously open-eyed and resigned. Although, with luck, they will stay together, there is no question but that staying together will hurt. This comes across as a small statement about life as well as about love:

> Life is sad,
> Life is a bust,
> All ya can do
> Is do what ya must.

Dylan's winging or whining voice, his innocuous tune and his plangent guitar make of that platitude something like urban folk wisdom. In the long run that may seem not so much less of an achievement than the finest of his visionary songs.

In *Planet Waves* Dylan had returned, after his country dream, to the reality of love, no longer evading its complexities. In that album love is his positive value, while in *Blood on the Tracks* merely human (sexual) love proves inadequate, its rewards illusory. In the next album, *Desire* (1975), Dylan explores similar themes but stands back from them objectively, presenting them in story form, dramatically and, more particularly, cinematically. Though the title, *Desire,* still emphasizes the sexual dimension, it may also carry Platonic implications of the Desire and Pursuit of the Whole, for no fewer than six of the story songs concern some kind of nemesis, and most of them exploit the guilt and retribution mythology of the cinematic Western, briefly touched on in the context of Dylan's film, *Pat Garrett and Billy the Kid.* The Western movie is a direct extension of the pulp Western novel of the nineteenth century, in which the hero was a progressively degraded descendant of the real but also legendary backwoodsman, Daniel Boone. He, as noted in the Foreword, had the curious dual identity of loner transcendentally communing with nature in infinite solitudes and of sower of civilization in savage realms. His successor, Kit Carson, again a real man, also became a legend, and in his mythical role was distinguished by superhuman strength and physical courage and by impeccable honour and chastity. However, since he lacked Boone's transcendental dimension, the image could and did soon tarnish. His descendants in the dime novels are trappers and mountain men whose freedom is not far from lawlessness and even criminality. The prototype is Buffalo Bill, also originally a real man; the nadir is the fictional Deadwood Dick, gargantuan in courage, appetite and virility, irresistible to women, and both crafty and ruthless in demolishing his enemies. He owed his popular appeal to his amorality, and perhaps even to the arbitrary confusion of his ethics. As both hero and villain, he shared the presumed savagery of the Indians and the brute cunning of the crooks who, in his later role as outlaw detective, were ostensibly his opponents. The female stereotype in the dime novels underwent a complementary change. Although still sometimes victim, or at least potential victim, she may also be a swashbuckling, two-shooting, hard-riding superwoman, beating the men at their own games, often in male disguise. Deadwood Dick is pursued by three betrousered but bosomy beauties simultaneously, a situation at which even he quails. The male attire assumed by these heroines is gaudy, like that of real cowboys, but tends to enhance rather than diminish their sexuality. Hurricane Nell, in particular, anticipates the Hollywood sex goddess. The better-known Calamity Jane is celebrated as much for character, craft and courage as for desirability.

In the dime novels neither heroes nor heroines show much respect for effete codes of honour, but rather demand an eye for an eye or, more pointedly, a scalp for a scalp. When Wild West mythology entered the movies it did not run to such grotesque extremes. 'Good' and 'bad' forces are at first again clearly identified; law and order are represented by the small-town sheriff, supported by the civilized white woman, usually the school-marm–a descendant of the just, genteel white woman hijacked, in Leatherstocking tradition, by the barbarians. In the early days of the western film there was never any doubt that the Indians were the representatives of evil, and the conflict was conceived in rudimentarily black (or rather red) and white terms. But ambiguity soon appears in the figure of the cowboy hero, who, acting as catalyst between good and bad, shares characteristics with both. He is honourable, courageous, sometimes even chaste; but also violent and not necessarily law-abiding in achieving his ends. After bloody battle, he does not so much effect change as conservatively restore the status quo. In the so-called Adult Western which evolved during the fifties and sixties the hero becomes, as white guilt surfaces, still more ambiguous. There is often an admission that the world *ought* to be changed, even though it is unlikely that it will be. The end of the movie is usually a relinquishment of the Adamic dream: the hero, his work as avenger or as potential redeemer done or undone, rides off alone, towards the setting sun.

The real Indian, although spiritually debased and enclosed in reservations as at best a tourist attraction, has surrendered little of his mythic potency. In a sense that potency may have been enhanced in that it has acquired positive as well as negative attributes, as the white hero seeks identification with, rather than opposition to, the aboriginal possessor of the American continent. In the pattern of law versus chaos, freedom versus authoritarianism, the roles played by goodies and baddies are now shiftily white, red and black. Just as the outlaw is simultaneously hero and villain, avenger and redeemer, so woman, white or red, may be both a victim (of skulking bad red or truculent bad white) and either a siren corrupting virtue or a goddess granting absolution.

These themes had been latent in Dylan's songs from his early days as adolescent hippy beatnik: a shaggy successor to the white hunter, frontiersman and pioneer who sought identity with his wild red brother even in the act of confrontation. In *Desire* these basic motifs are given increased dramatic punch and sharper visual definition. Instead of being youthfully involved in the stress of circumstances, Dylan is now cinematically outside it, regarding events with unflinching eye. He also hears with acute ear, for the western-country aura of *John Wesley Harding*, electrophonically treated, acquires a harsh, sunburned acridity apposite to the fierce and feckless tales the numbers tell. The Tex-Mex sonorities match the quality of border life more accurately than the relatively bland Tex-Mex music discussed in Part I. Dylan makes his harmonica wheeze like a distraught accordion; Scarlet Rivera scrapes Mexican folk fiddle with corybantic zest and with just the right degree of acid distonation; electric keyboards vividly emulate bar-room calliopes; Tex-Mex percussion, centred on bongos and other Latin-American instruments, is vibrant, yet as dry as the desert air.

The first number, 'Hurricane', catapults from the distonated fifth into a swinging Aeolian tune – Dylan's Tex-Mex music feels no need slavishly to adhere to its model's blatant diatonicism. The true story of the victimized Negro boxer, Rubin Carter, is told in eleven long stanzas, with much circumstantial detail and patches of vernacular dialogue. Although a few details might be considered grotesquely farcical, the story is presented without irony and with passionate indignation. Unusually for Dylan, conventional chronology is more or less observed. The modal music grows more formidable as with each stanza it is repeated as inexorably as fate; though Dylan's response to individual words and phrases – for instance the melismata on 'hot New Jersey night' and 'the all-white jury agreed' and the permutations of the 'champion of the world' refrain – ensure that the experience is fresh and vivid. The virtuosity of the Mexican percussion and fiddle, precise in pounding agility and soaring ecstasy, generates excitement; the folk-like immediacy is dependent on technical expertise. The enacting of the story shows creative imagination in both words and music, opening unsuspected horizons on a squalid tale. Compared with the victimization numbers of Dylan's early protest years this song has, by way of its cinematic objectivity, acquired the grandeur of a saga.

This is hardly less true of 'Joey', a song about victimization which is more complex because the hero or anti-hero is a gangster and outlaw. After a ten-year spell in prison for thefts and hold-ups, he gets himself murdered while eating with his family in a clam bar. Asked to account for his criminal ventures he grunts 'Just because': which suggests that he's dimly inarticulate rather than wicked, and perhaps that his outlaw's anti-creed is fatalistic. Dylan credits him with a rudimentary sense of honour according to his lights, with family feeling, with a distrust of guns, and with a bovine charm. If the story is told ironically, it is also told emotively. Whereas John Wesley

Harding, in the song of that name, is introduced as a Noble Outlaw who, as the song evolves, reveals feet of clay, Joey is a villain who turns into a victim, and the music underlines his dual status. The accordion-like sonority both wheezes and blazes; the unrelated diatonic concords in the refrain sound melancholy in their lack of direction, yet also rather grand in their euphony. While the number is not as musically impressive as 'Hurricane' it is, like its theme, subtler. Its epic dimension emerges gradually, along with the transformed perception of Joey. The final stanza and instrumental peroration have earned their nobility.

Not all the numbers are as down to earth as these two. 'Black Diamond Bay' rousingly recounts several stories simultaneously, in an appropriately cinematic manner. Indeed the number is about the confusion arising from vicariously living, courtesy of the media, several lives at once. The interlinked stories, set against a Constantinople-like background, concern an unsuccessful woman gambler and/or whore who 'wears a necktie and a Panama hat', but whose real identity is 'nothing like that'; a Greek suicide whom she mistakes, passing on the stairs, for the Soviet ambassador; a soldier engaged in mercantile and (probably) sexual commerce with 'a tiny man'. The human chaos of the shady tales is engulfed by various arbitrary acts of God in the form of thunderstorm, volcano and earthquake, not to mention a burst boiler consequent on them. In the last stanza it emerges that Dylan is in fact in Los Angeles, goggling at the television; from the seven o'clock Cronkite news he gathers that:

> There was an earthquake that
> Left nothin' but a Panama hat
> And a pair of old Greek shoes.
> Didn't seem like much was happening
> So I turned it off.

In this mutable flickering of images Pilate might well ask, 'What is truth?' How do we disentangle what really happens to us from what we see and hear on television, or desultorily read in newspapers? 'There's another hard luck story that you gonna hear,' but there is nothing to say about it that is worth the listening. Through all this confusion between appearance and reality the music remains impervious: the tune and the beat are jaunty, and recurrently permeated by a bar of four symmetrical crotchets harmonized IV–V–IV–V to I. This is the point: the most startling events, ingested by the media, become routine. Only the fact that each new stanza starts on the submediant instead of the tonic reflects the cinematic insubstantiality of the words.

If 'Black Diamond Bay' deals with real life phantasmagorically, 'Isis' reinvokes the magical landscapes of Dylan's psychedelic period. Its oriental mythology directly concerns the goddess theme investigated in 'Sad-eyed lady' and 'Shelter from the storm', again hinging on conflict between the patristic and the matristic. The tale-teller seeks a 'mystical marriage' with Isis, who is both woman and goddess. He marries her 'on the fifth day of May', but isn't able to 'hold on to her very long'. Cutting off his hair in order to assert his male dominance, he embarks on a heroic adventure or quest in order to prove himself to her. Coming to a symbolic 'high place of darkness and light', with a dividing-line running through the centre of town, he makes the conventional Western choice, hitches his pony to the light and right, and proceeds to a (purgatorial?) washing of his clothes. He is approached by a 'stranger' who asks for a *light*, but proves to be typical of industrialized adventurers in that he thinks he knows how to get rich quick. The Dylan-narrator throws in his lot with the stranger, and the two would-be patriarchs set off to the frozen North, far from Isis's warm South and the enveloping womb. Dylan gives the stranger his blanket, his only protection from the cold, receiving in return nothing but 'his word'. The narrator's dreams of wealth are conventionally of gold and diamonds, disturbed by transitory memories of Isis who, as moon goddess, must disapprove of his will-dominated quest; he 'can't remember the best things she said'. When Dylan and the stranger reach their goal it turns out to be an Alaskan Egyptian pyramid paradoxically embedded in ice. Since pyramids were tombs for dead kings, embalmed throughout eternity, the image suggests the ossification of dreams into materiality. The 'treasure' they are to dig for is not gold or silver but an immensely valuable and very dead, presumably mummified, body: 'If I carry it out it'll bring a good price,' the stranger mutters, recalling Stephano's and Trinculo's view of Caliban as a marketable commodity. But as they chop and chop through the frozen earth, from night until dawn, the stranger collapses, from desperation and/or exhaustion, and Dylan, hoping that what he died of 'isn't contagious', is left to dig on alone. When he opens the tomb he finds nothing, neither jewels nor body. Realizing that he has 'been had' and, in taking up the stranger's offer, 'must have been mad', he dumps him in the gaping tomb, says a 'quick prayer', and rides back to find Isis, not to establish any claims to her, but 'simply to tell her I love her'.

He has seen through his patriarchal illusions and is relieved to be back by the fourth of the month–the date of America's Fourth of July and the prelude to his wedding to Isis on the fifth of May. Even so his reunion with her is equivocal. Since he comes in 'from the East with the sun in my eyes' he seems to be still riding westward, and he briefly curses her and rides 'on ahead'. On the other hand the curse sounds rather like a kiss; and when at the end of a laconic conversation she asks 'You gonna stay?', he wails, 'If ya want me to, yes.' In the final stanza he addresses her as a 'mystical child'. 'What drives me to you is what drives me insane,'–so he is still shilly-shallying between submission to the moon goddess and trust in Western will and the song ends where it began. The music impressively incarnates this duality of male dominance with female mystery. Built over a remorseless I–VIIflat–IV–I ostinato, with no dominant, the Mixolydian vocal line is displaced, and suffers contortions at lines such as 'The wind it was howlin' and the snow was outrageous.' The ostinato makes musical flesh of the fact that wilfully he 'had to go on', while at the same time the 'outrageous' vocal roulades and the Dionysiac obbligatos on Tex-Mex fiddle and harmonica suggest that he 'must have been mad'. Both verbally and musically this number is highly wrought; Dylan is capable of a high degree of conscious art when he thinks it necessary. The poem's symbolic patterning cannot be fortuitous.

Although the saga is self-subsistent, the songs' moods are wide-ranging. 'Oh sister' adds to the country-western, Tex-Mex idiom something of the fervour of evangelical hymnody, with

Emmylou Harris as chorus, poised against Dylan's wistful voice and plaintive harmonica, and against Scarlet Rivera's sweetly penetrative folk fiddle. The slowly swaying G major tune arches around tonic and fifth, and the text, despite the Wild West setting, seems to be an appeal for love and understanding under the aegis of a ghostly father, rather than a straight love song. All the numbers are described as 'songs of redemption', and in this tender song redemption is achieved.

In 'Romance in Durango', an overspill from Dylan's western movie *Pat Garrett and Billy the Kid,* redemption, though called for, is not attained. The number overtly adapts Tex-Mex mythology, dealing with a man and his girl, resonantly named Magdelena, fleeing on horseback from law and order. The first stanza encapsulates both place and time, landscape and history. From 'the Aztec ruins and the ghosts of our people' we turn in the second stanza to the murderous violence that had precipitated their flight, echoing Lady Macbeth with a trite 'What's done is done.' The third stanza yearns wistfully for a haven where they will rest and 'drink tequila where our grandfathers stayed', an ancestral past embalmed in an eternal present. But the fourth stanza evokes 'the end' when 'the face of God will appear/With His serpent eyes of obsidian'. He sounds more like an Aztec agent of retribution than a Christian God of redemption; and this can be heard in the music also. The Tex-Mex tango rhythm, plain diatonic tune, burning accordion sonority and marimba-like quavering from mandolin start off perkily enough, but grow increasingly inimical as the refrain pictures the girl dancing a wild fandango in some liberated future. In final effect the music is no more euphoric than the words, which suggest that the law, equated with the serpent god, has caught up. The boy, it would seem, has been shot:

> Was that the thunder that I heard?
> My head is vibrating.
> I feel a sharp pain. . . .
> *We may not make it through the night.*

Retribution is in general as well as personal terms, and our sympathies are divided, since the central characters are simultaneously baddies and goodies: baddies as outlaws and possibly murderers, goodies in being young and vulnerable, and perhaps more *living*, as well as *loving*, than the law that pursues them. The end is even more than usually ambiguous. From one point of view doom may be not merely the sheriff in the present moment, but also an apocalyptic nemesis. On the other hand the music, though it grows savagely abrasive in sonority, remains basically cheerful in melody, rhythm and harmony, and the number merges without break into the next song, 'Black Diamond Bay', about the illusions of the media. 'Romance in Durango' may be a mini-tragedy, or it may be just another cinematic tale, like *Pat Garrett and Billy the Kid*.

'Mozambique', another semi-exotic number in Latin-American rhythm, offers light relief, comically dismissing the 'fabled dreams' of 'beautiful people' without totally discrediting their clichéd pleasures. The wit of the rhymes is gleeful:

> You turn around to take a final peek
> And you see it's so unique
> To be among the lovely people.

But the song is not as slight as it seems: the hammering beat grows slightly minatory as well as vivacious, while the alternation of tonic D major chords with chords of the flat seventh tends to undermine exuberance.

'Mozambique' may stand as a comic complement to the most remarkable song in the collection, 'One more cup of coffee': a mysterious, possibly tragic, love song about a girl with a daddy who's an outlaw (like Dylan). She is evoked in typically ambiguous, sad-eyed lady terms:

> Your pleasure knows no limits,
> Your voice is like a meadow lark,
> But your heart is like an ocean,
> Mysterious and dark.

Like her mother and sister, she is a fortune-telling gypsy who has never learned to read or write; she exists in her spontaneous instincts and, like Isis, makes Dylan and us laugh in freedom and at the same time tingle in fear. He cannot deal with her Cleopatra-like 'infinite variety'; and his balance between fascination and fright spills into music that might be described as American-Hebraic-Mexican-Moorish-Flamenco cantillation! There cannot be any direct link with the Hebraic-Spanish cantillation of New Mexican monody; but it is not fortuitous that this mysterious corner of the American continent should at last free the Jewish alienation theme latent throughout Dylan's work. Although his Orientalized vocal production sounds savage, yet also faintly risible, the end of the song, when after 'one more cup of coffee' he leaves for 'the valley below', is no laughing matter. The postlude's tonic minor triad, followed by major triads VII, IV, V and so back to the (Aeolian) tonic minor, rings like a knell. It is probably correct to sense doom in the offing. Biblically, the valley is the Valley of the Shadow of Death, which impartially demolishes the mirth and the danger of living and loving.

More oddly ambiguous is the song of personal redemption with which the cycle closes. This is ostensibly a straight love song, 'Sara', addressed to Dylan's wife. The mawkishness of the refrain might stick in the throat, were it not qualified by the particularity of the verses describing his children playing on the beach: the 'except for some kelp' phrase in the final stanza is masterly. The hyperbole of the refrains, contrasted with the particularity of the verses, reflects on Sara's dual identity in the song: she is both a flesh-and-blood wife and mother, and also Dylan's mythological moon goddess 'in a calico dress'. She is also equated with Diana, a moon goddess 'with arrow and bow' who is also a virgin huntress. Dylan recounts how he wrote 'Sad-eyed lady' for her, in the indubitable reality of New York's Chelsea Hotel. Musically there is a comparably uneasy balance between the hypnotic bleat of the refrain and the severe modality of the verses. The effect of both words and music is discomforting. Perhaps it is only with hindsight that one feels that Dylan may be trying too hard to assert the truth of his marriage. It had meant enough to make the song haunting in the hearing, lingeringly memorable in retrospect; and although the myth and the reality do not match, to a degree this must be true of any marriage.

It is interesting that Dylan should end the album with this intimate statement since most of these story songs are theatrically and cinematically presented, and make their impact through the contrast between the rawness of their material and the sophistication of its presentation. This is the first, and remains the only, album for which Dylan gives credit to a second creator. Jacques Levy helped with the verses of all the songs except 'Sara' and 'One more cup of coffee', though there is no indication of how much and in what direction. Perhaps his influence may be detected in the elaborately intellectual patterning of symbols in 'Isis' and in the cunning interweaving of stories in 'Black Diamond Bay', or even in the technical adroitness of the versification: the rhyme scheme of 'Hurricane', for instance, is aabbccdee, but the unrhymed line always rhymes internally with the next line. However, such effects are not unprecedented in Dylan's work and it may be that Levy's contribution is more general. As an experienced producer and man of the theatre, he may have encouraged Dylan to organize the often complex stanzas cinematically, thereby providing the basis for a saga that is Dylan's, the Wild West's and, vicariously, ours.

6
Towards Rebirth in a Legal Street

John Wesley Harding represented a revival and a deepening of the social, ethical and ultimately religious themes that had been latent in Dylan's work from the early years. The trinity of albums that followed – *Planet Waves, Blood on the Tracks* and *Desire* – tended to concentrate on story songs and on love songs with autobiographical overtones, though the religio-social dimension is not eradicated. It returns, further enriched, in the next album, *Street-Legal* (1978). It is possible that the strange title implies open statements in the marketplace, as opposed to illegal subversion in back streets. There is, however, no doubt that Dylan here relates personal preoccupations to public responsibilities, and so makes a step towards the total commitment to communal responsibilities which marks the 'conversion' discs. In the *Street-Legal* songs the art of the interwoven poetry and music is still more important than the message. However, that message is embryonic, waiting to be born.

If the songs in *Street-Legal* are related to the basic categories of monodic folk incantation, black blues and white march and hymn, an evolution from rejection to affirmation can be traced. An interesting new development is that the primitive elements now appear as a step towards a regeneration of the more sophisticated techniques. The simplest song, 'New pony', is a mean old, low-down, twelve-bar blues riddled with blue notes and with an opening phrase as primitive as any African tumbling strain. Dylan's vocal production is also at its rawest: his bleat, like Robert Johnson's, sears the senses; the blue notes are often painfully off pitch. This gives a twinge of venom to the words–a love song in that the ponies, new and old, turn out to be women. Although the sexual vigour of the song is affirmative, Dylan's plain words and abrasive vocal line have the toughness of the genuine black blues and, like them, deny personal involvement. Objectivity is encouraged because the solo line is answered by choric refrains in communal gospel style. This suggests that the first woman-horse that Dylan rides may be the world, the flesh and the devil–'I had a pony, her name was Lucifer'–and that her successor is related to a New Bride who is also a new birth. The refrain asks, with mounting fervour, 'How much longer?', as though he were waiting for the coming of the Lord rather than a new pony. Sexual energy is not lost in becoming communal, though it is 'placed', especially in the context of the other songs. One might almost say that it blows itself up by internal combustion! As the solo part grows more frenzied, with words that invoke voodoo magic, so the instrumental parts become more savage, culminating in a brilliant fuzz-buzz solo–an effect borrowed directly from the wilder types of African tribal music.

This cannot be called a gospel song: its sexual energy is too potent for the implications of the 'How much longer?' refrain to register. Even so, antiphony between solo voice and chorus is basic to it, as to most of the other songs. If, in 'New pony', the antiphony is that between shaman and tribe with no more than a veneer of Christianity, in 'Señor (Tales of Yankee Power)' the antiphony is that between gospel preacher and congregation. This magnificent song is the complement of 'New pony', an apparent affirmation which spells rejection; Señor is a rejection that proves to be affirmation. What is rejected is the American Dream, a Texan Way of Life in threatened ruin. A hazardous personal relationship seems to be involved too, though that is destroyed by a world's desuetude rather than by its own failure. The Señor addressed is an earthly lord, a head of state who may be held responsible for society's misery and chaos. But he is also surely the Lord, god and boss of the whole apparently meaningless show, with whom Dylan boldly attempts to establish a more meaningful relationship. The 'painted wagon' must belong to the Slow Train that is not far round the bend, transporting its 'trainload of fools' who will not accept the truth because, ravaged by the stinking tail of the dragon of the Book of Revelation, they cannot recognize it. After Dylan has 'stripped and kneeled' in humility and submission, another of his legendary figures, a 'gypsy with a broken flag and a flashing ring', plays the part of avenging angel, and we are left to 'disconnect these cables, overturn these tables',[1] because 'this place don't make sense to me no more'. The apparently destructive image, born of the anxiety, even dread, which the song induces, turns into affirmation as Dylan asks the Señor what he's waiting for: 'I'm ready when you are.' This difficult affirmation could not occur were it not for the music, which is both starkly primitive and highly sophisticated: primitive because the melody is a pentatonic folk incantation, this time destitute of blue notes, with an instrumental bass rigidly in the Aeolian mode; sophisticated because the instrumental sonorities, with chittering mandolin and whining guitar, are evocative of a precise Texan time and place while at the same time generating a cumulative, universal power. Dylan's voice, beginning with the 'speaking' minor third that addresses the anonymous señor, grows from intimacy to a deep resonance in low register, and finally to an almost hymnic majesty as, in the last stanza, on 'this place don't make sense', he descends from the song's highest note to the tonic. Throughout, the austere modal harmonization never compromises with chromatic alteration and it is that, rather than the music's steadily mounting dynamics, that lends conviction to the idea that religious affirmation may be the only answer to society's distress.

Rural folk hymnody, rather than the hymns of urban chapel or parlour, is evoked at the end of 'Señor'. However in 'No time to think', Dylan calls explicitly on the manner of the urban white hymn and parlour ballad, and produces a song of rejection without compensatory affirmation. This, I suspect, is intentional, for this long number is a message song, as were the talkin' blues of Dylan's early days. The poem consists of nine nine-line stanzas, metrically intricate with internal rhymes, and deals with the disparity between the cinematic mutability of modern life and the abstractions we think we live by:

[1] So printed, though Dylan sings the phrases in reverse order.

Socialism, hypnotism,
Patriotism, materialism
Fools making laws for the breaking of jaws
And the sound of the keys as they clink
But there's no time to think.

The 'no time' Dylan encompasses in a fatuous 6/8 tune that gyrates around itself in stepwise movement, breaking into choric ululations on long notes for each pair of abstractions in the refrain. The sonority whirls and wheezes, like a cross between a chapel organ and a fairground steam organ: the footling tune–entirely diatonic and non-modal though with a chapel-hymn partiality for subdominants and a reluctance to embrace the dominant–tonic relationship–chugs mindlessly around. Driven, always in strict time as though on a merry-go-round, it has no time for thought and precious little for feeling. And that is the point. Although this song debunks petty human deceits and this time offers no spiritual palliative in the music, it includes in the text some covert Christian references. We have no time to think because we are 'betrayed by a kiss on a cool night of bliss/In the valley of the missing link'.

If 'No time to think' is deliberately heartless, 'Baby stop crying' is passionately heartfelt, maturely balanced between desperation and hope. It seems at first to be a straight secular love song. The girl's sobs are broken, drooping in Lombard syncopations and in appoggiaturas. Dylan's approach to her begins conversationally ('You been down to the bottom with a bad man, babe'), acquiring lyrical nuance as the line drifts through pentatonic seconds, droops through a sixth, lifts again when he says he can provide no easy answers to the pain that makes her cry, since 'I can't tell right from wrong.' Through the antiphonies of the chorus private love song blossoms into public hymn. In the refrain the tempestuous crying seems to involve us all, reflecting the human condition, but is safeguarded from hysteria by the music's reiteration of an ostinato of I–III–IV–V–I triads, purely diatonic, and without blue notes. Although Dylan says in the last stanza that he 'don't have to be no doctor, babe' that, in effect, is precisely what he has been: he has renewed life from the acceptance of pain. The therapy of the blues is reinstated, in more sophisticated terms. In old-fashioned terminology this therapy could be called religious consolation, and it is not fortuitous that he invites his honey to go *down to the river*, and even promises to pay her fare.

In one song, 'Is your love in vain?', Dylan regenerates the white American hymn into spiritual grandeur. The verses–asking whether he can take his girl's protestations of love as true, whether she will allow him to be himself as well as her lover, and deciding to 'take a chance' and fall in love with her–sound somewhat self-regarding. But though an ironically queasy note remains–'Can you cook and sew? make flowers grow?/Do you understand my pain?'–the music demonstrates that he is asking fundamental questions that concern them both, and us all. It differs from 'No time to think', the only other number in which tonality is unambiguously diatonic major and rhythm squarely metrical, in being non-satirical. Although aware of human fallibility–consider the quavery little arabesque on 'in and out of happiness'–the tune, over a stable bass falling in dotted rhythm, is grave in its alternation of level repeated notes with scalewise-declining fourths; the texture, often in parallel tenths, is rich and solid. The instrumentation, resonantly organ-like, dominated by Steve Madaio's trumpet, is germane to this nobility, which ends in the kind of apotheosis white hymns achieved in the days when they were validated by experience. Dylan has won the right to see sexual love as heroic triumph, at least *in potentia*, in this religious as well as, or rather than, erotic sense.

Dylan's hymnic vein in *Street-Legal* is not usually as overt as this. More typical is 'True love tends to forget', which opens with hollering falling thirds, at first minor, from fifth to third, then major, from third to tonic. Yet the music is not simply euphoric. The five-bar phrases are oddly truncated, and the middle eight, as he 'lies in the reeds without oxygen', abruptly lurches to the triad of the flat seventh, and modulates to the minor of the subdominant before reinstating the tonic. After this hint of a darker reality the falling thirds recur, exuberantly decorated and sung with harsher vocal timbre. As climax they expand into (god-like?) fifths, reinforced by more animated percussion. The number is paradoxical, since its affirmation is real, yet humanly imperfect–unlike the love of God who presumably cannot forget. The same kind of paradox is present in 'We better talk this over', in which jazzy elements further compromise hymnic solemnity. It might be a song of loss in that its ambiguous thirds are very blue and its rhythms irregular, the four pulse alternating with uneasy fives. Dylan says he is 'displaced', and has a low-down feeling because his woman has been double-dealing; with nothing left except 'the sound of one hand clapping'–a marvellous image of separation and desolation–he has no choice but to leave tomorrow. Even so, the song's general statement is far from negative. 'Somewheres in this universe' there *is* a place that may be called home; and regret is dismissed when he invites her not to 'fantasize on what we never had', but to be 'grateful for all we've shared together and *be glad*'. Despite the rhythmic jitteriness of the 'tangled rope' that enchains them it is 'time for a new transition'–which can be heard in the winging freedom of the melody's peroration, and in Dylan's relatively open, songful rather than bleating, vocal production. There is another rejection here, but since it is a rejection of fantasy it may also be an acceptance of truth and a beginning of faith–such as is reflected in the grandeur of 'Señor' and 'Is your love in vain?' This receives an overtly religious metamorphosis in the first and last songs of the cycle.

The poems, in Dylan's partially surreal manner, are both very fine. 'Where are you tonight? (Journey through dark heat)' works verbally through a richly allusive technique related to the cinematic clip, juxtaposing snippets of a story without chronological sequence and at various levels of reality and myth. In the first stanza he is travelling in the familiar lonesome long-distance train, through the dark night; the rain on the window-pane merges into the tears he sheds for a woman apparently lost. But in the second stanza he is in a neon-lit bar of some seedy town, listening to 'laughter down in Elizabeth Street' in which he cannot share, and to a 'lonesome bell' in a 'valley of stone'. Into the hallucinatory haze flit sundry characters–a woman with a 'full-blooded Cherokee father', a 'golden-haired stripper', 'the guy you were loving', two 'strong men belittled by doubt', not to mention a lion and a demon. The triangular or quadrilateral relationships between humans and the mythic creatures remain, and are meant to remain, obscure: the separations of lover from beloved prove to be also a separation of self from self. The action is within the mind, precipitated from memory; probably the poet never really leaves the railway train he occupies in the first stanza. That the song concerns a longing for the undivided whole, a fundamental religious experience, validates the ecclesiastical flavour of the music. The vocal line, at first primitively in speech rhythms, oscillates between minor and major thirds and is unable to define a tune, while the harmony alternates between tonic and subdominant, the former often garnering a flat seventh to broach, but not to consummate, a full flatwards modulation. The flat sevenths, though indeterminate in pitch, forestall any dominant assertiveness. Not until the last clause, after three eights, is there a dominant triad and a change from the pendulum of tonic–subdominant in the bass, which now swings down the scale. In the middle section the melody's vacillating thirds turn into blue false relations, again indefinite in pitch as sung by Dylan, though flat enough to hint at the subdominant of the subdominant. Here the words refer explicitly to the divided self ('I fought with my twin, that enemy within,/Till both of us fell by the way'), and add, in the last section, that 'if you don't believe there's a price/For this sweet paradise,/Remind me to show you the scars.' Because he has come through, the reprise of the original music can grow grander as well as louder, until the splendour of the coda sounds like authentic religious experience in an age of unfaith. There is no deception, no retreat into Zen quietism, let alone into narcotic delusion. There is courage and strength, which may be related to Dylan's confrontation of a crisis in his own life – the failure of the marriage that, on the evidence of previous discs, would seem to have promised so much. But while personal crisis may have nurtured the further maturation of experience in *Street-Legal* the songs are not about that crisis. Dylan, true artist that he is, has rather used his own pain to investigate experience relevant to us all; and it is no accident that the remaining song – which Dylan placed first, under the significant title of 'Changing of the guards' – relates neurotic distress, expressed in mythological rather than personal terms, to the possibility of religious–and specifically Christian–conversion.

The opening of the visionary poem refers to the sixteen years of Dylan's musically creative life:

> Sixteen years, sixteen banners united
> Over the field where the good shepherd grieves;
> Desperate men, desperate women divided,
> Spreading their wings 'neath the falling leaves.

We are *all* divided selves, riding past 'destruction in the ditches/ With the stitches still mending 'neath a heart-shaped tattoo'. Yet through 'endless roads, empty rooms and the wailing of chimes,/The sun is breaking near broken chains'; and that good shepherd, turning into *the* Good Shepherd or Dylan standing in for him, addresses us as 'gentlemen', informing us that he doesn't need *our* organization:

> I've shined your shoes,
> I've moved your mountains
> And marked your cards.
> But Eden is burning.
> Either brace yourself for elimination,
> Or else your hearts must have the courage
> For the changing of the guards.

Dylan had issued similar appeals in early youth, in a social rather than religious context. The evolution has been both natural and inevitable; and Dylan's imaginative intelligence is shown in the fact that for this song, which is poetically dense and tightly wrought, he returns to basic musical simplicities. The tune is purely pentatonic, unsullied by even a tentative modulation, and has a lyrical grace recalling that of the folk-like numbers of his early years. The words, because of their complexity as well as their message, need to be audible, while the lilting phrases and the potent beat swell to apocalyptic fervour. The final stanza may suggest that the world is not yet ready for peace, tranquillity and 'splendour on the wheels of fire'; but the choric responses to Dylan's lyricism give a foretaste of gospel glory, while the brassy sonorities sublimate Salvation Army sanctity. The apocalyptic flavour of the song is thus, in a theological as well as musical sense, an annunciation for the first of the explicit gospel albums, *Slow Train Coming*, the aesthetic significance of which is, in the context of Dylan's work as a whole, independent of one's acceptance or non-acceptance of its Christianity.

7

Born Again

Primitive American gospel musics were the creation of people, black and white, who were deprived and alienated. The black man, in his adopted white land, was more palpably alienated than the white man; and in examining Dylan's roots I have shown how the black blues sprang from tensions and ambiguities–in more senses than one false relations–between the monodic vocal idiom the black man brought from Africa and the metrical and harmonic conventions given him by his new found land. Though the white Christian sources of black gospel music are clearly discernible, its vocal and instrumental use of them is, in modal ambiguity and flexibilities of rhythm and of pitch, no less black and sometimes blacker than the blues itself. This may be readily apprehended by listening to Roosevelt Charles[1] singing, alongside a traditional country number like 'The boll weevil' or a blues like 'Green dollar blues', evangelical numbers such as 'The ship of Zion', 'Jesus is a-listenin' ' and 'It's gettin' late'. These performances were taped while Charles was on parole from Angola prison, in 1959, yet the style he sings in, especially in the two tracks last named, sounds immemorially ancient. He ululates over a drone-like lower part provided by Otis Webster, the two voices functioning antiphonally. The under voice generalizes personal experience: it is not only Roosevelt who yearns for the alleviation of earthly deprivation and turmoil that only God–presumably of an indeterminate colour, neither white nor black–can offer. In the black gospel church the relation between the leader and/or the preacher and the congregation is similar: the audience *is* the congregation,

[1] *Roosevelt Charles: Meantrouble Blues.*

when two or three or two or three hundred or two or three thousand are gathered together. What results is half-way between art and ritual: as when Benj Bligen and the Moving Star Hall Singers[2] are Born Again.

Poor whites, if less obviously alienated, seem to have been, and perhaps in a few places still are, no less deprived than blacks. In any case they make the same kind of gospel music, on which I commented in Part I. They may sing communally, like Grandpa Ipsom Ritchie's congregation as they 'travel here below'; or they may sing individually, like Roscoe Holcomb with his extraordinary versions of hymns from the *Baptist Sacred Song Book*, which are often startlingly similar to Dylan in his early austerity. Sometimes, as in Doc Watson's version of gospel hymns, they may use their instrumental prowess to attain a relatively undeprived buoyancy–as Dylan does in an early march-hymn like 'When the ship comes in'. On the whole Dylan, in his gospel songs, owes more to alienated blacks than he does to deprived whites, and this may be a point of some significance. No white man of Dylan's time and place, omitting all consideration of his affluence, can be deprived and alienated as were the makers of the music mentioned above. Yet Dylan's point is precisely that in the most fundamental sense we are deprived of spiritual solace if not of material comforts, and are alienated from God if not from togetherness with the members of our tribe. In a way he is right, though we may deplore the fact that after the complex ambivalencies of the previous sixteen years–ambivalencies that had made him representative of his generation–he should now have found a definitive answer. Can he, can we, be born again as were those poor blacks and whites? Has he even earned the right to rebirth? In *Slow Train Coming* Dylan makes out a persuasive case that he may have.

Between authentic Gospel music and Dylan's Gospel numbers there is a technical bridge in the form of Motown music, flourishing from the sixties onwards. This black antiphonal music for a lead singer with backing voices electrophonically accompanied is dedicated to religious message (The Loving Sisters) or secular exaltation (Diana Ross and the Supremes) or a

[2] *Been in the Storm So Long.*

mixture of both (Gladys Knight and the Pips). Vocal techniques owe much to real Gospel music and to the blues, the idiom being appropriately termed Soul. The instrumental elements, however, are stream-lined and mechanized, thereby generating a Black Euphoria to complement the white variety. The Negro's growing self-confidence and economic viability made this feasible, both within vast urban communities like Detroit, from which the Motown company originally operated, and also in less developed West Indian communities, where the music came to be known as reggae.

In his Gospel songs from *Slow Train Coming* onwards Dylan consistently exploits Motown's antiphonal technique of an interchange between leader and chorus, thereby linking the individual with the tribe. In both cases the streamlining of traditional sonorities by microphone techniques and electric instruments is justified as a means of getting the ritual and the message across to audiences immeasurably vaster than the congregations at black or white evangelical churches. The medium is the message in the sense that large numbers of the spiritually if not materially benighted are enveloped within an aural womb from which rebirth may be possible. Yet despite this technical analogy, the experiential distinction between Motown and Dylan is obvious. Far from inculcating euphoria, Dylan's expertise enhances intensity, exposing the raw nerves of his religious aspiration, if not conviction. This may be why in *Slow Train Coming* the best–and often the simplest–songs are those closest to old Gospel tradition, black rather than white.

For instance, the opening number, 'Gotta serve somebody', has an almost pre-pentatonic melody over an ostinato bass undulating between pentatonic major seconds and minor thirds, with the electric piano twittering in (no less pentatonic) parallel fourths. This remains unchanged throughout the first eight and merely moves down a fourth when thoughts of the world and the devil momentarily hot up the harmony with a dominant seventh of G. When this is sequentially repeated a tone higher, the bass fleetingly acquires a chromatic note, but this is dispersed in the repeat for the second verse, so the modal folk incantation and the driving beat are not undermined. The words of the seven stanzas trenchantly and wittily put down the manifold deceits of the world, and Dylan enunciates with an intimacy that is half seductive, half wry: consider his weird stresses in phrases like 'high *de*gree thief', 'live in a *do*me', or 'with a *long* string of pearls'. However, when the verses merge into the chorus Dylan's voice is reverberantly confident, a clarion call echoed by the choric voices. The refrain is powerfully memorable, as a gospel song needs to be, but the forcefulness of the song remains if the specifically Christian message is ignored: it is an appeal to all sorts and conditions of men, including preachers along with city councilmen, barbers, construction workers, bankers, etc., that they should respect something, if not Somebody, beyond self-will. And no one could quarrel with that.

The title song, 'Slow train', works in a similar way but is musically more complex and poetically more particularized. The naughtinesses and hypocrisies of modern industrial civilization are castigated with a vigour that recalls Dylan's protest years; but though the pentatonic-modal incantation of the vocal line is comparable with that of 'Gotta serve somebody' and is likewise reinforced by stabbing parallel fourths from electric guitar, it is more jazzily fragmented. In particular Dylan's tumbling-strain-like ululations are emotionally fraught with blue notes on the fifth rather than third: the top notes are always sung flat, though not as flat as a whole semitone. This ambiguity makes the more telling the flat submediant major triad which announces the coming of the slow train. Again, the burden of the song is an appeal for human rather than divine sanctions:

> I don't care about economy,
> I don't care about astronomy,
> But it sure does bother me
> To see my loved ones turning into puppets.

The slow train, rhythmically and melodically, can reinstate humanity. 'When you gonna wake up' again teeters between social protest and religious affirmation, is again centred on a pentatonic-Aeolian A, and again chunters in parallel fourths on electric piano. Although there is a hint of a modulation to G major, the dominant of the relative, there is virtually no harmonic evolution in the song: many of the I, III, IV and (more rarely) V chords have no third, emphasizing their primitivism. On the other hand the melodic line is here more sustained, its forward thrust being reinforced by cross-rhythmed (3 plus 3 plus 2) ritornelli and by surging triplets that exhort us to 'strengthen the things that remain', despite the malpractice of 'Adulterers in churches and pornography in the schools,/Gangsters in power and lawbreakers making rules'. Nor is the point ethically loaded against evildoers who would be damned by any church. 'Karl Marx has got you by the throat/And Henry Kissinger's got you tied up in knots' applies to thousands who are not criminals, and one recognizes that Dylan is insisting–his voice here is forceful–that another and more fundamental truth is feasible. He does not attempt to define it, nor even claim that he possesses it: it is not public or private property in senses that a Marx or a Kissinger would appreciate. Verbally, Dylan's fundamentalist rhetoric of denunciation is richer and more powerful than the protest of his early years, though it is not notably more marked by the Christian virtue of charity.

The celebratory quality of these songs is reminiscent of some of the numbers from *Street-Legal,* though their pentatonic-modal folk vein shows little trace of the white hymn, except those 'white spirituals' which are almost indistinguishable from black gospel music. 'Gonna change my way of thinking' is also very black and formally a twelve-bar blues. Both tune and bass are purely pentatonic, the voice ejaculating brokenly. For the most part the chords eschew the third. Again primitivism is a means towards regeneration: 'There's a kingdom called Heaven,/A place where there is *no pain of birth.*' One has to go beyond or behind consciousness in order to be reborn: an Edenic quality would seem to be implicit, despite the nervous rhythm, in the music's total lack of chromatic alteration, in its consistent pentatonicism and in the electric guitar's unremitting parallel fourths. Disposing curtly of two fashionable but bogus attitudes, Dylan declares that he 'don't know which one is worse,/Doing your own thing or just being cool'. Again he is making an appeal for human responsibility, as he has done throughout his song-making career, and his vocal inflexions–for instance the wail on 'blood and water flowing through the land'–spring with committed spontaneity. There may be 'only one authority,/And that's the authority on high', but he has an intermediary in that 'God-fearin' woman' who can 'do the Georgia crawl' as well as 'walk in the spirit of the Lord'. Dylan adds that he can 'easily afford' her: a puzzling remark unless perhaps it involves a wry reference to the immense expense of his separation from his wife.

This God-fearin' woman must also be the 'Precious angel' who 'showed me I was blind', and 'how weak was the foundation I was standing on'. The harmony evades dominants in favour of plagal subdominants and shows an odd partiality for first inversions of the tonic, but the song is too jazzily syncopated and fragmented to be hymnic, at least in the early stanzas. The choric refrains, however, shine light on his blindness with cumulating fervour each time they are repeated, ending in corybantic ecstasy. The weighty part played by the choric voices here is pertinent to the theme since the point of the song is that 'I just couldn't make it by myself'. The young woman is not only a gateway to God but also to communion with other people.

There is a link between the God-fearing but Georgia-crawling woman of the gospel songs and the moon or earth goddess celebrated in earlier songs, though she has lost some of her darker and more mysterious aspects in becoming a servant of Christ. None the less her presence implies an equilibrium between the patriarchal and the matriarchal. This is touchingly evident in 'I believe in you', a love song addressed at once to the woman and to Jesus, who have become Janus-faced. This is the first song from the cycle to be in a diatonic major key–the traditionally Edenic E–and has a tune that begins with a descent down the scale through a fourth, answered by the scale's inversion, resolving the sharp leading note on to the tonic. If this suggests white hymnody it is counteracted by a metrical truncation of the phrase at the cadence, and by a substitution, in what starts as a repeat, of a chord of the flat seventh for the tonic. This momentary shiver reflects society's distrust of him in relation to God or the God-fearing woman or both, yet at the same time makes his belief seem more real, because more humanly precarious. Subtly, this shock chord of the flat seventh, originally prompted by alienation, becomes at the climax identified with the fact of belief: 'I believe in you even through the tears and the laughter.' Having heard it as a positive liberation, our response is modified when, in the last stanza, it is associated once more with 'pain' and the 'driving rain'. After the wild upward ululation at the end of the phrase 'even that couldn't make me go back' the song closes in gentle vulnerability. The amen (IV–I) cadence seems the less conclusive because it has been approached by way of the subdominant of the subdominant, that insidious flat seventh triad verbally associated with being 'a thousand miles from home'. It is becoming clear that many of Dylan's gospel numbers assert a *need* for faith but do not celebrate its total possession. He cannot always give the answer which he optimistically believes to be final.

The only number to exploit directly the style of the white hymn and parlour song is 'When he returns', in which Dylan is for the most part accompanied by Barry Beckett on a piano. The lurching 12/8 metre is as remorseless as the 6/8 lilt of *Street-Legal*'s 'No time to think', but I can detect no irony in this rhythmic rigour and unmodulating diatonicism. The number generates passion through its widely arpeggiated phrases and powerfully employs repeated notes in cross rhythms to express God's inexorability. Being inexorable he will seem to some rather nasty, despite the apparent conviction of the words. So two songs in which belief is, musically as well as verbally, tempered by wit can more readily be welcomed. 'Do right to me baby (do unto others)' incorporates a Christian message into its refrain but is basically a delightful appeal for compassion:

Don't wanna judge nobody,
Don't wanna be judged
Don't wanna wink at nobody,
Don't wanna be winked at.

It is ethical rather than religious, though in Dylan's songs human imperfection is usually a foil to divine perfection, since God is a yardstick beyond the fallible human ego. The song is notated in a very sharp B major, though the sevenths are always flattened. Moreover they are treated harmonically, in dominant seventh sequences veering between A and B, the harmonic point being marked by a metrical elision of half a bar. This gives an infectious jauntiness to the musical line which also makes a poetic point, since it comically stresses the verb in the capping phrases: 'Don't wanna *be* judged, Don't wanna be *winked* at', and so on. If the tune is sophisticated in being rhythmically displaced and harmonized in flickering sequential sevenths, it remains innocent in being a miniature tumbling strain. The chorus ('If you do right to me, baby,/I'll do right to you, too') piquantly introduces a major triad on the upper mediant and therefore in false relation, preparing for what promises to be the song's only real modulation: but isn't, since instead the bass substitutes E for the expected G, and leads into a da capo. This entrancing song, which combines the childlike openness of Motown with cunning wit, does indeed revive flagging spirits, without being Revivalist.

Nor can the engaging (and also reggae-like) 'Man gave names to all the animals', be called Revivalist, though the choric voices here function in traditional gospel fashion. Its manner is more explicitly childlike, since it is about the growth from pre-consciousness to consciousness and, in theological terms, about the Fall. Naming ceremonies are important for all primitive peoples, including children. *Infans* means 'unable to speak', and to evolve beyond the infant's inchoate cry is to learn to speak the identifying Names. Dylan whimsically allows man in Eden to name God's creatures in a snatch of tune that undulates between three consecutive notes of a pentatonic scale, appending the remaining two notes only at the tune's conclusion. The accompaniment is in the Mixolydian mode on E; the Motown-influenced percussion is light and lilting. However, cadential notes are sometimes sharpened, and this deliciously points the 'namings', especially since the 'I think I'll call it' phrase has been preceded by a risible false relation on the subdominant. The song ends with the relinquishment of Eden. After naming bear, cow, bull, pig and sheep, man sees 'An animal as smooth as glass,/Slithering his way through the grass'. The snake disappears by a *tree*, and the song abruptly ceases, rather than ends, on a dominant triad that, being unresolved, *dominates* nothing and *leads* nowhere. In this song Dylan's vocal production is open, warm, tender, faintly amused. So this unpretentious little song–in which the snake and the Fall obliterate Eden as consciousness acquires the identifying names–proves to be central to the cycle's theme. We have regressed to pre-consciousness–to Eden, to childhood, to the savage state–in order to be born again; we grow to consciousness and have knowledge of the Names; then, having fallen with the snake, we must make the Eternal Return, and the tale must be told again and again, as it was in the beginning, 'a long time ago'. This is why the song has to end *on*, but not *in*, the dominant.

With hindsight it can be seen that *Street-Legal* implies the Christian orientation, if not message, of the later discs, while preserving the poetic equivocations and musical complexities of the earlier songs. In *Slow Train Coming* the words surrender some of Dylan's resonant ambiguities, but maintain the moral-social fervour of his protest years. In *Saved*, the next disc, Dylan the poet is deliberately liquidated, and the words serve merely as triggers to release a response, as do the magic vocables of primitive shaman. 'Are you ready for the coming of the Lord?' is a question that permits of only two answers–and one of them is assumed to be wrong. The open-endedness which had always been typical of Dylan and had made him so forceful a spokesman for young people is obviated. Since he is, or seems to be, confident of the answer, poetic equivocation–which was still latent in *Slow Train Coming*–is no longer necessary. Here the medium is the message with total commitment. This puts an immense burden on the music. Dylan is sometimes, not always, equal to it.

Self-effacement in the sight of God is a precondition of salvation. Not only is there no picture of Dylan on the outside sleeve, except for a long shot with head bowed, face invisible, he also opens with a number that is not his own, presented as a gospel song, dealing, in blue intensity and immediacy, with what can be said for merely material satisfactions. This song, 'A satisfied mind', was originally a country number and is sung by Joan Baez on *Farewell Angelina* (1965) as a bucolic waltz. In gospelizing it Dylan demonstrates that the satisfactions it celebrates are illusory. He sings it superbly, with black virulence, using it as a springboard to launch him into a new but no less primitive gospel number, 'Saved', for which he shares credit with Tim Drummond. The words state that he has been saved by the blood of the Lamb; the music, notated in sharp B major though with persistently flattened third and seventh, tempers its modality only when he 'thanks' his Lord in a shift from B major-minor triads to a dominant seventh of A, and in one solitary cadence with sharp seventh. There is an element of frenzy, of course, in all gospel music, black or white, but this music, coming from a man who may be saved but is not and never was innocent in the sense that poor white and alienated black might be, has a slightly extravagant vehemence, as well as an uneasy edge. This is echoed in the weird choric refrains which, involving all the Saved (and potentially us) along with Dylan, whimper like grown-up babes.

There is a comparable fervour in 'Solid rock', a title which is a technical description of the music and also a pun. God's Rock needs to be very solid if it is to be a bulwark against the tempest raging in the beating music, which is blackly basic not merely in eschewing sharp sevenths but also in omitting the third from its diatonic chords. The cross-rhythmed repeated notes on 'Won't let go and I can't let go' sound desperate; Dylan seems to be working as hard to convince himself as he is to convert his audience, so even in this album equivocation may creep in by the back door.

Sometimes there is dubiety in the tunes themselves. 'Covenant woman', a homage to the woman who led him to be born again, begins with pastoral undulations in a pentatonic F, but then meanders unconvincingly over plagal-tending harmonies that, though simple in themselves, are weirdly distorted by the organ. Still odder is 'What can I do for you?' the 'you' being Jesus who, having given life and breath, has crowned his gift by 'choosing me to be among the few'. The self-righteousness of the words is fortunately belied by the misplaced rhythm, which inculcates a bemused bewilderment, echoed again in the choric refrains, sounding like the whining of lost children–not unexpectedly, since in Dylan's born again view that is what we all are. The instrumental postlude reinforces the song's strangeness, for over chapel organ harmony Dylan plays his 'natural' harmonica through its own microphone and amplifier in heavy Chicago blues style. The keyboard twitters black and blue arabesques, leaving the title's question unanswered. More gently, 'Saving grace' admits that the road to Calvary gets 'discouraging at times', pointedly contrasting the chapel organ-like sonority with Dylan's raspy voice and the acute wail of electric guitar; tonally, it teeters between its basic C major, the flat submediant A flat major, and that key's relative, F minor.

Nor is the *ecstasis* of the corybantic gospel numbers, 'Pressing on' and 'Are you ready?' altogether straightforward. The hammering beat bullies, rather than generating spontaneous assent; the rhythms, though orgiastic, are jittery in their permutations of 3 plus 2 plus 2 plus 3 quavers; tonality is deceptive, varying between voice part and instrumentals. Not surprisingly, the words too are equivocal, for the sign that 'comes from within' tells us that 'what's lost has been found, what's to come has already been'. We are advised to think for ourselves instead of 'following the pack'; yet are at the same time encouraged to submit to the will of God, in an act of communal assent! Presumably the reward for being born again is an ability to have it both ways.

Yet if such Dylan-like ambiguities were not latent throughout the cycle the finest number could hardly be so impressive. 'In the garden' deals simultaneously with personal experience and with a communal act. Jesus is presented as an individual human being, no less real because men and women for the most part could not see or misconstrued him. The key signature is B major. (Can there be a connection between 'late' Dylan's partiality for very sharp keys and the traditional association of sharpness with heavenward aspiration?) The pentatonic-diatonic tune is conceived in large, asymmetrical paragraphs. Tonality moves as early as the second bar from B major to its relative G sharp minor, then with a chromatic alteration to C minor, only to oscillate between diatonic major triads of G, F and E flat before shifting up to A major and so up again to B. An instrumental coda boldly asserts the tonic major, I–IV–V–IV–I, but is immediately dispersed for the wavery second stanza. In these incessant modulations, or rather tonal shiftings, there is no easy certitude, but there is a 'miraculous' annealing through musical growth, whereby the song generates both power and wonder. Even if one cannot swallow all the verbal implications, one can accept that in this gospel song Dylan's message is what it always was, with undiminished grandeur. This song seems to me as honest as it is affirmative: a summons to hope that remains aware of hazard.

The Dylan of the early eighties frequently refurbishes early numbers in post-gospel style. 'Masters of war', for instance, loses its satirical punch because the hubbub makes the words less comprehensible, and the song emerges as a venomously hymnic anti-hymn. 'Maggie's farm' is transformed from a wry story song into an assertion of the improbable togetherness of ill-assorted people. 'Blowin' in the wind' becomes furiously affirmative, though its answer, no longer vacillating, is not that which Dylan sought at the time he wrote the song. 'Mr Tambourine Man', electrophonically gospelized, becomes a very loud appeal that the Lord of Hosts should 'play a song for me', rather than an invocation of a magical pot-pedlar and Pied Piper who would act as guide through the mazes of youth's uncertainties. It is still a call for regeneration, and it still works, proving once more that Dylan's born-again manner is not a denial of his original postulates.

The ambivalent correlation between the tambourine man and the Son of God is echoed in the very title of the next disc, *Shot of Love*, an album which one finds oneself listening to simply as the latest stage in the Dylan canon, without reflecting on any proselytizing intent. The musical richness of the varied and densely written songs cannot be gainsaid; Dylan's obsession with the message *per se* needed to be no more than temporary. Some of the songs in *Shot of Love* carry on from the rawly authentic gospel manner of *Slow Train Coming*. The first number, 'Shot of love', recalls 'Gotta serve somebody', its melody being consistently pentatonic, while the rhythm is sharp and the sonority pungent. Dylan's timbre is both ripe and abrasive: appropriate to a song that effects an affirmation out of macabre threat by being musically sinewy. The sturdily descending bass in the refrain is potent in both a sexual and a spiritual sense; the sharp sixths of the Dorian mode deliver a 'shot' which, unlike heroin, proves to be no empty panacea. Similarly black in manner is 'Dead man, dead man', also entirely pentatonic in tune and unremitting in rhythm. Dylan's voice snarls as it sings, and electrophonic gibbers threaten the spiritually dead man much as they had haunted that earlier cypher figure, Mr Jones. Yet the number comes across as much more affirmative, partly because the paragraphs of the melody build up grandly, partly because the counter-rhythms of the inner parts are intricate, but mostly because the bass line is powerfully melodic, generating metrical drive and harmonic tension. This is a tightly written song, the musicality of which brings impressive rewards.

Less close to primitive gospel style is 'Property of Jesus', which arises out of the quotation from St Matthew which Dylan prints on the sleeve: 'I thank thee, O Father, Lord of heaven and earth, because thou hast hid these things from the wise and prudent, and hast revealed them unto babes.'[3] This time the tune is straight diatonic, avoiding anything like 'Dead man's' disturbance of its pentatonic simplicities by blue oscillations between the perfect fifth and the tritone. The verse is built over an unchanging ostinato on a tonic pedal, while the refrain has a firm bass descending from the submediant to the subdominant. The song is an assertion of the dignity of the man of God, though in worldly terms he may be a loser and a fool. Throughout the album basses that descend in metrical regularity form a rock that lost mortals may cling to. This is true even of the grimmest number, 'Trouble'. Here the beat thumps remorselessly and the sonority rasps, while Dylan's vocal line, lacerated with false relations, catalogues the terrors of the woeful world. Yet again the total effect is of vigorous affirmation: the major triad on the subdominant, suddenly injected into the Aeolian harmony, give a physical lift, and the beat seems not so much threatening as triumphant, since whatever horrors men inflict on men one may, given help from that rock, not only survive, but also sing.

Another group of songs is patently positive, generating a happiness that is never blindly and deafly euphoric. 'Hearts of mine', a love song that may also be religious, begins in country style, with gently plucked accompaniment. As in most country music, tonality is plain diatonic, and the atmosphere is cosy–or

[3] St Matthew 11:25.

it would be were not the music invigorated by the active bass line, hinting that although the song is about *not* roaming, the singer is aware of all that roaming implies. There is a comparable quality in the delightful 'Watered down love', a rejection of plastic substitutes that might itself sound mindlessly merry were not its rhythms so bouncy, its beat so precise, its sonorities so tingling. Pure love, opposed to the watered-down kind, is in no way evasive of earthly identity. Dylan has brought his white-black Jewish intensity to bear on this reggae-like, innocently rebellious music. The effect is even more jubilant than reggae itself, because it is more aware of what is at stake.

Three simple songs in ballad style justify the risks they take. The negative song of the group is a threnody for 'Lenny Bruce', written in the style of a parlour song, accompanied by *Hymns Ancient and Modern* harmony on the chapel piano. Lenny Bruce was hardly an obvious candidate for Christ, but neither was Dylan, who celebrates Bruce as 'an outlaw who told the truth'–as he did himself. Bruce may have been 'bad' but was also 'the brother you never had', and perhaps Dylan's own *alter ego*. The deep, almost parsonical register in which Dylan sings the number teeters between the minatory and the grotesque–as do the words: although Bruce told truths which some people did not want to hear, he 'never robbed any churches or cut off any babies' heads'. The musical as well as the verbal effectiveness of the song depends on a shamelessness precisely appropriate to the subject.

The two positive ballads reinstate Dylan's harmonica, with heart-easing effect. 'In the summertime' has a lyrical tune almost reminiscent of the Celtic flavour of 'Mr Tambourine Man'. Dylan's voice is gentle, without its usual abrasiveness. It is a love song addressed to a woman and/or to Jesus, and its clear major tonality and swinging lilt suggest an Edenic consummation. But again its simplicity is far from simple-minded: the paragraphs build up from the lyrical phrases in richly substantial continuity. Growth is latent within acceptance. This is true not merely of this song, but also of Dylan's born-again phase in general. Never have the distonations of his harmonica sounded more poignant–at once hopeful and frail–than in this number, unless in the final song on the album, 'Every grain of sand', another entirely diatonic major piece about the love of God and of man. This opens with calm parlour-style arpeggios over sustained organ triads, with a tune that finds confirmation in repetition–as do many love songs of ostensibly primitive peoples. The innocence of the harmonica postlude exists within the context of the musical maturity which typifies this unpretentious but unexpectedly complex album as a whole. Dylan's supporting musicians on guitars, keyboards, saxophone and drums, with the girlie chorus more discreetly used than on the previous gospel discs, are not only highly accomplished; they also generate an empathy that says much for human love, whether divinely inspired or not.

8

Dylan as Jewish Amerindian and White Negro

> In the language of archetype the Negro stands for alien passion and the Indian for alien perception. (Or perhaps this is only another way of saying that at the level of deep imagination the Indian is male and the Negro female.)
> Leslie A. Fiedler, *The Return of the Vanishing American* (1968)

Dylan's ability to grow is inseparable from his 'loneness' and from those elements in him that relate to folk tradition. Most pop music exists only in performance in the sense that the notations merely approximate to the sounds. None the less pop artists functioning in a commercial world must remain consistent in their stereotypes: a version of a number, especially a successful number, must be instantly recognizable to its public. An artist such as Dylan, who remains closer to folk origins, can however afford to make each performance a once-off, re-creating his songs according to the circumstances in which they are performed. I have mentioned the 1974 tour remakings of earlier material and his gospelized versions of recent years. His metamorphoses are not however restricted to such palpable examples of rebirth. The Isle of Wight version of 'Like a rolling stone', included in *Self Portrait*, is radically different from its ebullient original, meaner in its persistently distonated pitch and raggedly imprecise rhythm. On the 1978 Budokan tape, on the other hand, 'Like a rolling stone' is transformed from a gleeful song of rejection into a powerful, almost hymnic paean which has only a vicarious connection with the words: perhaps the music can make a positive asseveration because the words expose pretence, so that the paean is to freedom. The Budokan 'All along the watchtower', 'It's all right, ma (I'm only bleeding)' and 'Ballad of a thin man' are all performed faster than the originals. 'Watchtower' loses something of its grandeur, but becomes more nervously doomladen; this time the wind wildly 'howls' at the end. 'It's all right, ma (I'm only bleeding)' becomes angrier but also, in its enhanced rhythmic vivacity, more triumphant: 'Thin man' snarls in electric agility but attains, in this lighter texture, a near-humorous detachment which the heavy first version lacked. Even 'Forever young' grows chorically vigorous without surrendering the simplicity that made it sound convinced and convincing as a song addressed to Dylan's children. Occasionally a number is transmogrified to a degree that makes it almost a new song. 'One more cup of coffee', losing the hilarity of its 'Moorish-Flamenco-Hebraic' cantillation, comes across as unmistakably minatory; as does 'Oh, sister' which, shedding its evangelical tinge, emerges as a Tex-Mex number acrid in sonority and remorseless in tangoid rhythm, with gibbering and wailing voices off. The effect is sinister, perhaps because the song seems to have become a conflict between Dylan's Christian Father and his sad-eyed lady earth goddess. Some such tension is latent in many of the gospel songs; indeed the fundamental ambiguity which makes Dylan's work so rewarding is precisely this matriarchal–patriarchal synthesis or reconciliation.

In conclusion I shall consider whether any pattern emerges from the career of this poet-composer, performing musician and maker of myth, relating this to the speculations broached in the Foreword. Dylan began as an outsider, demolishing or castigating the industrial 'civilization' in which he lived and worked. At first his role as outsider-wanderer may obviously be related to his Jewish ancestry, even though in early youth he repudiated it by changing his name. In maturity, after the motorcycle accident, he took up the cause of Judaism, even to the point of working with the Jewish Defence League. Yet his hope that Israel might be one of the few places where life today had any meaning did not long survive; he approved in principle of a religion that found God within the self, but was disillusioned by the competitiveness and power struggle that corrupted Zionism no less than the left-wing radicalism of his earlier days. It remained true for him that 'My thing has to do with *feeling*, not politics, organized religion or social activity. My thing is a feeling thing. Those other things will blow away. They'll not stand the test of time.'[1]

So Dylan's Jewishness is in the last resort hardly a racial matter. Although a wanderer and an outsider he was at the same time an insider, in that he was a catalyst around which crystallized a new community: the young whose tribal values, Dylan would have said, contained the heart of the real America, before it was contaminated by industrialization and its concomitant economic evils. As a Jew Dylan was an outcast; as an American, he was aboriginal, if not patently Amerindian. His art functions, in reaction to modern American life, at levels far deeper than those at which the escapist country music industry exists; and although there is little direct musical evidence of his Jewish ancestry, the nasally inflected, melismatic style of cantillation found in extreme form in 'One more cup of coffee' is more pervasive than might at first be suspected. Particularly in the songs concerned with the landscape and mythology of the Wild West and of the Texan, Arizonan and New Mexican deserts, Dylan's singing may rediscover age-old links between the Hebraic, the Moorish and the Spanish, and may also reveal affinities with the starker musics of the Red Indians themselves. Dylan as authentic American has much in common with Henry Thoreau, who shared the Red Indian's at-home-ness in virgin woods and forests, as a backdrop to life in villages and small towns.

The science or quasi-science of cantometrics, explored by Alan Lomax and his associates, has much to tell us about the global village implications of Dylan's varied vocal techniques, through which contradictions seek unification. Lomax's

[1] Cf. also: 'What I write is much more concise now than before. It's not deceiving. . . .Deceiving means when I wrote a lot of those protest songs, they were written in a small circle of people. Then when they were brought to the outside, other people heard them, heard them in their own way. They could think something was happening which wasn't happening. But what I'm doing now, my stuff now is *me,* what seems to be happening in the songs is really happening.' Quoted in Anthony Scaduto, *Bob Dylan*, London, 1972.

findings suggest that cantillation of the Hebraic-Moorish-Spanish type, often latent and occasionally patent in Dylan's work, tends to be found in highly stratified societies. 'Where the fate of every individual depends on his relationship to the super-structure above him', the bard's output is 'elaborate, deferential, and suitable to a society made rigid by layers of privilege'.[2] For this reason he adopts a very tight vocal production, clearly distinguished from normal modes of utterance, and emphasizes his separation from *hoi polloi* by complex melismatic ornamentation. This establishes his exceptional status both because it disguises the basic melody and because it requires virtuosity in performance. Of its nature such cantillation must be sung by a solo voice, not by polyphonic choruses, though the magically mysterious properties of this solo voice may be highlighted by instrumental accompaniment, usually drone-based.

In Dylan's early work such styles are no more than covert, and when in later years they become vocally overt a near-Eastern flavour may sometimes be detected in the use of electric organs and bells. This has nothing to do with what Steve Reich has called 'the old exoticism trip'. It is rather that Dylan as Jewish outsider has some of the attributes of a priest: only by being separate, standing back from his experience, can he intuitively perceive the identity of apparent opposites. Using an ancient technique of musical alienation, he turns modern alienation against itself. And the near-Eastern, Hebraic-Spanish strain points to something more radical, for through the separateness of the Jewish outsider Dylan rediscovers the aboriginal Red Indian. There is no direct influence of Amerindian music on his work, except possibly in the wordless 'Wigwam', which might be construed as a parody–in the technical sense of a remaking as well as or rather than in the satirical sense–of indigenous material. None the less his later work, especially the Wild West songs, does reveal unconscious *affinities* with Amerindian musics; and the psychological and sociological relevance of this has become explicit in recent years, when young punks crop or topknot their hair in order to masquerade as those aboriginally red 'savages' whom modern technocracy had displaced. Musically, Dylan's affinities run much deeper;

[2] Lomax, *Folk Song Style and Culture.*

though he does not emulate Amerindian music, he creates song which at least has some technical properties in common with it.

According to Lomax, Red Indian musics reflect in extreme form the activity of a male-dominated, aggressive hunter society. Almost all the songs are chanted by men in fierce unison, banded in possessive togetherness. Rhythm is simple, an unremitting pulse without overlaying or underlying complexities, thumped on a single drum. Clarity of verbal message is unimportant; even if what seem like nonsense words once had meanings, these meanings were magical, 'a music of the vowels'. All that matters is the unisonal assertiveness of the vocal line, which sweeps irresistibly onwards, with frequent open intervals of third, fourth and fifth. To a more extreme degree than in any other music, vocal timbre is characterized by 'nasality' and 'rasp', these being technical terms in cantometrics. Vocalization is strictly syllabic, modified only by quavering and glottal shakes, probably intended to induce awe. Though Dylan has not consciously called on such techniques, he frequently sings tumbling strains, in high, strained, rasping timbre, often on meaningless vocables; and he frequently accompanies his vocal ululations by furious one-beat percussion, with no or minimal harmonic support. The primitivism of his singing is certainly Poor White more overtly than it is Red; none the less it is not extravagant to suggest that the red lay hidden behind the white, biding its time: as D. H. Lawrence had prophesied nearly sixty years ago when he wrote:

> Assuredly the dead Indians have their place in the souls of present-day Americans, but whether they are at peace there is another question. . . . It is presumable, however, that at length the souls of the dead red man will be one with the soul of the living white man. Then we shall have a new race.[3]

Certainly in Dylan's Wild West numbers the hero as Jewish outsider and as rediscovered Indian insider became deeply interrelated. If it is accepted that Amerindian song[4] is the most

[3] D. H. Lawrence, *Studies in Classic American Literature*, London, 1924.

[4] There are many recordings of Amerindian musics, among which *Songs of Love, Luck, Animals and Magic: Songs of the Yurck and Tubura Indians* may count as representative. *Songs of Earth, Water, Fire and Sky: Songs of Nine Amerindian Peoples* is especially interesting in the context of Dylan since Indian melodies

extreme musical instance of male dominance, it can be said that in evoking the Amerindian Dylan is stripping to its bare bone contemporary industrialized aggression and paternalism. In so doing he is able to ameliorate its rigour by fusing it with imported African traditions.

Again according to Lomax's findings, African hunter groups, in their indigenous state, display some similarity with, but more difference from, the Amerindians. With the Africans clarity and particularity of text are again unimportant: consonants are slurred and refrains used repetitiously; line is again unornamented and beat is steady as a rock. But whereas Amerindians sing in a wild (and therefore not entirely congruent) unison, overriding any opposition to the tribal will, African hunter groups sing chordally and antiphonally, with two or more lines often freely overlapping, as blithe as birds chattering in consort. Although nasality, rasp and yodel may be resorted to for special effects, they are not the basic sonority, which is clear and liquid. The more extreme techniques are called on, if at all, as playful rather than painful extensions of the norm. The overall impact of African styles is, in Lomax's words, 'multi-levelled, multi-parted, highly integrated, multi-textured, gregarious and playful voiced'. Through their music as through their other social customs, African hunter groups seek not dominance, but an easy reciprocity and solidarity.

It follows that, whereas Amerindian male-assertive musics are unisonal and unimetred, African musics tend towards polyphony, or at least heterophony, and polymetre. Although black Africans enslaved in white America could hardly be expected to preserve the jolly, socio-musical interchange of their native communities, they did not totally abandon it but

---

are, in the modern 'Rabbit dance', combined with English words. Modern permutations of traditional material also occur on *Comache Peyote Songs* and *Round Dance Songs of Taos Pueblo*. A Red Indian rock artist may be heard on Norton Buffalo, *Desert Horizon*.

I should perhaps add that a few, but not many, Indian peoples complement the patriarchal masculinity of their music by allowing women to sing chants of their own, usually associated with domestic occupations like weaving and basket-making. Their tunes are gently undulating and stepwise moving, springing from the rhythm of the words rather than from muscular physical activity. Unlike African peoples, Amerindian men and women never sing in consort.

rather adapted their mores to those of the Christian Church. In black gospel music the incantation of preacher and congregation overlaps in traditionally African style; and congregations include women along with men, as do most indigenous African ceremonies. The Negro gospel service becomes a model of egalitarian human interaction. Word content matters greatly; vocal lines are speech inflected and normally move in narrow compass, without aggressive leaps, except for special effects. Although nasality, rasp and yodel may be employed to expressive ends, the basic timbre is sonorous, warm and liquid. Whereas the Red Indian sings straight and as loudly as possible, the Negro cultivates a varied expressivity, which may flower into melismatic ornament, and into relatively complex rhythm. The same distinction is evident in dance style. The Red Indian moves with his trunk as a single element, battering and pounding the earth; the Black American experiences his body as a dual identity divided by the pelvis, and thereby generates the erotic, simultaneously male and female quality of his dance. Red Indian culture is sexually restrictive, black American culture is not; if the quasi-Red Indian strain in Dylan's songs exposes the tough root of *our* restrictiveness, the far more powerful black American strain may represent a search for a politically, economically and sexually more egalitarian society.

In his songs Dylan's balance between patristic and matristic impulses is delicate. In his life it seems to have been less so, for he has been cruel to many of the women who have loved him–not merely to casual chicks picked up in a life of hippydom or superstardom, but to deeply involved lovers such as Suze Rotolo, Joan Baez and Sara. (His marriage to Sara looked hopeful because she was a 'laid-back' type well into Zen and uninterested in competition.) Biography is not our concern and is ultimately irrelevant to an artist's work. Even so, it is worth noting that compassion must have mingled with cruelty in Dylan's complex love life, and that many people detected in him androgynous qualities–a fusion of male aggression and abrasiveness with an almost female softness and sensitivity. His ambiguity, we are told, extends even to his physical appearance, which may seem sinewy at one moment, frail at the next. In his music we cannot crudely equate male and female with red and black elements, but we may suggest that Dylan, at once a Jewish Amerindian and a White Negro, discovers through his Hebraic cantillation unexpected links between the *ecstasis* of a Navaho Night Chant and the corybantic continuity of Negro gospel music. Interestingly enough Francis Parkman, travelling the Wild West, was reminded by Indian song and dance simultaneously of 'savage' orgy, of black gospel music, and of Jewish cantillation, remarking that

> The Indians in concert raised their cries of lamentation over the corpse, and among them Shaw clearly distinguished those strange sounds resembling the word Hallelujah which, together with some other accidental consequences, have given rise to the absurd notion that the Indians are descended from the lost tribes of Israel.[5]

Genetically, the notion may be absurd, though, as noted in the Foreword, it was vigorously canvassed in the seventeenth and eighteenth centuries. A Jewish writer, Manasseh ben Israel, published in 1650 an *Origen de los Americas; Esto es esperanza de Israel*[6] which, translated into English by Moses Wall, became a bestseller, reinforced by an English work published in the same year by Thomas Thorowgood: *The Jewes in America, or, Probabilities that the Americans are of that Race.*[7] However scientifically dubious, the authors give their case a certain symbolic logic, tracing parallels between Indian and Jewish myths, rites, customs and speech, and relating the hardships suffered by the Indians to those biblically prophesied for the Jews. The Red Indians' discovery of Christ may be equated with the ultimate conversion of the Jews; and this millennialist approach is not altogether irrelevant to Dylan's apocalyptic epiphany. As a young man in the Village Dylan once said, 'Did I ever tell you I got my nose from the Indian blood in my veins? Well, that's the truth, hey. Got an uncle who's a Sioux.'[8] It probably wasn't the truth but one of the tales Dylan invented to mystify people. Even so, the myth points to the identity of Dylan as an abori-

5 Francis Parkman, *The Oregon Trail*, New York, 1849–1892.

6 Santiago Pérez Junquera (ed.), Madrid, 1881.

7 Quoted in Huddleston, *Origins of the American Indians*, Texas, 1967.

8 Quoted in Scaduto, *Bob Dylan*. The fascinating story of a young actress who thought Dylan was Jesus is told on pp. 238–40.

ginal American who has found Christ and has, indeed, been regarded by some of his wilder fanatics as Christ reincarnate! This is not of course Dylan's view, though he has spoken of himself as one of the Chosen People.

This Jewish-Red Indian connection helps us to understand why Dylan, whose attitude to the world may seem in its matriarchal and magical aspects opposed to the historical process of Christianity, should have experienced, and should want us to experience, a Christian conversion. Evangelical Christianity is in origin Hebraic, biblical and historical. It is not mystical, but is concerned with events presumed to exist in historical time, past, present and future. In mysticism 'the eternal is sought', in John Oman's words, 'as the unchanging by escape from the evanescent'.[9] Despite his flirtings with Oriental religions, this has never been the core of Dylan's creed. His is a religion of Revelation, 'the unveiling', as Reinhold Niebuhr puts it, 'of the eternal purpose and will underlying the flux and evanescence of the world',[10] the expectation being fulfilled in both personal and historical terms. The boy Dylan inherited from his evangelical background a lively sense of sin, the consequence of which he saw grossly magnified in the corruptions of industrial civilization. At first, a bold young Goliath, he attacked the dragon of evil in the world outside. Gradually he discovered that dragons fumed within himself, and the confrontation of guilt proved too much for him in that, after the fear-ful *John Wesley Harding* album, he seemed to retreat from battle. He returned to it by unflinchingly grasping the historical sense of doom bequeathed by his Hebraic ancestry. If Dylan is regarded, throughout his career, as deeply representative of young American democracy, the words which, some a hundred and fifty years ago, Alexis de Tocqueville wrote in what is still the most brilliant, and prophetic, book ever written about America may be to the point: 'For my part, I doubt whether man can support complete religious independence and entire political liberty at the same time. I am led to think that if he has no faith he must obey, and if he is free he must believe.'[11]

[9] John Oman, *The Natural and the Supernatural*, New York, n.d.

[10] Reinhold Niebuhr, *The Nature and Destiny of Man*, vol. 1, New York, 1941.

[11] Alexis de Tocqueville, *Democracy in America* (1839–48), translated by George Lawrence, J. P. Mayer (ed.), New York, 1966.

Belief, of course, is not necessarily an asset: it depends on the kind and quality. De Tocqueville was as usual acute about the dangers inherent in the fact that

> Although the desire to acquire the good things of this world is the dominant passion among Americans, there are momentary respites when their souls seem suddenly to break the restraining bonds of matter and rush impetuously heavenward. . . . Forms of religious madness are very common there. . . . If their social condition, circumstances and laws did not so closely confine the American mind to the search for physical comfort, it may well be that when they came to consider immaterial things they would show more experience and reserve and be able to keep themselves in check without difficulty. But they feel imprisoned within limits from which they are apparently not allowed to escape. Once they have broken through these limits, their minds do not know where to settle down, and they often rush without stopping far beyond the bounds of common sense.[12]

There is still some truth in those 150-year-old words; and it may be tempting to dismiss some aspects of Dylan's gospel ethic as beyond the bounds of common sense, not to mention common charity. Yet the evolution of American industrial technocracy during that period has produced a situation that not even de Tocqueville could have foreseen. This situation may be one with which common sense is incompetent to deal; and the belief which Dylan has stumbled towards through his creative life cannot be encapsulated in an evangelistic formula; it is still true that, as he tersely put it in conversation with Anthony Scaduto, 'I'm not part of no Movement.' It is not so much an accredited creed as an inescapable necessity that has led Dylan to his present position, in that the sense of doom under which we labour cannot be gainsaid. It is now within our power to extinguish the human race. In insisting that there is no answer to doom that does not involve some concept of faith Dylan reinforces the words from de Tocqueville quoted above. The freedom he has pursued throughout his life is, in de

[12] Ibid.

Tocqueville's sense, inseparable from belief. This message need not be interpreted in narrowly Christian terms, even by Dylan himself. And though the Christian answer may be the most valid in that it is both historical and revelatory, it must be seen as a beginning rather than as an end. To return to the theme of the Foreword, any belief we arrive at must be pertinent to an American culture of which the roots are simultaneously white, red and black. Dylan is on the mark in implying that if we are not, in this creative interfusion, born again, our vaunted civilization, whether Christian or pagan, is finished; and will deserve its fate.

Afterword

FOLK SONG, ART AND TECHNOLOGY

Writing words about music is a hazardous occupation and is at its trickiest in the areas of folk, country and folk-pop music which are the subject of this book. These areas resist definition since, neither flesh nor fowl, they exist in limbo. About real folk music the most we can risk saying is that it is 'music of necessity' made to fulfil some specific social, religious or magical function, which function is achieved in the act of making. Presumably we sing in order to communicate; yet the question of the kind of communication we seek remains unresolved. It is clear that all primitive song offers a low density of information. Information is not its main concern, since as soon as man sings he embarks on an activity that carries him beyond mere personal expression. When his words become music–even in the rudimentary form of the incanted and enchanted utterance of a single-pitch tone or the alternation of two pitches–he enters a different dimension. His purpose is no longer only, or even mainly, to convey a message. On the contrary, song tends to destroy linear and temporal progression and to put the singer into a mystical communion with something other than himself–whether God or the state or his children. In primitive song words are often replaced by magical or nonsensical vocables, as in the musics of such disparate groups as the waulking women of the Outer Hebrides or the horse-breaking Amerindians of the Southern Plains. All forms of oral song use repetitions, refrains, hollers and borrowings from previously established songs in order to enforce a togetherness that effaces the self. All oral songs depend on living within given assumptions, while being at the same time outside them. Different *données* are evolved for different kinds of song, from ritual incantation to work song to narrative ballad. All types operate by virtue of their conventionalism. When conventions have outworn their social or magical meaning we call them clichés, although they may still have a limited efficacy. Of its nature song seeks transcendence. In the words of Victor Zuckerkandl,

> The singer who uses words wants more than just to be with the group: he also wants to be with things, those things to which the words of the poem refer. Tones remove the barrier between the person and the thing, and clear the way for what might be called the singer's participation in that of which he sings.[1]

Both singer and audience, if there is one, become the song. Whereas speech and, by corollary, written verse and prose are a linear process existing in time, song is not a process but a state, by its nature circular and atemporal.

We have little difficulty in accepting this in reference to so-called primitive song: there must have been at some time an original maker or germinator of tunes which in various permutations have become songs of the folk. But to a degree it is true also of songs which are called art songs because they are created by artists who are recognized as distinguished by superior talents. Somewhere, and to define the line is difficult, there is a distinction between a folk singer who is more creatively enterprising than most, and an art composer of songs which are a product of civilization in the sense that their forms and structures may mirror the organizing faculties of the human imagination. Trained vocal technique–in Europe pre-eminently bel canto–emphasizes this distinction between achieved artefacts and the raw material of experience. Even so, European art song does not function as a linear ratiocinative process. The American scholar Mark Booth has brilliantly demonstrated how

> The dependence of singing on right hemisphere (brain)

[1] Victor Zuckerkandl, *Man the Musician*, Princeton, 1973.

> activity sheds light on the nature of songs as marriages of music and words and also on the nature and function of the patterns in addition to music that have been discovered binding oral compositions. 'Time-independent', 'appositional' and '*Gestalt*', characterizations of the right hemisphere, the part of the brain on which song primarily depends, indicate that the binding of song words into patterns above the flow of discursive syntax is what distinguishes song and related phenomena from speech.[2]

Post-Renaissance art songs do, of course, tend to have beginnings, middles and ends, as primitive song types do not; yet the meaning of the song overrides that temporal progression–as Booth indicates in his analysis of Thomas Campion's 'I care not for these ladies', in which 'wanton Amaryllis' is always available and accommodating, unlike those fine ladies who may be occupied with other men and other events, at another time and place. They live in time, aware of 'what is past, and passing, and to come'; whereas Amaryllis is folk-song-like in living in the existential moment.

Whatever account one gives of European art song, there is no doubt that in our time song as a manifestation of existential moments has re-emerged, bringing with it a rejection of those complex formalizing principles which, in post-Renaissance music, represent the triumph of civilization through the human will. We cannot evaluate a song by Bob Dylan by the same standards as are applicable to a song by Gabriel Fauré or Hugo Wolf. Indeed to approach a Dylan song is in some ways more difficult, because whereas with Fauré or Wolf there is a notated artefact which bears some recognizable relation to the song in performance, with Dylan, or any modern folk-pop singer, the relation between artefact and performance is of its nature ambiguous. Asked in an interview which track on a new album he considered the best, Dylan parried with another question: 'Song or performance?', implying that each performance is a re-creation and in that sense also a *com-position*. A new technique of analysis is called for, and its nature is demonstrated in a highly intelligent and revealing book on Dylan's songs as *Performed*

[2] Mark Booth, *The Experience of Songs*, Yale, 1981.

Literature, written by Betsy Bowden. Bowden analyses in detail a number of Dylan songs in various performances, demonstrating how the open-ended nature of the poetry lends itself to the transcending quality of song, and how the same or nearly the same words can produce different, even totally disparate, experiences in their collusion with music. She is concerned mainly with the music inherent in the singer's voice: the translation of a smile into a snarl, a bark into a chortle. Such an approach can be only empirical, tested by the arduous process of listening and relistening to each version of a phrase, and collating the alternatives. The process is exhaustive and exhausting; had she gone on to discuss musical characteristics *per se*–the contour of a melodic phrase, the shift of a rhythm, a change of gear in harmony or tonality–the operation would have become unmanageable, though it is only on such an integrated poetical-musical basis that one could claim to offer an adequate analysis of how a Dylan song works. Such a technique would not have been feasible in a book covering as wide a scope as this. Intuitively–my book was finished before I came across Betsy Bowden's work–I have aimed at a compromise, commenting, if only briefly, on the relation between poetic meaning and manner of performance and relating both to the (composed) musical events. I have not, however, resorted to musical notation, as I did in my book on the Beatles, because I now accept that in relation to such music it is more misleading than illuminating. We come back to the point often made glibly and complacently: that the analysis of popular musics is unhelpful, risible, and even morally suspect. Obviously I do not accept that: Dylan, say, is a creator whose motivations are not radically distinct from those of Shakespeare or Beethoven, although his *means* to his ends may be different. Betsy Bowden's book is important in that it attempts to define those means, or some of them. It is valuable in that it shows us what to listen for in Dylan's and related musics. Understanding more inwardly how it works, we may the more readily hear what is there to be heard. This is true in a general sense, as an approach to Dylan's songs. I doubt however whether one should use her book as a companion to the songs. To listen to the five or six versions of a song on which she comments, to read her revelatory words, and then to add one's own gloss on the musical events collateral with the verbal ones, would be a task that left one without the imaginative and intellectual stamina to respond to any, even much simpler, words and music.

In treating Dylan as an aural-oral poet-musician Bowden recognizes that he usually employs electronics in the interests of his folk-like ends. This is only superficially paradoxical: whereas electrophonics are in an obvious sense a product of the head, intellect and science, they have often been used self-destructively, at several different levels. At the lowest level, tribal pop has made of electrophonics an aural womb-tomb in which consciousness, that starry crown of the West, may be obliterated. Such submission to mindlessness is dangerous not because it is politically subversive, but because it may become totally amnesiac. Much punk rock offers amnesia as the only alternative to what its practitioners purport to hate, while the effect of some chart-dominated pop on the minds and senses of the pre-teenage and teenage children who are its public is hardly distinguishable from that of Muzak: a manufactured product *designed* to be not listened to but merely to undermine resistance to commercial pressures, to make us conform to a vacuous solidarity or, if we're a bit older, to assuage our (technologically induced?) stresses and distresses.

At a higher level, technology has been used against itself in more rewarding ways: as in the magical electrophonics at the Court of the Crimson King, or in the science fiction extravaganzas of Pink Floyd, Yes or The Who. Such musics succeed in creating a ritual through which it is possible to re-enter those existential moments with which primitive musics are concerned. Indeed the electrophonic fade-out is a technique which, in denying temporal progression, is dedicated to that end: technology achieves what occurs in real primitive music when the activity does not conclude, but simply stops. The same thing is hinted at in jazz performance when a blues singer or pianist leaves the cadence unresolved on a dominant seventh–a chord normally associated in Western music with an approach to harmonic consummation.

Dylan's crucial significance is not unrelated to the fact that he stands between these extremes. His early numbers, purveying a message in narrative form, sometimes have beginning, middle and end. None the less most of his albums have been produced from within the factory of the pop music industry, often at Nashville itself, and all have used electronics not to ballast the 'patriarchal' aspects of his work but to enhance its 'matriarchal' magic. Fade-outs are as prevalent in the late gospel as in the dream-and-nightmare songs of the middle years; Dylan calls on technological sophistication to give *mind*-boggling immediacy to his most primitively black music. He is a highly articulate poet whose words are a modification, not a denial, of the head's articulateness; and his truth is synonymous with the dimension his music adds to his words. Dylan is a folk poet, but he is more than that: his mind and his sensibility have become representative of, even responsible for, a generation. That he should have reached middle age and still be vigorously creative is encouraging, for it suggests that the beat generation was not, after all, beaten. Dylan's songs, balanced between body and soul, head and heart, may be a more revealing pointer to our future than the work of many 'serious' poets and composers, for they may imply the evolution, as well as the survival, of a myth. They may herald the beginning of a words-and-music-making era that will help to shape our turbulent lives. The light at the end of the tunnel may not, after all, be the oncoming train.

Discography

Recordings by Bob Dylan appear under the heading of the chapters in which they are discussed. All other recordings are assigned to the chapters in which they are first mentioned.

I The Backdrop: From the Appalachians to Nashville

1 The Word and the Body: The Legacy of the Old World

Music of Scottish Tradition, Volume 3: Waulking Songs from Barra, Tangent Records, 1972, TNGM 111

Columbia Library of Folk Music, Volume 1: Scotland, collected and edited by Alan Lomax, n.d., AKL 4941

Columbia Library of Folk Music, Volume 6: Ireland, collected and edited by Alan Lomax, n.d., AKL 4946

Music of Scottish Tradition, Volume 2: Music from the Western Isles, Tangent Records, 1972, TNGM 110

Jeannie Robertson: The Great Scots Traditional Ballad Singer, Topic, 1959, 12T96

Jean Redpath, Philo, 1975, Philo 2015

Isla St Clair Sings Traditional Scots Songs, Tangent Records, 1972, TGS 112

Scottish Bagpipe Music Played by Pipe Major John A. MacLellan, Folkways, 1951, FW 6817

The Classical Music of the Highland Bagpipe, BBC Records, 1968, REB 48M

John Burgess, King of Highland Pipers, Topic, 1969, 12T199

Billy Pigg the Border Minstrel, Leader, 1971, LEA 4006

Music of Scottish Tradition, Volume 4: Shetland Fiddle Music, Tangent Records, 1972, TNGM 117

A Tribute to Niel Gow by Ron Gonella, Lismor, 1978, LILP 5085

Aye on the Fiddle: Bobby Harvey, Waverley-EMI, 1967, LP 2086

Music of Scottish Tradition, Volume 6: Gaelic Psalms from Lewis, Tangent Records, 1975, TNGM 120

Discography

2 The Old Heritage in the American Grain

I'm on my Journey Home, New World Records, 1978, NW 223
Almeda Riddle: Ballads and Songs from the Ozarks, Rounder Records, 1972, Rounder 0017
Old Love Songs and Ballads from the Big Laurel, Folkways, 1964, FA 2309
Aunt Molly Jackson, Library of Congress Recordings, vol. 7 no. 4, collected by Alan Lomax, Rounder Records, 1961, Rounder 1002
A Girl of Constant Sorrows: Sarah Ogan Gunning, Topic, 1967, 12T171
Nimrod Workman: Mother Jones' Will, Rounder Records, 1976, Rounder 0076
The Gospel Ship: Baptist Hymns and White Spirituals from the Southern Mountains, Alan Lomax (ed.), New World Records, 1977, NW 294
Old Harp Singing of Eastern Tennessee, Folkways, 1951, FA 2356
White Spirituals from the Sacred Harp, New World Records, 1976, NW 205
Brighten the Corners where you are: Black and White Urban Hymnody, New World Records, 1976, NW 224

3 The White Euphoria

Early Shaker Spirituals from Sabbathday Lake, Maine, Daniel W. Patterson (ed.), Rounder Records, 1976, Rounder 0078
Hymns and Carols: Andrew Rowan Summers, Folkways, 1951, FA 2361
Sara Cleveland: Ballads and Songs of the Upper Hudson Valley, Folk-Legacy Records, 1968, FSA 33
Brave Boys: New England Traditions in Folk Music, New World Records, 1977, NW 239
Child Ballads in the Southern Mountains, Sung by Jean Ritchie, Folkways, 1961, FA 2301
Hedy West: Pretty Saro and Other Appalachian Ballads, Topic, 1966, 12T146
Frank Proffitt: Northern Carolina Songs and Ballads, Topic, 1966, 12T162
White Gospel Songs, Sung by Harry and Jeanie West, Kenneth S. Goldstein (ed.), Folkways, 1957, FA 2357
That's my Rabbit: Traditional Southern Instrumental Styles, New World Records, 1978, NW 226
Echoes of the Ozarks, Volume 1: Arkansas String Bands 1927–1930, County, 1970, County 518
Old Time Music at Charlie Ashley's, recorded by Eugene Earle, Ralph Rinzler and Mike Seeger, Folkways, 1961, FA 2355
Fiddlin' John Carson: The Old Hen Cackled, the Rooster's Gonna Crow (1923), Rounder Records, 1973, Rounder 1003
Georgia Fiddle Bands, vol. 2, County Records, n.d., County 544

Music of the Louisiana Acadians, recorded by Harry Oster, Arhoolie, 1960, Arhoolie 5105 and Arhoolie 5013
J. P. and Annadeene Fraley: Wild Rose of the Mountain, Rounder Records, 1973, Rounder 0037
Bluegrass for Collectors, remastered by Randy Kling, RCA Records, 1974, APMI 0568
Going Down the Valley, New World Records, 1977, NW 236
Uncle Dave Macon, the Dixie Dewdrop, Folkways, n.d., RF 51 and Vetco, n.d., Vetco LP 101
Dock Boggs, Mike Seeger (ed.), Folkways, 1964, FA 2351 and FA 2392
Hobart Smith: The Old Timey Rap, Topic, 1969, 12T187
Doc Watson and Son, Ralph Rinzler (ed.), Vanguard, 1965, VSD 79170
Doc Watson, Vanguard, 1964, VSD 79152
Roscoe Holcomb and Wade Ward, Folkways, 1962, FA 2363
Roscoe Holcomb: The High Lonesome Sound, Folkways, 1968, FA 2368
Mountain Music of Kentucky, Folkways, 1968, FA 2317

4 The Liquidation of Tragedy and Guilt

Hills and Home, 30 Years of Bluegrass, New World Records, 1976, NW 225
Flatt and Scruggs, Don Law and Frank Jones (eds.), Columbia, 1962, CL 1830
The Cowboy: His Songs and Brag-talk, Folkways, n.d., FA 5723
Back in the Saddle Again, Cowboy Songs in Two Traditions, Authentic and Commercial, New World Records, 1977, AF31–2
Cisco Houston, Folkways, n.d., FA 2022 and FA 2042
Country Music South and West, New World Records, 1977, NW 287
Dark and Light in Spanish New Mexico, New World Records, 1978, NW 292
Texas Mexican Border Music, Chris Strachwitz (ed.), Folklyric Records, 1974, Folklyric 9003
Western Swing: Historic Recordings, vol. 3, Chris Strachwitz (ed.), Old Timey, 1975, Old Timey 117
Bob Wills Anthology, Columbia, n.d., KG 32416
Ernest V. Stoneman and the Blue Ridge Corn Shuckers, produced by Mark Wilson, Rounder Records, n.d., Rounder 02144
Ola Belle Reed and Family, Rounder Records, 1977, Rounder 0077

5 The Family, the Loner and the Radio Networks

Famous Country Music-Makers: The Carter Family, 2 discs, John Atkins, (ed.), RCA Records, n.d., DPM 2046

The Carter Family: Original Recordings, produced by Don Laws and Frank Jones, Columbia, n.d., HL 7280

Let the Circle be Unbroken, 3 discs, United Artists, 1972, UAS 9801

Famous Country Music-Makers: Jimmie Rodgers, John Atkins (ed.), RCA Records, 1972, DPS 2021

Country Music in the Modern Era 1940s–1970s, New World Records, 1976, NW 207

The Best of Merle Travis, SM 2662

The Ernest Tubb Story, Decca, 1970, MCA 2–4046

Roy Acuff's Greatest Hits, Columbia, CS 1034

The Collector's Hank Williams, vol. 1, MGM, 1975, Select 2353 118

Hank Williams: Forty Greatest Hits, 2 discs, produced by Fred Rose, MGM, 1978, 2683 071

Elvis's Golden Records, RCA Records, 1970, SF 8129

Big Mama Thornton: Mama's Pride, produced by Ed Bland and 'General Hog' Wyler, Vanguard, 1975, VPC 40001

Kings of Country Music, vol. 2, Hallmark Records, 1975, SHM 863–4

Shake, Rattle and Roll: Rock and Roll in the 1950s, New World Records, 1977, NW 249

Chuck Berry's Golden Decade, Chess Records, n.d., vol. 1: 2–Chess 6641018, vol. 2: 2–Chess 6499185

Charlie Rich: I'll do my Swingin' at Home, Embassy, 1975, EMB 31212

The Country Side of Jim Reeves, Camden RCA, 1969, CDS 10000

II Bob Dylan: Freedom, Belief and Responsibility

1 Grass Roots

J. B. Smith: Ever Since I have been a Man Full Grown, Bruce Jackson (ed.), Takoma, 1972, Takoma B1009

Angola Prisoners' Blues, collected and edited by Harry Oster, Arhoolie, 1959, Arhoolie 2011

Angola Prison Spirituals, 77 Records, n.d., 77 LA 12/13

Blind Willie Johnson, His Story Told, Annotated and Documented by Samuel B. Charteris, Xtra, 1970, Xtra 1098

Classic Jazz Masters: Robert Johnson 1936–7, Philips, n.d., BBL 7359

Woody Guthrie: Library of Congress Recordings, Elektra, 1964, EKL 271–2

2 Protest and Affirmation

Bob Dylan, CBS, 1962, CBS 62022 (reissue: 1981, CBS 32001)

The Freewheelin' Bob Dylan, CBS, 1963, CBS 62193

The Times They are A-changin', CBS, 1964, CBS 62251 (reissue: 1981, CBS 32021)
Pete Seeger: We Shall Overcome, CBS, 1963, CBS 62209
Another Side of Bob Dylan, CBS, 1964, CBS 62429 (reissue: 1981, CBS 32034)
Bringing It All Back Home, CBS, 1965, CBS 62515 (reissue: 1983, CBS 32344)

3 Between Vision and Nightmare

Highway 61 Revisited, CBS, 1965, CBS 62572
Blonde on Blonde, CBS, 1966, CBS 66012 (reissue: 1982, CBS 22130)
In 1966 There Was, Bootleg LP, 1971
Bob Dylan and The Band: The Basement Tapes, CBS, 1975 (recorded 1967), CBS 88147
The Band: Music from the Big Pink, Capitol, 1968, ST 2955
Rock of Ages: The Band in Concert, Capitol, 1972, SABB 11045
John Wesley Harding, CBS, 1968, CBS 63252

4 The Country Dream: The Private and the Public Life

Nashville Skyline, CBS, 1969, CBS 63601
Self Portrait, CBS, 1970, CBS 66250
New Morning, CBS, 1970, CBS 69001 (reissue: 1983, CBS 32267)

5 Love and Loss, Redemption and the Myth of the Wild West

Pat Garrett and Billy the Kid, CBS, 1973, CBS 69042 (reissue: 1982, CBS 32098)
Dylan 1973, CBS, 1973 (recorded 1969–70), CBS 69049 (reissue: 1983, CBS 32286)
Planet Waves, Island Records, 1974, ILPS 9261 (reissue: 1982, CBS 32154)
Bob Dylan/The Band: Before the Flood, Island Records, 1974, UDBD 1 (reissue: 1982, CBS 22137)
Blood on the Tracks, CBS, 1975, CBS 69097
Desire, CBS, 1976, CBS 86003

6 Towards Rebirth in a Legal Street

Street-Legal, CBS, 1978, CBS 86067

Discography

7 Born Again

Roosevelt Charles: Meantrouble Blues, recorded by Harry Oster, Vanguard, 1964, VRS 9136
Been in the Storm So Long, Folkways, 1967, FS 3842
Slow Train Coming, CBS, 1979, CBS 86095
Saved, CBS, 1980, CBS 86113
Shot of Love, CBS, 1981, CBS 85178

8 Dylan as Jewish Amerindian and White Negro

Songs of Love, Luck, Animals and Magic: Songs of the Yurok and Tubura Indians, New World Records, 1977, NW 297
Songs of Earth, Water, Fire and Sky: Songs of Nine Amerindian Peoples, New World Records, 1977, NW 246
Comache Peyote Songs, Indian House, 1969, Indian House 2401
Round Dance Songs of Taos Pueblo, Indian House, 1966, Indian House 1001
Norton Buffalo: Desert Horizon, Capitol, 1978

Bibliography

MUSIC OF THE OLD COUNTRY

Bronson, B. H., *The Ballad as Song*, Berkeley, University of California Press, 1969

Buchan, David, *The Ballad and the Folk*, London, Routledge & Kegan Paul, 1972

Collinson, Francis, *Traditional and National Music of Scotland*, London, Routledge & Kegan Paul, 1966

Johnson, David, *Music and Society in Lowland Scotland in the Eighteenth Century*, London, Oxford University Press, 1972

Lord, Albert B., *The Singer of Tales*, Harvard, Atheneum, 1959

O'Canainn, Thomas, *Traditional Music of Ireland*, London, Routledge & Kegan Paul, 1978

THE AMERICAN EXPERIENCE

Adams, Andy, *The Log of a Cowboy*, Boston, University of Nebraska Press, 1983

Barkhofer, Robert F., jun., *The White Man's Indian*, New York, Random House, 1978

Fetterman, John, *Stinking Creek: The Portrait of a Small Mountain Community*, New York, Dutton, 1970

Huddleston, Lee Eldridge, *Origins of the American Indians*, Texas, Institute of Latin American Studies, 1967

McCallum, James (ed.), *Letters of Eleazor Wheelock's Indians*, Hanover, NH, Dartmouth College Publications, 1932

Browne, R. B (ed.), *Frontiers of American Culture:* Purdue University Studies, Indiana, Purdue Press, 1968

Rourke, Constance, *The Roots of American Culture*, New York, Harcourt Brace, 1942

Smith, Henry Nash, *Virgin Land: The American West as Symbol and Myth*, Harvard, Harvard University Press, 1950

Tocqueville, Alexis de, *Democracy in America*, trans. George Lawrence, J. P. Mayer (ed.), New York, Doubleday, 1966

MUSICS OF THE NEW FOUND LAND

Abrahams, Roger D., *Anglo-American Folk Styles*, New Jersey, Prentice Hall, 1968

Booth, Mark W., *The Experience of Songs*, Yale, Yale University Press, 1981

Jackson, George Pullen, *White Spirituals in the Southern Uplands*, New York, Dover Press, 1933

Lomax, Alan, *Folk Song Style and Culture*, New Jersey, Prentice Hall, 1968

Malone, Bill, *Country Music U.S.A.*, Texas, American Folklore Society, 1968

Malone, Bill, and Judith McCulloh (eds.), *Stars of Country Music: Uncle Dave Macon to Johnny Rodriguez*, Illinois, Illinois University Press, 1975

Sandberg, Larry, and Dick Weissman, *The Folksong Source Book*, New York, Knopf, 1976

Bowden, Betsy, *Performed Literature: Words and Music by Bob Dylan*, Bloomington, Indiana University Press, 1982

Dylan, Bob, *Writings and Drawings*, London, Jonathan Cape, 1973

Guthrie, Woody, *Bound for Glory*, London, J. M. Dent & Sons, 1969

Herdman, John, *Voice without Restraint*, Edinburgh, Paul Harris Publishing, 1981 and New York, Delilah Books, 1981

Klein, Joe, *Woody Guthrie: A Life*, London, Faber and Faber, 1981

McGregor, Craig, *Dylan: A Retrospective*, Sydney, Angus and Robertson, 1972 and New York, William Morrow, 1972

Porterfield, Nolan, *Jimmie Rodgers: Life and Times*, Illinois, 1972

Ritchie, Jean, *Singing Family of the Cumberlands*, New York, Oak Publications, 1955

Scaduto, Anthony, *Bob Dylan*, London, W. H. Allen, 1972

Tharpe, Jac. L. (ed.), *Elvis: Images and Fancies*, Jackson, University of Mississippi Press, 1979

Index

Authors of books and composers of music and songs are shown in round brackets; performers of songs and recordings in square brackets.

Index

Index

Index

Index

Index

Index

Index

Index

Index

Index